Sexual Boundary Trouble in Psychoanalysis

Inspired by the clinical and ethical contributions of Muriel Dimen (1942–2016), a prominent feminist anthropologist and relational psychoanalyst, *Sexual Boundary Trouble in Psychoanalysis* challenges the established psychoanalytic and mental health consensus about the sources and appropriate management of sexual boundary violations (SBVs).

Gathering contributions from an exciting range of analysts working at the cutting edge of the field, this book shatters normative professional guidelines by focusing on the complicity and hypocrisy of professional groups, while at the same time raising for the first time the taboo subject of the ordinary practicing clinician's unconscious professional ambivalence and potentially "rogue" sexual subjectivity. *Sexual Boundary Trouble in Psychoanalysis* uncovers the roots of SBV in the institutional origins and history of psychoanalysis as a profession. Exploring Dimen's concept of the psychoanalytic "primal crime," which is in some ways constitutive of the profession, and the inherently unstable nature of interpersonal and professional "boundaries," *Sexual Boundary Trouble in Psychoanalysis* breaks new ground in the continuing struggle of psychoanalysis to reconcile itself with its liminal social status and morally ambiguous practice.

It will appeal to all psychoanalysts and psychoanalytic psychotherapists.

Charles Levin, PhD, FIPA, is a training and supervising analyst, Editor-in-Chief of the *Canadian Journal of Psychoanalysis*, and Director of the Canadian Institute of Psychoanalysis. He has edited and authored several analytic books and many articles on clinical, ethical, and cultural topics.

RELATIONAL PERSPECTIVES BOOK SERIES

ADRIENNE HARRIS,
STEVEN KUCHUCK & EYAL ROZMARIN
Series Editors

STEPHEN MITCHELL
Founding Editor

LEWIS ARON
Editor Emeritus

The Relational Perspectives Book Series (RPBS) publishes books that grow out of or contribute to the relational tradition in contemporary psychoanalysis. The term *relational psychoanalysis* was first used by Greenberg and Mitchell[1] to bridge the traditions of interpersonal relations, as developed within interpersonal psychoanalysis and object relations, as developed within contemporary British theory. But, under the seminal work of the late Stephen A. Mitchell, the term *relational psychoanalysis* grew and began to accrue to itself many other influences and developments. Various tributaries—interpersonal psychoanalysis, object relations theory, self psychology, empirical infancy research, feminism, queer theory, sociocultural studies, and elements of contemporary Freudian and Kleinian thought—flow into this tradition, which understands relational configurations between self and others, both real and fantasied, as the primary subject of psychoanalytic investigation.

We refer to the relational tradition, rather than to a relational school, to highlight that we are identifying a trend, a tendency within contemporary psychoanalysis, not a more formally organized or coherent school or system of beliefs. Our use of the term *relational* signifies a dimension of theory and practice that has become salient across the wide spectrum of contemporary psychoanalysis. Now under the editorial supervision of Adrienne Harris, Steven Kuchuck, and Eyal Rozmarin, the Relational Perspectives Book Series originated in 1990 under the editorial eye of the late Stephen A. Mitchell. Mitchell was the most prolific and influential of the originators of the relational tradition. Committed to dialogue among psychoanalysts, he abhorred the authoritarianism that dictated adherence to a rigid set of beliefs or technical restrictions. He championed open discussion and comparative and integrative approaches, and promoted new voices across the generations. Mitchell was later joined by the late Lewis Aron, also a visionary and influential writer, teacher, and leading thinker in relational psychoanalysis.

Included in the Relational Perspectives Book Series are authors and works that come from within the relational tradition, those that extend and develop that tradition, and works that critique relational approaches or compare and contrast them with alternative points of view. The series includes our most distinguished senior psychoanalysts, along with younger contributors who bring fresh vision. Our aim is to enable a deepening of relational thinking while reaching across disciplinary and social boundaries in order to foster an inclusive and international literature.

A full list of titles in this series is available at www.routledge.com/mentalhealth/series/LEARPBS.

1   Greenberg, J. & Mitchell, S. (1983). *Object relations in psychoanalytic theory.* Cambridge, MA: Harvard University Press.

Sexual Boundary Trouble in Psychoanalysis

Clinical Perspectives on Muriel Dimen's Concept of the "Primal Crime"

Edited by Charles Levin

Routledge
Taylor & Francis Group

LONDON AND NEW YORK

First published 2021
by Routledge
2 Park Square, Milton Park, Abingdon, Oxon OX14 4RN

and by Routledge
52 Vanderbilt Avenue, New York, NY 10017

Routledge is an imprint of the Taylor & Francis Group, an informa business

British Library Cataloguing-in-Publication Data
A catalogue record for this book is available from the British Library

Library of Congress Cataloging-in-Publication Data
Names: Levin, Charles, 1950– editor.
Title: Sexual boundary trouble in psychoanalysis: clinical perspectives on Muriel dimen's concept of the "primal crime" / edited by Charles Levin.
Description: New York: Routledge, 2020. |
Series: Relational perspectives book series |
Includes bibliographical references and index. |
Identifiers: LCCN 2020017634 (print) |
LCCN 2020017635 (ebook) | ISBN 9781138926806 (hardback) |
ISBN 9781138926813 (paperback) | ISBN 9781315682969 (ebook)
Subjects: LCSH: Sex (Psychology) | Psychoanalysis. |
Psychologists–Professional ethics. | Psychotherapists–Sexual behavior. |
Psychotherapy patients–Sexual behavior.
Classification: LCC BF692 .S4339 2020 (print) |
LCC BF692 (ebook) | DDC 150.19/5–dc23
LC record available at https://lccn.loc.gov/2020017634
LC ebook record available at https://lccn.loc.gov/2020017635

ISBN: 978-1-138-92680-6 (hbk)
ISBN: 978-1-138-92681-3 (pbk)
ISBN: 978-1-315-68296-9 (ebk)

Typeset in Times New Roman
by Newgen Publishing UK

"Sexual boundary violations carry not only the dread of rupture, but also a haunting of the uncanny, of the unthought known—an echo of the big bang that was muffled by all our fallen progenitors who married their patients in an attempt to morally domesticate the forces they could not resist.

As therapists, we all have been (or still are) patients—wounded healers with visceral sense memories of those times our own treatments failed, or worse, collapsed around us. Every accusation of a boundary violation disturbs the unsettled peace each of us has made with our own treatment history—each revelation serving as a stark reminder of the ultimate fragility of analytic work, no matter how honorably conducted.

That is why this book hurts. Wrapped in the melancholy of Muriel Dimen's passing, and fueled by a commitment to redress the isolation she endured as a whistle-blower, the contributors to this volume exhaustively wrestle with the hydra-headed pathogen that Dimen labeled 'the primal crime'.

'Monumental,' 'egregious,' 'catastrophic,' 'demonic'—this is a forlorn sampling of the adjectives these anguished and gifted authors feel moved to deploy so as to capture the tsunami of destruction that results from the treachery of a sexual boundary violation.

For the analysand, an erotic enactment spells the collapse of the state of enchantment that suffuses the 'real/not real' tension of transitional space, which is what gives imagination a chance. Coming out of this perverse scenario (a state of mental enslavement) is like escaping from a cult—instead of being helped by therapy, the patient has been consumed by it.

For the community, the revelation of a boundary violation destabilizes everyone within earshot (rumor and gossip travel fast), causing serious moral harm, but also placing a moral demand upon a professional collective not schooled—or prepared—to think and act as a group. Demonization and banishment (Dimen's 'Rotten Apples'), serve to defensively separate 'us' from 'them,' even though each of us battles a queasy state of identificatory dread—there is always the criminal within.

Modeling what it takes to think under fire and against shame, these papers shine with such deeply considered analytic insights. Painful and discerning in equal measure, they document and theorize the unfolding of an abomination—and by articulating what has been lost or spoiled, the authors rethink what is crucial to an analytic experience—what is sacred.

In taking up the darkness of this open secret, they reclaim the analytic project in all its vulnerability and daring."

Virginia Goldner, PhD, Faculty member, NYU
Postdoctoral Program in Psychotherapy and Psychoanalysis,
and Co-Executor of Muriel Dimen's literary estate

"Sexuality has always been at the heart of psychoanalytic theory. It is ironic, in this regard, that sexual acts between analyst and patient have historically been undertheorized. For the most part, such transgressions have been covered up, ignored, denied, or simply not discussed under the umbrella of 'confidentiality.' By courageously writing about her own experience with her male analyst, Muriel Dimen opened the door for theorizing in a way that has enlightened the entire profession. Charles Levin had the wonderful idea of collecting some of the leading thinkers in psychoanalysis to share their perspectives on this ongoing problem in our field. This superb set of essays, devoted to the memory of Muriel, reflects the current state-of-the-art in psychoanalytic discourse. *Sexual Boundary Trouble in Psychoanalysis* is an extraordinary book that should be read by psychoanalysts, psychotherapists, and all others who care about the future of the psychoanalytic enterprise."

Glen O. Gabbard, author of *Boundaries and Boundary Violations in Psychoanalysis* (2016)

In memoriam: Muriel Dimen (1942–2016)

Contents

Contributors

Mark J. Blechner, PhD, is Training and Supervising Analyst at the William Alanson White Institute, and Professor and Supervisor at New York University. He has published three books: *Sex Changes: Transformations in Society and Psychoanalysis* (2009), *The Dream Frontier* (2001), and *Hope and Mortality* (1997). He is former Editor-in-Chief of the journal *Contemporary Psychoanalysis*.

Andrea Celenza, PhD, is Training and Supervising Analyst at the Boston Psychoanalytic Society and Institute, Faculty member of the Massachusetts Institute for Psychoanalysis, and Assistant Clinical Professor at Harvard Medical School. Dr. Celenza has consulted with, evaluated, supervised, or treated over 350 cases of therapist-patient sexual boundary transgressions. She has authored and presented numerous papers on the evaluation and treatment of therapists who have engaged in sexual misconduct, with a focus on training and supervisory issues. Her book, *Sexual Boundary Violations: Therapeutic, Supervisory, and Academic Contexts*, was published in 2007. Dr. Celenza is the recipient of several awards, including the Karl A. Menninger Memorial Award, the Felix & Helena Deutsch Prize and the Symonds Prize. Her most recent book is *Erotic Revelations: Clinical Applications and Perverse Scenarios* (2014). She is in private practice in Lexington, Massachusetts.

Muriel Dimen, PhD, was a pioneer in the feminist transformation of the psychoanalytic landscape. Originally trained as an anthropologist, she undertook her personal analysis early in her adult life and progressed to become a major clinical contributor to the rise of relational psychoanalysis in New York. She retired as Professor

Emeritus of Anthropology at CUNY and became Adjunct Professor of Clinical Psychology at New York University, teaching and supervising regularly in the NYU Postdoctoral Program in Psychotherapy and Psychoanalysis. She was Associate Editor of *Psychoanalytic Dialogues*, Principal Editor of *Studies in Gender and Sexuality*, and a founding board member of the International Association for Relational Psychoanalysis and Psychotherapy (IARPP). Muriel passed away in 2016.

Dianne Elise, PhD, is a Personal and Supervising Analyst and Faculty member of the Psychoanalytic Institute of Northern California, a Training Analyst member of the International Psychoanalytic Association, and a member of the Center for Advanced Psychoanalytic Studies (CAPS), Princeton. She is Associate Editor of *Studies in Gender and Sexuality*, and has served on the editorial board of the *Journal of the American Psychoanalytic Association*. Her practice is in Oakland, California.

James P. Frosch, MD, is a Training and Supervising Analyst at the Boston Psychoanalytic Society and Institute. He has taught and published papers on narcissism, on the treatment of difficult patients, and on Mafia movies. He has served on the editorial boards of both the *Journal of the American Psychoanalytic Association* and the *International Journal of Psychoanalysis*. He is on the faculty of Harvard Medical School.

Orna Guralnik, PhD, is a clinical psychologist and psychoanalyst. She is on the faculty at the National Institute for the Psychotherapies (NIP), St Luke's Roosevelt Hospital, and the Stephen Mitchell Center, and is a visiting scholar at the Psychoanalytic Institute of Northern California (PINC). She is also Co-Editor of the Psychoanalytic Dialogues blog, and an associate editor of *Psychoanalytic Dialogues* and *Studies in Gender and Sexuality*. She co-founded the Center for the Study of Dissociation and Depersonalization at the Mount Sinai Medical School, and publishes on the topics of dissociation, depersonalization, and culture. She is a graduate of the NYU Postdoctoral Program in Psychotherapy and Psychoanalysis.

Charles Levin, PhD, FIPA, is a member of the Canadian Institute of Psychoanalysis (CIP) and Director of the CIP-affiliated English psychoanalytic training program in Montreal. He is Editor-in-Chief of the *Canadian Journal of Psychoanalysis/Revue canadienne de psychanalyse*, and author, editor, and collaborator on many psychoanalytic books and articles addressing clinical, ethical, and cultural topics, including *Confidentiality: Ethical Perspectives and Clinical Dilemmas* (2003) and *Art in the Offertorium: Narcissism, Psychoanalysis and Cultural Metaphysics* (2012)

Joyce Slochower, PhD, ABPP, is Professor Emerita of Psychology at Hunter College & the Graduate Center, CUNY. Joyce is a faculty member and supervisor of the NYU Postdoctoral Program in Psychotherapy and Psychoanalysis, the Steven Mitchell Center, the National Training Program of NIP (all in New York), the Philadelphia Center for Relational Studies and the Psychoanalytic Institute of Northern California in San Francisco. She is on the editorial boards of *Psychoanalytic Dialogues, Ricerca Psicoanalitica* and *Perspectives in Psychoanalysis* and is on the board of the IARPP. Joyce has published over 80 articles on various aspects of psychoanalytic theory and technique. Second editions of her books *Holding and Psychoanalysis: A Relational Perspective* (1996) and *Psychoanalytic Collisions* (2006), were released by Routledge in 2014. She is also Co-Editor, with Lew Aron and Sue Grand, of *De-Idealizing Relational Theory: A Critique from Within* and *Decentering Relational Theory: A Comparative Critique*, both published by Routledge in 2018. She is in private practice in New York City.

Juan Tubert-Oklander, MD, PhD, was born, studied medicine, and trained as a group therapist in Buenos Aires, Argentina. Since 1976 he has lived in Mexico City, where he trained as a psychoanalyst, and where he now works in private practice. He is the author of numerous papers and book chapters, published in Spanish, English, Italian, French, Portuguese, Czech, and Hebrew. His books include *Theory of Psychoanalytic Practice: A Relational Process Approach* (2013), *The One and the Many: Relational Psychoanalysis and Group Analysis* (2014), and (with Reyna Hernández-Tubert) *Operative*

Groups: The Latin-American Approach to Group Analysis (2004). Among other affiliations, he is a full member of the Argentine Psychoanalytic Association and the International Psychoanalytical Association, Honorary Member of the Group-Analytic Society International, Founding Member of the International Field Theory Association, and Member of the IARPP.

Acknowledgments

Muriel Dimen and her work were the inspiration for this book, which is dedicated to her memory. I will always cherish the friendship we had. I am also very very grateful to my collaborators, the contributors to this book, many of whom were close to Muriel. They have been brilliant, generous, diligent, and kind.

This collection of essays came together through much dialogue among the participants, and with a great deal of personal struggle on their part, in response to some of the most difficult clinical and ethical issues facing our profession. In the end, it proved impossible to contain their number and enthusiasm in one volume of tribute to Muriel's work, and so the project had to be split in two. The present collection, *Sexual Boundary Trouble in Psychoanalysis: Clinical Perspectives on Muriel Dimen's Concept of the "Primal Crime"* emphasizes clinical issues. Its companion, *Social Aspects of Sexual Boundary Trouble in Psychoanalysis: Responses to the Work of Muriel Dimen*, emphasizes the systemic nature of the ethical problems in psychoanalytic groups and communities. Each of the chapters in both collections grew from a remarkable sense of purpose and mission, of which I was the privileged witness and beneficiary.

I want to thank in particular Adrienne Harris, whose sympathy, patience, encouragement, and dedication have been essential to me in the preparation of this work. I am also very grateful to the Executors of Muriel Dimen's literary estate, Virginia Goldner and Avgi Saketopoulou, for their gracious assistance and guidance in the editing process.

The idea that it would be a good thing for the analytic community, which includes our patients, to publish a discussion inspired by Muriel

Dimen's (2011) account of her own "training" analysis, owes much to the International Association for Relational Psychoanalysis and Psychotherapy (IARPP), and also to Mark Blechner. At that time, Blechner was the editor of *Contemporary Psychoanalysis* and was willing to publish Muriel's seminal text, "*Lapsus linguae*," featured in this volume, when other editors found it too long and controversial. Muriel's efforts, the fruit of many years of reflection and self-examination, changed the psychoanalytic landscape, being one of the first—and certainly the most comprehensive—examples of a psychoanalyst daring, in a non-sensational way, to discuss the morally less savory details of her own analysis in public.

In 2011, the IARPP held an internet colloquium on the topic of Muriel Dimen's paper. Katie Gentile and Eyal Rozmarin were the brilliant moderators of that powerful and contentious, sometimes stormy, colloquium. All the people involved in that IARPP project deserve a great deal of credit. Not least among them are the many analytic patients who contributed important and illuminating personal accounts of their own analytic experiences. Many of them, like Muriel, were also analysts. The whole IARPP community, as gathered for that occasion, did something very special and unusual that prompted me to conceptualize this book.

I am not the only author and editor in our field who is indebted to Kate Hawes at Routledge and her remarkable team working on the psychoanalytic book series. Kate is a bit of an enigma to me. How can she be so patient, and so forgiving? What I have learned is that she is personally very dedicated to keeping psychoanalysis happening and growing. Kate's staff at Taylor & Francis, especially Hannah Wright, whose editorial stewardship has been impeccable, reflect this embracing spirit. I also want to mention the editors of the Relational Perspectives Book Series, Adrienne Harris, Steven Kuchuk, Eyal Rozmarin, and the late, great Lew Aron.

The editors of *Contemporary Psychoanalysis*, *Psychoanalytic Dialogues*, and *Psychoanalytic Psychology* were very generous in granting permission to republish the material appearing in the following chapters.

Chapter 2 was originally published in *Contemporary Psychoanalysis* 47 (1): 35–79 (2011). Reprinted by permission of the William Alanson

White Institute of Psychiatry, Psychoanalysis & Psychology and the William Alanson White Psychoanalytic Society (www.wawhite.org).

Chapter 6 was originally published in *Psychoanalytic Dialogues* 25 (5): 557–571 (2015). Reprinted by permission of Taylor & Francis, LLC (www.tandfonline.com).

Chapter 7 was originally published in *Psychoanalytic Psychology* 34 (2): 195–200 (2017). Copyright 2017 American Psychological Association. Reproduced with permission.

Chapter 8 originally appeared in *Contemporary Psychoanalysis* 50 (1–2): 23–33 (2014). Reprinted by permission of the William Alanson White Institute of Psychiatry, Psychoanalysis & Psychology and the William Alanson White Psychoanalytic Society (www.wawhite.org).

One more thing: thank you, Kathi, my darling.

Chapter I

Introduction

From "Eew" to We: an overview of Muriel Dimen's contribution to psychoanalytic ethics

Charles Levin

The essays collected in *Sexual Boundary Trouble in Psychoanalysis* reflect a basic consensus within the psychoanalytic profession: that analyst-patient sexual relations constitute an extremely serious violation of professional ethics; firstly, because they are so harmful to the psychic life of the patient, thus violating the Hippocratic Oath; secondly, because they are an egregious breach of social trust, placing the profession in disrepute; and thirdly, because they do a great deal of damage to the psychoanalytic community, which includes other patients, prospective patients, colleagues, students, and all their relatives and friends.

Yet at the same time, the contributors to this volume express discomfort with this consensus—not because they disagree that sexual relations with a patient are ethically unacceptable, but because the consensus itself seems to have been formed in a rather superficial way, as a response to crises of public confidence in the closing decades of the twentieth century. We may all agree that sex with patients is "bad," but has psychoanalysis really dealt with the issue? Does the prohibition reflect genuine self-understanding, or just a blind sense of danger to the profession? Is the consensus credible as a reflection of the ethical state of psychoanalysis?

Part I: Muriel Dimen's "*Lapsus linguae*": from Eew! to We!

In voicing their discomfort around these questions, the contributors to this volume have taken inspiration from Muriel Dimen's remarkable psychoanalytic memoir (Dimen 2011), reprinted as the first part of this book. "*Lapsus linguae*" is an unusually personal but also conceptually profound exploration of the experience that we so neatly categorize as "sexual boundary violation" (SBV). In that essay, Dimen notes the immaturity of our group response to this problem: our tendency to act out the familiar (and familial?) dynamics of shame, such as cover-up and denial, self-exculpating disavowal, and stigmatization of the transgressor, whose moral dirtiness becomes an emblem of our own analytic purity (see also Dimen 2016). She draws our attention to what can only be described as our professional sociopathology, in which the "unpast" (Scarfone 2006, p. 811) of our psychosexual history as a group endlessly repeats itself. As a profession, we manage the symptoms of this syndrome with ethical codes (thus answering to public morality) and with valiant, though unfortunately isolated, individual efforts to raise awareness (and to help deal with the devastating loss of trust within certain beleaguered analytic communities, e.g., Gabbard & Peltz 2001; Celenza 2007); but we rarely ask ourselves any clear questions about what is behind this symptom of our group life, or why we keep falling into the same neurotic pattern of isolating, externalizing, and denying the significance of the disturbances in our behavior. The standard rationalization is to simultaneously individualize and depersonalize the phenomenon of sexual misconduct—to treat it as a statistically inevitable reflection of our population, something to be managed, through education and sanction, but otherwise accepted as a fact of human nature.

Muriel Dimen's work invites us to think about these and many other issues in a new vertex, inspired by her background in anthropology and contemporary feminist thought. We might call this new vertex the "We! factor," echoing her not unrelated study of the "Eew! factor" (Dimen 2005), in which she identified sexual and other forms of countertransference disgust as a problem for the analytic group rather than just the individual clinician. Writing of the Eew! factor, Dimen stated that her interest in "clinicians' sexual unease is part of a larger project, individual and collective, of reconsidering sexuality postclassically, beyond but not exclusive of the oedipal, inclusive of narcissism but registering culture too" (p. 4). She might very well have said the same about the "We! factor" in her work on sexual boundary violations. Just as in psychoanalysis "sex talk is also sexy talk ... which may threaten to violate ethics" (p. 4), so talking openly about sexual misconduct in the analytic community may be experienced as a kind of violation—an ominous disruption, rarely defined explicitly, spreading with "affective contagion."

Dimen's work can be read as an invitation for "us" to consider a new kind of "psychoanalytic we," not of the "royal" or in-group variety, but expressing psychoanalysis as a larger community, including patients. This may sound like an obviously good thing that "we" can all support, but in practice it would require analysts to make painful changes to our professional identity, our sense of who "we" are, and how we relate to each other and the interested world. To become a truly ethical community, we would have to acknowledge the Eew! at the heart of our sense of who "we" are, and put this acceptance into self-critical practice as a group, rather than merely "applying" it to our patients as knowledge already supposedly mastered.

The primal crime

With regard to the question of SBVs, Dimen finds us in a kind of ethical abyss of unresolved transference to our own profession—in the full mode of what Marx called alienation, or what might be described in intrapsychic terms as "inner estrangement" (Levin 2010). To capture this uncanny, haunted quality of our relationship to ourselves, Dimen resorts to an historically loaded phrase: "the primal crime of sexual transgression." It would be a misunderstanding to read a moralistic tone into this choice of words. Her aim is not to indict and excommunicate individual analysts who "transgress" but rather to locate the social dynamics of transgression in the origins of the profession itself. In her echo of Freud's speculative anthropology of the psyche, with its language of primal horde, primal father, and primal scene, Dimen is not trying to generate scandal or moral panic, but to disturb our professionally self-serving assumptions about the otherness of the unethical in our midst. She is suggesting that our analytic rituals are invested in the ancient logic of sacral repetition and expiation. Our general practice remains tied to mythic assumptions that tragically limit the potential for internal communication, negotiation, dialogue, and reparative (as opposed to retributive) justice (Levin in press, a,b).

If analysts' SBVs represent something "primal," as Muriel Dimen suggests, then they cannot be morally and/or ethically extraneous to psychoanalysis, i.e., "*un*psychoanalytic"; they must have been present at the origin, implicit in the formation of the psychoanalytic idea, constitutive of the profession. In effect, Dimen is drawing our attention to an embarrassing inconsistency in our self-understanding. Given that psychoanalysis is a way of thinking that established its origins in the discovery of sexual repression, how could we fail so massively, and for nearly a century, to be curious about our own sexual behavior?

The essays in this volume all in their various ways question the level of certainty implied in the confident language of SBV. The words seem to suggest not only that we have a handle on highly elusive phenomena but, more importantly, that the violation we are referring to is not something we originally intended, is not linked, in some deep and primary way, *to what psychoanalysis is really about.* The fact that certain instances of SBV are very clear—to paraphrase what the supreme court judge said of pornography, "we know it when we see it" (Greenberg 2008, p. 889)—fosters a comforting illusion that these are secondary phenomena, "aberrations," thus perpetuating the broad pattern of collective dissociation from our traumatic origins as a profession.

The concept of a sexual boundary

Swimming against this current, the thinking in this volume struggles to move behind or underneath the closure of deontological truisms. Muriel Dimen's metaphor of the primal crime becomes a new point of departure in psychoanalytic ethics, envisaging the possibility that the very idea of psychoanalysis was already a monstrous "transgression" long before the clinically specialized (as opposed to conventional social) construct of a "sexual boundary" was invented. From this perspective, indeed, the very concept of boundary seems problematic, an evasion of what is fundamentally difficult in the psychoanalytic enterprise.

A significant problem with the assumption of a sexual boundary is that it tends to privilege a behaviorally concrete definition of the ethical challenges we face. To borrow a phrase from an important French study of SBV (Urtubey 2006), the boundary approach reduces the conundrum of sexuality in the countertransference to the striking image of "l'analyste qui passe à l'acte"—the analyst who crosses over into the realm of action. On the one hand, as we know in psychoanalysis, it is impossible to establish a clear distinction between speech and action, the psychic and the somatic, the internal and the external, or the analyst and the analysand. On the other hand, in the world of actual practice and professional self-regulation, it is not realistic to dispense with behavioral definitions of what constitutes analyst abuse of professional power. We all need a moral superego image of what it is that "we *know* when we see it." Nevertheless, superego morality is not ethics; such images may simply obscure the fact that overtly sexual forms of bad practice often originate in more covert processes that may alternatively express themselves in other, less easily identifiable forms of patient coercion.

The ethical problem is not that we explicitly deny the complexity and ambiguity of our working situation; but rather that we haven't been able to find better ways to talk about them, even amongst ourselves. The ubiquitous literature on countertransference since 1950 amply illustrates this point: it ventures into the territory of what is therapeutically contraindicated (e.g., the concept of projective counter-identification; Grinberg, 1962); but it rarely engages the implications of the analyst's inevitable transference to the patient, which may be entirely malignant without being in the least way sexual in the explicit sense. Nor has there been any clear acknowledgment in our literature of an obvious related problem—what might be termed the *institutionalized negative countertransference to the patient population*, passed down through knowing words in supervision and training programs for generations. We see this first in Freud's casual denigrations and his (1937) characterization of the typical patient as a "poor helpless wretch" (*Hilflöse arme Person*—notice how Strachey converted *Person* into wretch). Some intriguing allusions to this phenomenon can be found scattered in the general literature (e.g., Langs & Searles 1980), but they have never been followed up.

In "*Lapsus linguae,*" Muriel Dimen illustrates the moral complexity of the analytic situation, and of her own first analysis, in exquisite detail. She and her analyst tumbled into a problematic and ambiguous, sexually charged physical exchange at the end of the last session before a long weekend—but it turns out that this was just a surface phenomenon signaling a much more serious relational deformation. For Dimen, the ethical problem had more to do with the fact that her analyst did not acknowledge in any emotionally helpful way that this sexually explicit interaction had even occurred. In her recounting of the event and its aftermath, Dimen struggles over the fact that she was also unable to speak about it, or even to think about what was really happening in her analysis. What she emphasizes, in her painful but lucid reflections on her own history, is that the physical slip of the tongue was not the ultimate locus of the psychic invasion she suffered as an analysand. The analyst's literally intrusive sexual behavior was "over the line," as we say, but only briefly "out of control." What Dimen suffered was more profound, something potentially more troubling for us: a betrayal more massive and surreptitious than the analyst's symptomatic parapraxis.

How to describe this more consequential invasion of the analysand's psychic life? Is it really best characterized as a *sexual* boundary violation? Is the matter in question even "sexual"? Or is it a manifestation of another kind of "boundary trouble" that goes unrecognized, though it lies at the heart of the entire psychoanalytic enterprise? Dimen's anxiously nuanced reflections on her own experience suggest that while the problem in this, her first analysis, was obviously related to sexual dynamics, something much more insidious than sexual attraction, sexual desire, or transference love was at work.

An attentive reading of her text strongly suggests that the toxic factor in her analysis was not the sexual interplay but rather the analyst's programmatic deployment of the analytic setting as a stage for the rationalization of his unexamined (and I would argue professionally sanctioned) narcissism. The beauty of Dimen's account is that she renders moot the speculative question of whether her analyst's narcissism was malignant and/or predatory, or merely neurotic and circumstantial. (In online discussions of her paper [IARPP Colloquium, 2011] there was a lot of debate about this.) Rather, she makes a persuasive case, without directly stating it, that his analytic style was probably a fairly typical instance of the prevailing patriarchal culture of psychoanalysis, regardless of the "school" in which he was trained and practiced. The slip—and, more importantly, the failure ever to acknowledge it—were revealing symptoms, not so much of the analyst's precise character structure as of the organization and practice of psychoanalysis itself.

How can we even begin to contemplate the implications of such a radical proposition? The answers elaborated in this book bring varied methods and perspectives to bear on that question, but all agree that the problems facing psychoanalysis cannot be resolved by appeal to, or by mere application of, an outward facing ethics or deontology. The issue is not whether there should be rules and moral standards, codes and sanctions—these are necessary and inevitable because no profession can function ethically as an autonomous social entity (Michels 1976). The question is whether the analytic community should continue to function internally as if such principles and procedures are sufficient from a psychoanalytic perspective.

The difficulties of ethical self-reflection in the group

The import of the papers gathered in this collection can be summarized in the following way. First, that "the primal crime of sexual transgression" is not just something that psychoanalysis objectively identifies, uncovers, and analyzes; it is something that psychoanalysis actually does without realizing that it is doing it. Second, that the only way for psychoanalysis to come to grips with this deeply embarrassing but potentially useful and constitutive fact is to surrender and accept failure of mastery in its own domain. Third, we need to reimagine psychoanalysis as a way of trying to understand not only individuals, but individuals in "groups," the group in the individual, and collective phenomena in their own right; notably (in the inaugural traditional of self-analysis; Freud 1900), we need to overcome the inhibition/prohibition against revealing our collective fantasies and "analyzing" them together. This is the new We! factor.

We need to acknowledge that Freud's "discovery" of the unconscious does not establish an exclusive and privileged object domain, accessible only to the properly trained analyst according to an exclusive method. If Laplanche (1997), following Macalpine (1950) and others, is right that psychoanalysis requires a seduction of the patient, the latter cannot be ascribed simply (and self-exculpatingly) to infantile regression induced intentionally by the setting, and under the control of the analyst. This is not just a pleasant Winnicottian trope. If there is a generic regression involved in analysis, it most certainly involves both parties (Scarfone 2010). In Laplanche's terms, the "otherness" of the unconscious, and its origins in the enigmatic sexual messaging of the adult world, do not stop with the patient. The patient is also other to the analyst, and the analyst too is struggling with enigmatic messages which cannot be reduced to "counter" transference. The embedded history of the "primal crime" in psychoanalysis (Gabbard 1995) challenges us to question the adequacy of any particular version of analytic technique, because it opens up the further question, not only of the analyst's intrapsychic life, but also of his or her potential immersion in transpersonal, social, and energic fields of force—the barely explored psychic dimensions of collective life. As Dimen tried very hard to help us understand, we still lack the metapsychology of culture required to work these problems through at the institutional level, in our training, our practice, and our self-governance (see also Grand 2017).

Within the presumptive context of an individual unconscious capable of containment, it once made sense to define sexual misconduct in roughly the same manner that traffic violations are set by an explicit code with clear geographic demarcations and quantitative limits. Within that context, the appeal to the unconscious effectively reinforces the validity of psychoanalytic-ethical "rules," favoring but not necessarily requiring an authoritarian and exclusionary style of enforcement. There is an issue of personal responsibility, and given the human capacity for self-deception (Gabbard 2008) resistance to the one-person model faces problems of credibility, not to mention seemingly insurmountable administrative and legal impediments. As Dimen (2005, 2016) has shown, the Eew! factor manifests as individual psychology but actually functions surreptitiously at the group level. It naturally hinders recognition of the group's responsibility, and the secondary gain for the group of its exclusionary dynamics. Without a capacity for collective self-reflection, the potential for a responsible "We!" remains dominated by the dynamics of "Eew!"

If we now consider the unconscious as an intersubjective or transpersonal phenomenon, it is all the more puzzling that the traditional one-person ethics have not been reviewed at the level of the group. One problem is that the currently fashionable two-person model does not necessarily translate into serious thinking about groups any more than does the so-called one-person model. Object relations theory and self psychology, even intersubjective systems theory, all maintain the unconscious as internal to the individual—or internal to a primary dyadic constellation of the individual. This makes it easy for us to continue conceptualizing SBV as highly localized in the personalities of individual patient and analyst, ignoring the larger group dimension. But there has been a silent revolution in analytic theory which goes beyond the usual focus on universal mental contents or developmental processes. I am thinking of implicit modifications still relatively unformulated, in the countertransference revolution of the 1950s, beginning with Heimann (1950) and Racker (1968); the related emergence of field theory, stemming essentially from the marriage of Marx and Bion in Latin America (Baranger & Baranger 2008); the advent of relational thinking, as an organized response to medical authoritarianism in the profession (Mitchell 1988); and, perhaps most tellingly, the shift from an "archeological" model of the unconscious to what Levine (2010), for example, calls the "transformational or constructive model of analytic interaction" (p. 1388).

In the latter conceptualizations of the analytic relationship, it is tacitly recognized that the analyst's suggestion (read seduction), both conscious and unconscious, necessarily comes into play from the very beginning of the process, even during the evaluation of the patient's suitability for analytic therapy (or the candidate's suitability to become an analyst). As Levine states, "Once the analyst's conviction is implicated as a motivational element in the process of recommending and helping patients to accept the recommendation to enter analysis, we are forced to recognize the extent to which these processes are dependent on factors which are unconscious, intersubjective and co-determined" (p. 1391). The question then remains: where does the "analyst's conviction" come from? Is it based only on clinical experience? Or is it pre-constituted by the social environment and the educational culture in which the analyst was "trained"? What other factors in addition to therapeutic conviction enter into the analyst's unconscious messaging to the patient at the outset of analysis?

Searching for the responsible "We": the problem of love in psychoanalysis

The analyst as co-participant in the analytic process belongs to what Cooper (2010), with intentional *double entendre*, has described as "a disturbance in the field." Recent relational reformulations of the analytic relationship and process hint strongly that the psychoanalytic enterprise is socially determined and that best practice is relative to the cultural ground that is always already shifting under our feet (Dimen 2012). The idea of an unconscious "field" seems to throw every aspiration for clear ethical boundaries into question. Whatever a sexual boundary might turn out to be, we can be sure, given our present knowledge, that psychoanalysis had already crossed it as soon as Freud dared to turn his investigation of unconscious phenomena into a paid service, provided by a professional agent who was interested in the sexuality of his patients. Indeed, psychoanalysis could fairly be described as a technically sophisticated, socially sanctioned, interpersonally self-conscious attempt to *operationalize human boundary trouble.* Or, to modify Muriel Dimen's phrase, psychoanalysis is *"organized primal crime"!*

The proximity of psychoanalysis to the erotic love relationship is, of course, central to Freud's original contributions. But when he remarked (Freud 1909) that the Rat Man's doubt was "in reality a doubt of his own love—which ought to be the most certain thing in his own life ... A man who doubts his own love may, or rather *must*, doubt every lesser thing" (p. 241), Freud was also invoking a dimension of love that we now imagine more confidently than he as fundamental (if not always available) to human development (Natterson 2016). Though variant in their accounts, all schools of analytic thought, from Klein to attachment theory, seem to agree in principle with Freud's (1914) proposition that while "strong egoism is a protection against falling ill ... in the last resort we must begin to love in order not to fall ill, and we are bound to fall ill if ... we are unable to love" (p. 85).

As organized primal crime, psychoanalysis deliberately sets out to experiment with the philosophical theory of love as a generative category, to play with loving feelings as organizers of human life. Unlike religion, we do not try to mobilize this love into large and potentially dangerous groups (Freud 1921). But psychoanalysis does place every patient's love on the existential brink—one might even say on the sexual boundary—by demonstrating love in action as a kind of category mistake (transference), an inherent conflation of logical levels and psychological layers. Love in psychoanalysis unwittingly becomes a narrative amalgam of needs and cultural conventions whose positive valence ("love makes the world go round") still somehow maintains a slim hold on faith in the cultural evolution of humankind.

In *"Lapsus linguae,"* Dimen locates the highest expression of the analyst's love for the patient in the capacity to contain and abide transference (in both directions). Agreeing in essence with Benjamin (1988), Freud (1915), Gabbard and Lester (1995), and Celenza (2007, 2014), among many others, she frames the patient's love for the analyst as a struggle for recognition and individuation, which at all costs must never be co-opted or exploited by the analyst. In this, Dimen comes as close as we have seen in conventional terms to the true meaning of a sexual boundary in psychoanalysis.

> One of those predictable life wounds that Freud warns about, the suffering of unrequited love, is also key to a certain freedom: having endured it, one both gains oneself and is spared the unbelievable confusion attendant on one's desires being granted by the very other from whose desires one is trying to free oneself. One is granted the room to create oneself as if one were autonomous.
>
> (p. 60; this volume, p. 51)

Dimen's eloquent elaboration of this emotional-developmental insight sheds new light on Hans Loewald's (1960/2000) description of the analyst as guardian of "the patient's emerging core." In proposing this, he had redefined the "essence" of objectivity and neutrality in psychoanalysis as "love and respect for the individual and individual development" (p. 229).

Speaking of the hypnotic ambiguity of love in psychoanalysis, Lear (1990) stated that it is "only from an external perspective that what we have [in the love relationship] are two people ... it is not that he [the patient] is falling in love with another person; he is falling in love with a world that infuses him" (p. 198). The pervasiveness implied in Freud's "Introduction of Eros" (Lear 1998) positions the analyst at the radical joint between "narcissism and socialism" (Bion 1992, pp. 104–106), loss of boundaries and creation of boundaries, "destruction as cause of coming into being" (Spielrein 1912/1994). Ultimately, what Lear seems to be hinting at is an idea of love as a cultural infusion of psychic life—a Freudian variation on field theory. Does our reluctance to pursue these ethically ambiguous propositions about psychoanalysis reflect an underlying sense of social and historical guilt? Could it be that in our offer of psychoanalysis we are implicitly asking our patients to violate culturally regulated definitions of significant boundaries—not just sexual in the behavioral sense—including the socially acceptable limits of personality and thought?

To compound the embarrassment of our failure to be curious about these uncanny dimensions of the "primal crime," Dimen nudges the analytic reader toward another outrageous idea: that all psychoanalysts inherit and recreate, at the professional level, through their idealizing aspirations and their disappointing experiences of analytic training (Levin 2014), an identity disorder. This disorder expresses something very troubling for our conventional self-understanding, yet at the same time it is central to it: that psychoanalysis is practiced by people who, for whatever reason, need to embody a cultural crisis. That we are so positioned is intelligible in terms of Freud's patriarchal master narrative of infantile wishing and paternal infanticide, or the idea that every child is somewhat violently "seduced" into an "adult" world, and we can make sense of it as a phylogenetic crisis if we reread *Oedipus* through Claude Lévi-Strauss (1949/1969): the incest taboo as an undecidable "boundary" between nature and human culture. In his essay on transference love (Freud 1915), Freud implicitly reframed this cultural crisis as that nagging question so pervasive, yet difficult to pose, in human experience: is *love* real?

Part 2: boundary trouble in the psychoanalytic process

Andrea Celenza's contribution searches for an answer to this question, delving right into the enigmatic messaging systems of professional ethical evasion. Her extensive clinical experience working with sexual transgressors (Celenza 2007) enables her to provide a unique window on psychoanalytic boundary trouble. Conceptualizing the history of psychoanalysis as "a series of erasures," she provides a comprehensive taxonomy of willful and unconscious self-blinding in the field. Her chapter integrates multiple dimensions of the analyst's working situation, ranging from biases in competing ideals of the analytic stance (and the associated liabilities of the analyst's concordant and complementary identifications with these) to questions of institutionalized power that feed into various perverse scenarios underlying SBV. Celenza's work in this area, in coordination with a handful of pioneers, represents the best of the ethics revolution in late-twentieth-century psychoanalysis: clinically based research that generates basic ethical principles from the inherent characteristics and aims of the treatment situation itself. From its inception (Gabbard 1989, 1996), this research tradition has placed the problem of love at the center of our concerns. Fittingly, Celenza (2014), arguably our leading authority today on the use and abuse of erotics in psychoanalysis, concludes her essay with an original reflection on the ambiguous place of love in the analytic process.

Staying with the problem of unrequited love as posed by Muriel Dimen in "*Lapsus linguae*," Orna Guralnik sharpens the focus, entering what readers may experience as a kind of virtual dialogue with Celenza. For both writers, the realization of love in the analytic process relies critically on the analyst's commitment to the frame, which Guralnik likens to a social contract. Its collapse into SBV turns the analyst's love into what Celenza calls the "fundamental violation"— not so much the sex but rather "the lie," a kind of poisoned gift. Guralnik highlights the social dimension of the primal crime:

> Every seemingly private instance of the analyst's violation is actually a cultural and social action that reverberates throughout the contractual web [of society], corroding the ethical specificity of psychoanalysis as a discipline that in its pure form is about suspending rather than enacting normative assumptions about relations of power.

Echoing Celenza's concern with the intrapsychic life of the analyst, Guralnik zeroes in on the precise nature of the analyst's commitment to protect the analytic space of "enchantment." For Guralnik, the object of desire is always socially constructed and never pre-discursive. This means that the analyst's sexual desire for a patient cannot be merely natural, an instance of rogue true love expressing authenticity and independence from the prevailing culture or the "social contract" (a frequent rationale for SBV). Rather, it signals a failure to internalize the analytic boundaries that define patients as sexually unavailable, just as post-Oedipal desire desexualizes infantile objects so that "they do not need to be renounced over and over" (Guralnik, this volume). To remain true to the therapeutic promise of analysis, the analyst needs to be deeply, almost characterologically identified with the frame; as

Guralnik puts it, one cannot really do analysis through the medium of an "unintegrated super-ego introject." If the analyst is pretending, if the analyst is an "as if" analyst, then the transitional, "as if" quality of the pretend space that we try to create and curate—the space that allows the emergence of unconscious life—will be compromised.

Thus both Guralnik and Celenza arrive at similar conclusions, though perhaps from different starting points. Guralnik emphasizes that psychoanalytic work requires a profound internalization and identification with vocational discipline. This would imply that psychoanalytic training should aim for a significant change in the personality, which she compares to the dissolution of the Oedipus complex. Some might question whether this degree of internalization of the analytic ideal is desirable or realistic. Nevertheless, both Guralnik and Celenza understand psychoanalytic identity as the product of a loving, rather than authoritarian, process of education, fostering the deconstruction of identifications with power and authority, rather than strategies for hiding behind and exploiting them.

James Frosch continues the investigation of inherent tensions in analysis, exploring in greater depth the theme of the analyst's "denial of limits." Assuming that no analyst, regardless of character and training, is exempt from the lures and traps of ordinary narcissism, Frosch places the transgressing analyst on a continuum with all analysts. Arguing that a critical factor in the event of boundary trouble is the *analyst*'s capacity to mourn the loss of an ideal object or ideal self, Frosch extends this consideration to psychoanalysis *per se*: even the most careful attention to ethical guidelines (seeking consultations, for example) may be insufficient to avoid unresolvable impasses. As Frosch demonstrates in his clinical examples, boundary trouble occurs in all kinds of ordinary ways that elude our capacity for self-analysis and self-monitoring. Psychoanalysis necessarily involves the cultivation of a problematic "uneasy intimacy," a term Frosch borrows from Crastnopol: "it always has powerful elements of the desire to seduce and be seduced." Reflecting on Muriel Dimen's experience with her analyst, Dr. O, and echoing her call for the integration of skepticism in the analytic ethos, Frosch concludes with a plea for moderation in theory and practice: "the best one can hope for is that the acceptance of the existence of such narcissistic desire can pave the way for an understanding of the enactments it creates."

This grouping of chapters concludes with Dianne Elise's unusual clinical report and devastating portrait of "collateral damage" (Wallace 2010; Young 2014) in psychoanalytic communities affected by SBV. This has been a neglected area in both our clinical and ethical literature, and Elise comes to it fully prepared to break new ground, drawing on personal experiences and extensive analytic work with patients abandoned by their former analysts, who had either ceased to practice or been suspended by their institute following the substantiation of an ethical complaint against them—"a unique pairing in a very troubled circumstance."

As the "subsequent analyst" in the wake of various kinds of analytic betrayal, Elise was faced clinically with the very delicate task of helping patients to overcome inevitable splitting and to somehow integrate "what was good about the treatment relationship with the former analyst while being able to trust one's experience about what was problematic and harmful." The difficulty of the situation for the individual analyst (in parallel with the entire analytic community, as Elise recognizes), is compounded by the traumatic loss of trust in psychoanalysis itself. Proceeding from an insightful reading of Dimen's "*Lapsus linguae*," Elise explores the extensive psychic damage incurred through such iatrogenic disruptions of the analysand's faith in goodness, both internal and external: there is a dislocation in time, with confusion of autobiographical memory, and loss of both past and future as vital dimensions of ongoing life; there is also severe disorientation in social space, with loss of relational spontaneity, and a loss of trust in one's own reality testing, moral judgment, and security of person. Such analysands deeply suspect not only the subsequent analyst but also their own analyzability.

Part 3: boundary trouble in the analytic community

Joyce Slochower, writing—like most contributors to this volume—from painful personal experience, develops a comprehensive perspective on what she describes as "the malignant underbelly" of our professional ideal. With careful attention to all sides of this question, the reasons—good and bad—for our disavowals, our silences, and our rationalizations around SBV, she builds a picture of our community that highlights the binding (but also double-binding) power of idealization. Meanwhile, in conjunction with the powerful force of idealization, silence and gossip (*lashon hara*) go hand in hand. Legal constraints on open discussion combine with private shame and paranoia to create an atmosphere of mystification and even a kind of self-inflicted gaslighting of the "wider professional community and, particularly, candidates in training." She suggests pointedly that "we in the community fail to contain violations because we're invested in them." Notice again the emphasis on the first person plural—"we in the community." "No analytic theory entirely protects us … protection … lies instead in community." But Slochower's appeal for us to break the silence, she admits, implies another kind of idealization—an "ideal speech situation" (Habermas 2001) that may still seem impossible in practice. "Can we find a way," she asks, "to create our own version of the South African Truth and Reconciliation Commission? … We need to revisit our relationship to our personal and professional ideals and make peace with the limitations of this profession."

Mark Blechner's "Dissociation among psychoanalysts about sexual boundary violations" clinches all the foregoing arguments for collective responsibility with a factual discussion of a "primary inconsistency" in our thinking about SBV—"the disconnection between the official and private attitudes of members of our profession." Blechner documents collective dissociation of SBV as the historical norm for psychoanalysis. He outlines three basic ethical positions, two of which are pervasive, although they contradict the official psychoanalytic prohibition on sexual relations with patients. One of these is an attitude of acceptance of SBV, either through relativistic arguments (e.g., sex with a patient is ethically justified if the analyst marries the patient) or through advocacy of the therapeutic value of sexual relations with a patient. The second is what Blechner cogently describes as "the empathic-sentimental position," in which unofficial sympathy for "romance and true love" serves as a fuzzy rationalization for a history of boundary violations involving many idealized figures within the profession and many dissociative responses at the local level.

If our boundary troubles call into question the way we conceptualize the foundations of psychoanalysis (see especially Levin in press, a,b), how do we square this with the standard prohibition on SBV? In his "Do we really need boundaries?" Juan Tubert-Oklander struggles to find a satisfying answer. He begins with a reflection on the unconscious, viewing it in Matte-Blanco's terms as the massive and largely ungovernable presence of symmetrical thinking in what is otherwise supposed to be, in the analytic setting and frame, an asymmetrical helping relationship: "Most of the analytic relationship will be necessarily symmetrical, unbounded, and non-ethical. It is up to the analyst, standing in the no man's land between symmetry and asymmetry, to strive to preserve the former, while always taking into account the latter." Recognizing the need for clear rules with respect to the analyst's temptation to exploit the patient—as Guralnik (this volume) observes, these are built into the very idea of the frame, and need to be understood as a kind of social contract—Tubert-Oklander adds that analytic work cannot be grounded in such a rule; nor can it rely on a good enough training analysis to shield the analyst from self-deception. He suggests rather that it be "part and parcel of every analysis" to revisit the question, "why should the analyst abstain?" The analyst needs to stay in that interzone, leaving the constitutive questions open and unanswered, requiring in each case "a major ethical reflection." Like Saketopoulou (in press), Tubert-Oklander does not mean by this that we should dispense with the prohibition against sexual relations with patients; the important issues lie on another level— the ethical nature of the analytic process itself. For Tubert-Oklander, as I read him, this requires something equivalent to Bion's "without memory and desire." Given the need to engage the symmetrical unconscious with each patient, there is a beneficial sense in which the analyst would try to begin every analysis without remembering the rules or desiring to be a "good" analyst. In a good enough analysis, everything we think we know in order to provide a good analysis needs to be relearned in relation to this particular patient, including psychoanalytic ethics. To paraphrase Adam Phillip's popular aphorism (but giving it a very different meaning): "psychoanalysis is what happens when two people discover the reasons why they didn't have sex."

Like Frosch, Slochower, and others in this volume, Tubert-Oklander also addresses "the high incidence of other kinds of abuse ... the aggressive, economic, political, academic, or narcissistic exploitation of patients ... frequently more subtle than sexual acting out ... but ... no less noxious." His discussion sheds sober light on the history of analytic training institutions. He singles out Muriel Dimen's striking portrait of the abjection of the analytic patient, an emblem of the devaluation of care for both self and other, as reflected in the perverse idealization of individual self-sufficiency that still permeates psycho-analytic ideology and contemporary neo-liberal politics.

References

Baranger, M. & Baranger, W. (2008). The analytic situation as a dynamic field. *International Journal of Psychoanalysis* 89: 795–826.
Benjamin, J. (1988). *The bonds of love: Psychoanalysis, feminism, and the problem of domination*. New York: Pantheon.
Bion, W.R. (1992). *Cogitations*. London: Karnac.
Celenza, A. (2007). *Sexual boundary violations: Therapeutic, supervisory, and academic contexts.* New York: Jason Aronson.
Celenza, A (2014). *Erotic revelations: Clinical applications and perverse scenarios*. London and New York: Routledge.
Cooper, S. (2010). *A disturbance in the field*. London and New York: Routledge.
Dimen, M. (2005). Sexuality and suffering, or the Eew! factor. *Studies in Gender and Sexuality* 6: 1–18.
Dimen, M. (2011). *Lapsus linguae*, or a slip of the tongue? A sexual violation in an analytic treatment and its personal and theoretical aftermath. *Contemporary Psychoanalysis* 47 (1): 35–79.
Dimen, M., Ed. (2012). *With culture in mind*. London and New York: Routledge.
Dimen, M. (2016). Rotten apples and ambivalence: Sexual boundary violations through a psychocultural lens. *Journal of the American Psychoanalytic Association* 64 (2): 361–373.
Freud, S. (1900). The interpretation of dreams. *The standard edition of the complete psychological works of Sigmund Freud* (vols. 4 & 5). London: Hogarth Press.
Freud, S. (1909). Notes upon a case of obsessional neurosis. *The standard edition of the complete psychological works of Sigmund Freud* (vol. 10, pp. 151–318). London: Hogarth Press.
Freud, S. (1914). On narcissism: An introduction. *The standard edition of the complete psychological works of Sigmund Freud* (vol. 14, pp. 73–102). London, Hogarth Press
Freud, S. (1915). Observations on transference love. *The standard edition of the complete psychological works of Sigmund Freud* (vol. 15, pp. 159–171). London: Hogarth Press.
Freud, S. (1921). Group psychology and the analysis of the ego. *The standard edition of the complete psychological works of Sigmund Freud* (vol. 18, pp. 69–143). London: Hogarth Press.

Freud, S. (1937). Constructions in analysis. *The standard edition of the complete psychological works of Sigmund Freud* (vol. 23, pp. 255–269). London: Hogarth Press.

Gabbard, G.O. (1989). *Sexual exploitation in professional relationships.* Washington, DC: American Psychiatric Press.

Gabbard, G.O. (1995). The early history of boundary violations in psychoanalysis. *Journal of the American Psychoanalytic Association*, 43: 1115–1136.

Gabbard, G.O. (1996). *Love and hate in the analytic setting.* New York: Jason Aronson.

Gabbard, G.O. (2008). Boundaries, technique, and self-deception: A discussion of Arnold Goldberg's "Some limits of the boundary concept". *Psychoanalytic Quarterly* 77: 877–881.

Gabbard, G.O. & Lester, E. (1995). *Boundaries and boundary violations in psychoanalysis.* New York: Basic Books.

Gabbard, G.O. & Peltz, M. (2001). Speaking the unspeakable: Institutional reactions to boundary violations by training analysts. *Journal of the American Psychoanalytic Association* 49 (2): 659–673.

Grand, S. (2017). Selective excess: Erotic transformations, secret predations. *Psychoanalytic Psychology*, 24(2): 208–214.

Greenberg, J. (2008). Right destination, wrong path. *Psychoanalytic Quarterly* 77: 883–890.

Grinberg, L. (1962). On a specific aspect of countertransference due to the patient's projective identification. *International Journal of Psychoanalysis* 43: 436–440.

Habermas, J. (2001). *On the pragmatics of social interaction: Preliminary studies in the theory of communicative action.* B. Fultner (Trans.). Cambridge, MA: MIT Press.

Heimann, P. (1950). On countertransference. *International Journal of Psychoanalysis* 31: 81–84.

IARPP (2011). *Colloquium 18: Muriel Dimen's "Lapsus Linguae, or a Slip of the Tongue?".* May 9–22. Retrieved from http://iarpp.net/colloquium/muriel-dimens-lapsus-linguae-or-a-slip-of-the-tongue-a-sexual-violation-in-an-analytic-treatment-and-its-personal-and-theoretical-aftermath/

Langs, R. & Searles, H. (1980). *Intrapsychic and interpersonal dimensions of treatment: A critical dialogue.* New York: Jason Aronson.

Laplanche, J. (1997). The theory of seduction and the problem of the other. *International Journal of Psychoanalysis* 78: 653–666.

Lear, J. (1990). *Love and its place in nature: A philosophical interpretation of Freudian psychoanalysis.* New York: Farrar, Straus & Giroux.

Lear, J. (1998). The Introduction of Eros: Reflections on the work of Hans Loewald. In *Open minded: Working out the logic of the soul* (pp. 122–147). Cambridge, MA: Harvard University Press.

Lévi-Strauss, C. (1949/1969), *The Elementary Structures of Kinship.* New York: Eyre & Spottiswode.

Levin, C. (2010). The mind as a complex internal object: Inner estrangement. *Psychoanalytic Quarterly* 79 (1): 95–127.

Levin, C. (2014). Trauma as a way of life in a psychoanalytic institute. In R. Deutsch (Ed.), *Traumatic ruptures: Abandonment and betrayal in the analytic relationship* (pp. 176–196). New York: Routledge,.

Levin, C. (in press,a). Social preconditions of psycho-sexual violations in psychoanalysis: Reflections on the ethics of Muriel Dimen. In C. Levin (Ed.), *Social aspects of sexual boundary trouble in psychoanalysis: Responses to the work of Muriel Dimen.* London and New York: Routledge.

Levin, C. (in press,b). Boundary trouble in the psychoanalytic republic: Reflections on Muriel Dimen's concept of the primal crime. In C. Levin (Ed.), *Social aspects of sexual boundary trouble in psychoanalysis: Responses to the work of Muriel Dimen.* London & New York: Routledge.

Levine, H. (2010). Creating analysts, creating patients. *International Journal of Psychoanalysis* 91: 1385–1404.

Loewald, H. (1960/2000). On the therapeutic action of psychoanalysis. In *The Essential Loewald: Collected Papers and Monographs.* Hagerstown, MD: University Publishing Group, pp. 221–256.

Macalpine, I. (1950). The development of the transference. *Psychoanalytic Quarterly* 19: 501–539.

Michels, R. (1976). Professional ethics and social values. *International Review of Psychoanalysis* 3: 377–384.

Mitchell, S. (1988). *Relational concepts in psychoanalysis: An integration.* Cambridge, MA: Harvard University Press.

Natterson, J. (2016). The loving self: A theoretical and practical concept. *Canadian Journal of Psychoanalysis/Revue canadienne de psychanalyse* 23 (2): 337–356.

Racker, H. (1968). *Transference and countertransference.* Madison, CT: International Universities Press.

Saketopoulou, A. (in press). Does the sexual have anything to do with sexual boundary violations? In C. Levin (Ed.), *Social aspects of sexual boundary trouble in psychoanalysis: Responses to the work of Muriel Dimen.* London and New York: Routledge.

Scarfone, D. (2006). A matter of time: Actual time and the production of the past. *Psychoanalytic Quarterly* 75: 807–834.

Scarfone, D. (2010). In the hollow of the transference: The analyst's position between activity and passivity. *Sitegeist* 4: 7–20.

Spielrein, S. (1912/1994). Destruction as the cause of coming into being. *Journal of Analytical Psychology* 39: 155–186.

Urtubey, L. de (2006). *Si l'analyste passe à l'acte*. Paris: Presses Universitaires de France.

Wallace, E. (2010). Collateral damage: Long-term effects of losing a training analyst for ethical violations. *Canadian Journal of Psychoanalysis/Revue canadienne de psychanalyse* 18: 248–254.

Young, C. (2014). Collateral damage: the fallout from analyst loss due to ethical violations. In R. Deutsch (Ed.), *Traumatic ruptures: Abandonment and betrayal in the analytic relationship* (pp. 109–125). New York: Routledge.

Part 1

The primal crime

Chapter 2

Lapsus linguae, or a slip of the tongue?

A sexual violation in an analytic treatment and its personal and theoretical aftermath

Muriel Dimen

Introduction: the hug and the hard-on

When I was a graduate student in anthropology, long before I thought of becoming a clinician, I entered treatment with an impeccably credentialed psychoanalyst. I was 26 and it was 1968, an era of political, personal, cultural, and intellectual change, but in which women's sexual subjectivity was still officially less than their own. In November 1973, I was about to attend an annual anthropology conference (I was by then an assistant professor), set on sleeping with a man I'd met the previous year. Off and on, I'd been sharing this plan with Dr. O and was now relating my excitement, fear, and adulterous guilt. Though I'd often discussed sex, I see, looking back, that this was the first time I was owning my sexual intentionality. Doubtless, feminism and the so-called "sexual revolution" (aided by the 1960s birth-control pills and New York State's 1973 legalization of abortion) were, for me, synergizing with psychoanalysis to recuperate a way of self-knowing that had been closed off for too long, an unthought-known reason I'd sought treatment.

The session ended, Dr. O walked me to the door, I said, "I'm scared, I want a hug." (This was not the first hug: in the spring of the preceding year, when I was grieving my father's death, he sat on the couch to put his arm around me.) As I was ending the embrace, I kissed his cheek; I do not know whether there'd been a kiss before, but I don't think so. And then he said, and this was a definite first—and last—"No, how about a real kiss?" So—it wasn't even a question, because, as the quip goes, there's a "trance" in "transference"—I kissed his mouth. He returned the favor with his tongue—at which point, I recall—as I write—a feeling of shock, and then a feeling of ignoring the shock.

He chuckled: "Oops, I'm getting a hard-on, I better stop." In me, nothing or, rather, awareness of nothing. Call it a confusion of tongues.

I left, went to the conference, had disappointing intercourse, never saw the guy again, returned to analysis, did not speak of the hug or the hard-on or the French kiss, and never did anything like it again in a treatment that lasted for seven more years. Dr. O did not mention it either.

Dr. O's professional background made his silence odd. Had he been classically trained, we might deem his lack of speech technically mandated: no matter what the analyst does, it's the patient's perception of it that matters and is in need of investigation (Brenner, 1979). The ordinarily loquacious Dr. O, however, held the analyst to be a person just like the patient: the analyst is not a cipher but a contributor to the relationship. And he regarded the patient as responsible, an adult like the analyst. He believed the psychoanalyst should routinely acknowledge and sometimes even discuss the patient's reception of the analyst's particular presence. Had Dr. O stuck to his last, however, the treatment would have soon ended. Instead, it was prolonged by the silence vitiating it.

Dr. O, you should know, fed me well. His voice and cadence, familiar to me from my mother's, were a comfort. And, unlike my father, whose narcissism took a different path, Dr. O listened. *A man who listened.* O brave new world! That was enough, a phallic presence with a mothering heart. Gender and power were never more beautifully married, a solution that, needless to say, became a problem. My transference neurosis—call it penis or, better, phallus envy—was that his masculinity would free my own voice. Nestled in this powerful patriarchal transference—was it love?—I grew. In the idealizing glow of his care and modeling, an engaged, engaging, vocal self, abandoned early on, returned. My confidence burnished, I wrote my first book (Dimen-Schein, 1977), switched careers from anthropology to psychoanalysis, and left my marriage.

All this took place next door to a profound dissociation. I would go to sessions with what I privately called "hopeless hope." Blind faith, I would call it now that I can think. Unconsciously, that's where I wanted to stay, and indeed could stay, because, absent symbolization, *nothing* had happened and no time had passed. Sometimes I think of myself as having been a Lorenz gosling (Brigandt, 2005), as one is in deep analysis. Except that's how I was from the initial phone call and apparently that's how I wanted to remain, in a state of total trust and worship, that necessary but dangerous state of attachment (Bowlby, 1982) we call "imprinting" (Brigandt, 2005). Dr. O's silence not only enhanced dissociation and protected me from the shame that blankets fear, it drew on and intensified the originary trance.

I always remembered the hug and the hard-on, I always recalled that tongue slipping into my mouth, but I couldn't sort any of it out. The memory lived without affect, as though in two dimensions. Post-Dr. O, whenever I tried to go beyond the mere recounting of who did what to whom, I would feel only hunger and an overwhelming sadness that led to an obsessive questioning of every other turning point in my life. Attempting to manage this painful flood alone, I could not locate a chain of significance. More precisely, what happened between Dr. O and me had not been an object of knowledge until I wrote about it and had the exchange afforded by writing and speaking with the psycho-analytic community and others. It simply *was*. In the absence of mutu-ality (Aron, 1996; Benjamin, 1988), feeling could not be contained (Bion, 1962/1967), knowledge (Ogden, 1994) could not coalesce, nor could there evolve an "I" to hold the self-shards together (Bromberg, 1996; Rivera, 1989).

Because an enormous ambiguity surrounds and infuses Dr. O's lapse, it seemed sensible to entitle this article "*Lapsus linguae.*" Literally this phrase translates as "a slip of the tongue," an expression giving my second title, which I have in turn put as a question, because what went on in that treatment is not at all limpid (indeed, were it so, this long article would have been unnecessary). In psychoanalysis, we apply the rather concrete Greek *parapraxis* (an act or deed gone wrong; Freud's *Fehlleistung* (faulty action; Strachey, 1901/1960) to that which *lapsus linguae* connotes.

The Latin, in contrast, simmers with imagery; according to the *Oxford Latin Dictionary* (Glare, 1982, p. 1002), "*lapsus* can have sev-eral senses [in historical order]: (1) simply falling down or slipping; (2) a smooth gliding motion, e.g., slithering, creeping; (3) a fall from favor or high rank; (4) the fact of falling into error or misconduct, fail-ing, lapse" (Schein, 2010). This layer-cake of meanings seems apt: the slithering tongue, the fall from grace, the creepy misconduct. Happily, *lingua* puns too, signifying "tongue" as organ and speech (Glare, 1982,

p. 1032–1033), a doubling whose special relevance to this familiar, albeit unique, situation will become clearer later on.

In this article, I want to restore depth and time to an instance of a phenomenon that happens frequently when the person in need is young and female (but also sometimes male), and is seeking help from an older male (but also sometimes female) authority. This ongoing violation of trust is barely thinkable in the vocations marked and marred by it—from the religious and spiritual to the medical and secular, including, I must emphasize, all brands of psychoanalysis. So I want to try to think about that fragmented experience, to repair and fill it in by drawing on my own history, as well as on profession-wide ideas and practices that have evolved exponentially since my treatment with Dr. O (who, it should be said, is no longer alive). I hope this project will also contribute something to the discourse on boundary violations.

To do this, I must disclose, selectively, a bit of myself. Autobiography is, of course, subject to various dangers: one is not one's own best historian, and memory is not a value-free scientific method (not to mention the problem with self-analysis, which is, as they say, countertransference). But autobiography is all I've got. Here was the classic trauma, which I kept from myself: the only one I felt could help me was the one who had harmed me, whom I needed, and in whose trustworthiness I therefore urgently had to believe. For Gabbard and Pope (1989, p. 118), sexual boundary violations by analysts may sow doubt, inclining patients to "postpone [...] grief work and hold on to the fantasy that someday [...] [incestuous] wishes will be gratified." Indeed, one prod for staying in treatment as long as I did may have been a dissociated hope for a repeat performance: a few years past the treatment's second and final end (not recounted here), I was startled to discover a fantasy that Dr. O was to have been waiting for me at the end of termination road. My struggle in writing this account has been to balance my loss, grief, and fear of shame with the capacity to think (Bion, 1962/1967; Fonagy et al., 2002). Indeed, perhaps I became an analyst—a process I will later assess—to help me think about something that did not bear thinking, to speak the unspeakable, and to grieve while speaking.

In what follows, I consider the roots of Dr. O's lapse in this strange treatment, which can be deemed both a success and a failure. His transgression issued from the mix of what he, as I perceived him, and

I, as I perceive myself, brought to it; conceptual lacunae and technique poorly used; and dangers inherent to psychoanalysis. In Part I, I trace how my muteness wed Dr. O's silence, fashioning an analysis laced with an incestuous streak, a matter I take up theoretically as well as clinically in Part II. In the Conclusion, I reflect on psychoanalysis's collective dilemma: the primal crime of sexual transgression.

Throughout, I will be bearing in mind the professional, intellectual, and cultural contexts in which the analysis took place and in which my reflections have emerged. In that sense, this article may be read as an account of an era in which the deep structure of psychoanalysis began to change. My treatment with Dr. O bridged the late 1960s and the early 1980s, an epoch that generated patients' rights, democracy in the consulting room, the acknowledgment of parental sexual abuse of children, and of course, what preceded them all, women's liberation.

I. The sounds of silence

Reinvented by *Nachträglichkeit,* memories are uncertain possessions. When I first began this article, I believed the most shocking piece of Dr. O's betrayal to be his sexual transgression. In reaction, I had shattered: one part of me flourished in its attachment to psychoanalysis, the other lived in terrible, mute remembrance. Writing this article has set these two parts of me in conversation with each other and with the psychoanalytic world. This colloquy has in turn revised my estimate of Dr. O's most stunning perfidy: in the context of the talking cure, his resounding silence, as much as his intrusive act, broke his compact and my heart. Ferenczi (1933), of course, taught us this a long time ago, but it's one thing to read and another to live.

Breaking my own silence has recast the past. Crucially, a seemingly unique moment—indeed, it had been fabricated by dissociation *as* a single instant—now appears as, so to speak, *primus inter pares.* Dr. O's *lapsus linguae* was one among many more mundane clinical missteps in my work with a man whose character put a particular spin on a particular sort of treatment, for good and for ill. At the same time, it remains not only a symbol of profound betrayal, but the thing itself: signifier, signified, and referent in one. If, in my memory, the hug, the French kiss, and the hard-on came to stand for the analysis' corruption, the event also stood out because it entailed a sexual act whose repair would have required sexual speech from a self whose pre-Oedipal shell had, at the time, barely cracked.

Looking back, I think that it actually was my silence that I wanted psychoanalysis to cure. And in this treatment I did in fact encounter the new, speaking experience I sought, as well as the same old stuff I didn't know I needed to get rid of. In ways both generative and destructive, Dr. O's countertransference matched my transference all too well. When I was in treatment with him, there emerged a voice that felt more true to myself than any I'd so far heard come out of my mouth or onto paper. At the same time, however, as I began to speak, Dr. O advanced his desire, and then neglected to speak of it, and so a small but vital piece of me just shut right up, went dumb, continued on its silent way. In no treatment is everything aired. But his silence, enhanced by my muteness, fit a pattern in which mutual reflection—on who I was, who he was, what was (not) going on in our relationship, how we might mutually map it—had no place.

Dr. O's help: mourning my mother

Oddly enough (or perhaps not oddly at all), only with Dr. O did I begin to comprehend how damaging silence can be. One of the underlying troubles that drew—or drove—me into treatment was my inchoate response to my mother's unexpected death. Except that she had died when I was 20, nearly six years before my first visit to Dr. O, and I was silent about this loss from January 1963 to December 1968, almost six years. It's not that I never spoke of it at all. But I was emotionally silent. I did not know how to grieve, and neither did anyone else in my family. We just went about our lives. For me—as, I suspect, for others in this culture— "process" would become a verb of intimacy only a decade later, in the 1970s, when therapy became a household word in the United States. My family—and friends, and graduate school peers, and husband—did not know that talk was helpful; some still don't find it so.

When, early on, Dr. O asked me how my mother had died, I replied in black and white: "She was a statistic." Nonplussed for what would be only two or three times in the years I knew him, he managed to ask me what I meant. As though reading an obituary of someone remotely familiar, I explained that she'd died after a major routine surgery—removal of her thyroid—but that my father had not ordered an autopsy—had preserved the silence—and so the cause of her death was unknown. All my family knew, from some random nurse's notes, is that in the wee hours my mother, unable to breathe, rang for help. After a tracheotomy, she rang again but—somehow we know this—no one answered. Silence in the dark hospital night.

Responding in Technicolor, Dr. O exclaimed: "That's not a statistic, that's a catastrophe!" I do remember the honor I felt upon hearing Him, whom I held in awe already, use such a big word about my little life. The certainty with which he spoke—and with which, we will have to acknowledge, I must also already have endowed him—was a blessing. Looking back, I see that he had properly mirrored my suffering's magnitude, for which I will always be grateful. I had determined to dry my tears with probability because, lacking both the hard facts that would have been produced by an autopsy and the embrace of a family comfortable with mourning, I could not bear her death's meaninglessness.

But, in Dr. O's office, where emotion was knowable and meaningful, this abrupt loss was no longer just one of those things, an insignificant statistic in the history of a population: it mattered. It would never have occurred to our family to place an obituary anywhere, but now, with Dr. O's assured protest supporting me, my mother's death made it into *The New York Times* of my mind. My cry, my grief, my attachment mattered. Having received the recognition I didn't know I was waiting for, I became able to recognize myself, my needs, and my wants. I even began to allow myself to want to know, to investigate my loss, and naïvely phoned my mother's cousin, a physician himself, for enlightenment. That he could have had no information to offer after so many years was irrelevant: the point is that knowing and wanting to know finally felt safe.[1]

The newspaper metaphor is no accident. With Dr. O, I began to (re)find my own voice. I was already claiming possession of it with the encouragement offered by the feminist world I was helping to build as I inhabited it. Still, Dr. O's authorization of my interior life's newsworthiness played no small role in the (re)discovery of my literary self. Writing had come easily before high school, but until midway through my treatment with Dr. O it was a source of terror and paralysis. Likewise with public speaking: facing an audience, I would go mute for a minute as all meaning shredded, the muteness recapitulating my regular, more sustained silences in class throughout college and graduate school. Speech, writing, and voice returned to me both imperceptibly and in sudden leaps even as that flawed treatment proceeded so unevenly.

Dr. O—and, to be sure, psychoanalysis itself—filled a void with meaning: instead of a blank in time, there was tragedy. Without fear of mockery for, as my family usually sniped, "taking yourself too seriously," I could begin to treat myself with delicacy. I know this seems a contradictory experience to have had with a man who confessed to be a bull in a china shop. In fact, he once recounted, with glee and delight, that his supervising analyst had signed off on his training with the words: "If he can't get in the front door, he'll use the window." But second-story men are not necessarily unkind. Once, after a tearful session capped by recovery and reconstitution, Dr. O smiled: "I feel like a parent who's just put his kid in her snowsuit and tied her scarf, and is sending her out to play." That he was the subject of the sentence and I the object may be one reason it sticks in my mind. Still, some tenderness made it past the self-involvement that consistently wizened his technique.

His identification as a nurturing parent made an indelible impression. Its strength goes some way toward explaining why I stayed in treatment after his egregious transgression, why I overlooked the selfishness (or shall we call it narcissism?) of his desire, why I kept the faith for so long. It was not only that I fell for him—became imprinted like a gosling—when, having rung him for an appointment, I first heard him speak. What sacrifice—of speech, knowing, self—would you not make on behalf of a man who grasped what you could not, your horrified and helpless vision of your mother drowning in her own blood?

Who spoke when your father did not? I knew the immensity of my father's grief: as the funeral home emptied, I spied him, alone facing a corner, his body caved in by tears. But I did not go to him. I never mentioned his pain and neither did he. After the funeral, someone—I don't know who—handed me my mother's wedding band, as well as a pearl ring given her by my father when he'd risen a bit in the world. Intentionally, I refrained from telling him I had the jewelry, because I feared mention of it would hurt. Meanwhile, he was frantically searching for the rings, because, of course, he knew they'd been in the hospital safe, and he wanted me to have them.

Word and deed

Will it now seem ungrateful if I notice what Dr. O did not do? Speaking where there was silence, Dr. O helped me mourn. Stepping in instead of abandoning me to my grief, as we in my family did to each other, he named the tragedy and empathized with the anguish it entailed. This "corrective emotional experience" (Alexander et al., 1946) was itself good. But a little inquiry would have come in handy. Speaking from long clinical experience, I wish that, at some point, he had also helped me wonder how unthinkable it had been to register my loss as tragic. Psychoanalysis is not about just ameliorating the patient's state. As I have learned from my own work and subsequent treatments, it is about helping the patient know what helps, which provides at least some of the wherewithal to make a life.

To know what helps in turn depends on recognition, and so it is up to the analyst, in recognizing the patient and receiving her recognition in turn, to assist her self-recognition (Benjamin, 1988). This process entails guiding her through, by participating in (Sullivan, 1953) a reflective process that takes place in a relationship, which itself becomes the object of that reflectiveness as well (Ogden, 1994). This mutually contemplative process by the two knowers in the room (Mitchell, 1997) aims to enhance the patient's self-understanding in a healing way.

To do this, however, analytic technique demands a little humility, a virtue not in great supply in Dr. O's particular consulting room. The certainty with which he pronounced on the immensity of my mother's sudden death had its downside. For example, during some turbulence in my outside life or within the treatment, he would often report, with a sagacious air, that he had sailed these perilous passages before. Of course he had. But it was his absolute self-confidence that he had already charted this territory that would totally reassure me. On reflection, however, it would have been better had Dr. O at least noted how hard it was for me to bear my fear and doubt, instead of simply telling me not to worry because he knew what he was doing.

Perhaps, though, the pleasure in being able to supply what I craved, to embody omniscience, proved too enticing. In this regard, he resembled his peers: Which analysts, trained in the 1960s like Dr. O, did not regard themselves as already *knowing* the map of psychoanalysis? Forget whether they were classical or, like Dr. O, postclassical: prior to that magical cultural shift called the Sixties, the Doctor Knew, the patient did not, and most providers and consumers accepted and relished this hierarchy. After all, it was only in the 1990s that analysts began querying what the analyst really knows (Mitchell, 1997; Chodorow, 1996).

It goes without saying that the context for my treatment with Dr. O was a hierarchy skewed by sex. Not only as a doctor but as a (heterosexual) older man, Dr. O occupied a prestigious social and economic position. Not only as a patient but as a (heterosexual) younger woman, I was awed. He talked down, in a way once styled as avuncular but that now, in the light of feminism, can be named for what it was: patriarchal. And, an admiring girl glowing in the eroticized light of an older man's brilliance, I ate it up, while keeping my feminist activism mostly out of the room, protecting it from his casual contempt, and preserving for myself the glory and soothing of his certainty.

Dr. O's sins of commission and omission were due, then, in part to his era and the state of psychoanalysis at which I first encountered it. To history and gender hierarchy, however, we must add character, and here we find a deep and damaging contradiction. Dr. O was a brash and cocksure man who would wax fulsomely on uncertainty. True to his psychoanalytic philosophy, he would focus on my fear of not knowing: he often emphasized that, if only I could accept the inevitability of uncertainty, I would be far less anxious. Not a bad idea, either, if he had not been so certain about it. Surely my current appreciation of the limits to knowledge has something to do with his influence: when I entered analysis I believed anthropology ought to aspire to truth-producing science, but by the time I terminated, I was in the throes of proto-postmodernism. Still, it is ironic that, given Dr. O's evident intelligence, as well as his inclination to reveal himself, he never took note of the mordant contradiction between what he said about uncertainty and the certainty with which he acted, between his words and his deed.

In this instance, and in general, Dr. O seemed content, even determined, to *do,* to act. Sometimes his action was concrete and gestural— the granted hug—but just as often it was symbolic and linguistic

(Harris, 2005). Indeed, maybe his erection, an action if there ever was one, did not spring only from testosterone. Maybe it (and the hormonal flow) arose from his use of his tongue, as an organ first of speech and then of Eros and power. Remember how his speech act turned the hug into the hard-on: he redefined the terms of my embrace by labeling the "real" kiss, thereby, through his eroticized authority, invalidating the buss I'd given him and dignifying the kiss he demanded. Transforming my active reach for shelter into passive submission to his word, Dr. O found his way back to doing, not to mention (patriarchal) power. Was he unsettled by my claim on that amoral, impersonal sexuality about which *Three Essays* is so passionate? Was he threatened and excited by my anticipated adulterous foray into an earthy and explosive sexual milieu remote from his office? Either way, he resorted to what he himself might have deemed a security operation—which was also a power move to preserve a patriarchal masculinity (Corbett, 1993) whose foundations were being shaken by a feminist earthquake (Frosh, 1993; Goldner, 2003).

I think that Dr. O generally saw himself as a warm, generous Daddy-Mom: his expressiveness and volubility went a long way to make up for my mother's depressive coldness. "Healing in the maternal transference/countertransference" might describe this crucial aspect of my treatment with him. However, in my view, the analyst is not another parent; his or her job may be to soothe, but not only by doing. Analysts should also think with patients about healing so that patients can notice something about their own needs. This is not exactly a matter of interpreting or not interpreting the positive transference or not. Rather, we would say now that it is about reflecting on the repair, on finding the new in the old or, even, the new in the new (Boston Change Process Study Group, 2008). In helping you to re-represent your experience, the analyst offers the means to reclaim and regenerate your own life.

Whether he acted soothingly or sexually, Dr. O usually did so without processing. I think he mostly shot from the hip. The high-calorie emotional diet he served was crucial to my psychic malnutrition and I devoured it. But it lacked a critical nutrient: shared self-reflection. Clinicians are familiar with that stubborn resistance to processing the "unobjectionable" (Stein, 1981) transference: things are proceeding apace, the patient appears to be improving or having insights or progressing in one way or another, the analyst is proud. It is harder to hold on to the advice Sullivan allegedly gave—"God keep me from a therapy that goes well [...]!" (Levenson, 1982, p. 5)—than to savor the feeling, "If it ain't broke, don't fix it."

Sotto voce

Psychoanalysis runs on the ordinary silent energies by which people stumble their way to each other (Coles, 1998). It puts projections and counterprojections to work, turns them into tools, systematizes them, and makes them explicit. Assessing this complexity, Levenson (1983, p. 72) argues that the analyst and the patient always do what they are talking about: "every verbal exchange [...] every interpretation, consists of a piece of behavior with the patient and then a commentary, in speech, on that behavior. The commentary, the content of the interpretation is [...] the metamessage." Clinical theory then directs the clinician to decode this recursiveness—transference and countertransference—into voice, with the patient, this pattern that, first informally established in the family kitchen, repeats in the different lexicon of the consulting room.

Recursion suggests, in a funny way, that silence, or at least what is unspoken, is inevitable and even vital to the talking cure (Stern, 1997). On the one hand, the important thing about free association (if there really is such a phenomenon) is when it stops—when silence breaks the flow, and the repressed or dissociated signals its presence. On the other hand, sometimes we do what we say before we can say what we do, because, in some cases, we cannot know what we have to say until we materialize it by enacting it. Then, according to current enactment theory (see Leary, 1994, for a review), our raw material comes alive before our eyes in a tangible drama. In the analyst's and analysand's collective hands, enactment becomes fodder for conversation, from which they create the liberating analysis. Then again, sometimes silence is merely about private space, the clinician's or the patient's, and as such ought to be left alone (Winnicott, 1971; Khan, 1974).

The silences between me and Dr. O, however, constituted one big recursion. In other words, silence that reflects anxiety (i.e., not talking about an enactment) can itself be an enactment. One thing you could say about the me who came to see him: I did not speak very much, which is probably a surprise to those who know me now. The habit of wordlessness, as I learned from my second analysis, was not exactly innate. Or if I tended toward silence, I also made it a way to survive. Many years ago, friends would experience my quietude as withholding, even hostile. Maybe the sound of inhibition inverts the unconscious attack, but I was aware mainly of the fear of sounding stupid. Shame was my constant companion. Now, casting my eye back, I see that quieting myself—dissociating what I saw and felt and knew—helped me manage my internal life. I was making a strenuous effort to wrangle emotions, passions, and thoughts that felt too noisy in my family and the world.

Family rules authorized loudness for my father and brother, while my mother tiptoed around, whispering the words *"sotto voce,"* and I was what they called "quiet." Which I knew wasn't a good thing, even if my mother, leaning on Italian (which no one spoke, but which perhaps seemed refined, not coarse like her parents and husband), urged everyone to hush. The failures subtended by quietness—tantamount to being good—heightened my sense of a core defect. My silent manner stumped my parents. That I knew, with the same dissociation with which I knew they settled for it in the face of more obtrusive troubles—my father's brittle narcissism, my mother's depression, and my brother's near-delinquency. Anyway, the social worker to whom my mother took us for family therapy said, "She's okay, leave her alone." My brother was the identified patient, while my father's fearful and selfish, if gender-normal, refusal to attend sessions ruined my mother's brave intervention.

Within the blankness that lulled my teeming mind and was also meant to calm my storming family, I was lonely (as, I now think, I was with Dr. O, though neither of us realized it). Unfortunately, under the indirect rule of *sotto voce,* any expression of distress would come across as, and sometimes indeed was, merely obstreperous. My own expressiveness would, in turn, further reduce both my mother's self-esteem and my own; my failure to validate her inflamed my shame. Only my father had the privilege of apparently shame-free, wordless self-expression—the smack here, the shake there, the storming out the door for the rest of the day. His brutality, mantled by silence, was unveiled only when I began peeking: my second analyst's hunch caused me to query extant kinfolk (my father's death followed my mother's by nine years) about family violence. When I was 18 months old, said a cousin 20 years older than I, she overheard her mother speaking to my mother, who was worrying that my father was being "too rough" with me. Did "rough," I asked, mean hitting or shaking? "Oh, not hitting, I think, just shaking," replied my cousin.

Three points to note: my father was shaking me; my mother may or may not have been stopping him, or trying to; and she wasn't sure anything was wrong. Of course, a third-hand report about an event from over a half-century ago needs many grains of salt. That my father also brutalized my brother (who attests to this) proves his capacity for violence, which I must have witnessed. Surely both culture and character were active here. In my parents' immigrant families of origin, beatings and verbal abuse were routine, a legacy of cultures where corporal punishment was standard and immigration brought economic hardship as well as political and cultural safety. That my father seemed to have no hesitation about physical abuse and that my mother appeared to question but nevertheless put up with it—this difference may have had also to do with gender as well as character. Certainly the blue-collar chip that he wore on his businessman's shoulder had something to do with his attractive cockiness, defiance, and tendency to bully.

A quiet girl patient must have been a mixed blessing for Dr. O. He never addressed my paralyzed silence as such—and to have done so at the times of my most shameful muteness would have been tactless—but even then, I could tell from his repeated efforts to work around my voicelessness how trying he found it. Clumsily persistent, Dr. O would often ask, "What's in your head?" Perhaps making him toil gratified me, but mostly I felt helpless. It may be that all those years with him laid the groundwork for my second analyst's success in helping me to put words to my silence. Or it may be that my second analyst eventually addressed directly that which held my stubborn muteness in place, the helpless shame I wore like a *burka,* which, hidden in plain sight, Dr. O never mentioned, at least not until it was too late.

Pre-Oedipal delight, Oedipal shame

Writing this article has gradually heightened my awareness. Now I see that, at the same time as the pre-Oedipal, maternal failure was being repaired, an uninterpreted Oedipal and (mostly) paternal repetition was taking place. If the one signals the success of the treatment, the other marks its failure. Even if it is generally recognized now that pre-Oedipal and Oedipal matters and themes show up in a mix, separating them helps me think. For example, it allows me to put into its proper context Dr. O's denigrating response to my admiration for a professor who'd researched the ritual use of hallucinogens among the Jivaro of the Brazilian Amazon: "Aw yeah, he's an academic, he'd *have* to do those drugs." My puzzlement upon hearing his castrating words emerges now clearly as a life-preserving but also stubborn defense against dismantling the savior-mother so as not to unveil the destroyer-father.

If my silence obstructed Dr. O, the scope it offered his self-expansion must have been a delight. Or so I guess. This was a man full of himself, I can now safely say. From the vantage point of an altered psychoanalysis and a changed me, I can avow the appeal of this off-putting quality to me, a person whose self seemed like something no one would want, let alone be full of. When Dr. O spoke, he seemed to enjoy himself, to stretch out into his words and ideas. Looking back, I see myself enjoying his (macho display of his) enjoyment. I see myself watching in both imprinted awe and heterosexual wonder someone so apparently free and happy in his expressiveness. I see myself craving such delight and pride. Now, as a clinician, when I find this yeasty pleasure rising (Smith, 2000), I try to take such (hierarchical) self-indulgence as a warning: Why is the room filling up with my voice, not my patient's? But as a needy patient, I was inspired to imagine myself a free speaker who liked herself while speaking.

If my silent rapture was implicated in a heterosexual gender hierarchy, it may also have been part of an uninterpreted pre-Oedipal (maternal and/or paternal) transference. It was a joy to be spoken to, and with, and in front of by him. I was always happy to be with people who spoke fluently, because then I had to be neither lonely nor verbal. But, with Dr. O, this safety had wings of ecstasy. When Dr. O mused on ideas and philosophy, he seemed to take me into his confidence. If little of what he said has lasted, I do recall my (unstated and unanalyzed) bliss. His flattering implication of a mutual intellectual footing resumed a trajectory I'd lost when my mother died (and never had with my father). He offered a life of the mind that she'd pined for and, judging, for example, by our memorable museum trips, wanted to share with me. Inferring from my own experience of patients who are excited to be with me, my rapt attention encouraged him, and the pleasure he took in me was likely fueled by my intensity.

Perhaps each patient brought him this pleasure. But I felt special, a treasure bought with silent shame. Fascinated, if also slightly repelled, I swallowed his "stick-with-me-kid" insinuations. When, on occasion, he used that patronizing cliché, he may have been playing, but irony is not the best dialect to use with a five-year-old excited by an idealized grown-up. Needless to say, our habit of engaging without noting the quality of our interaction would have fed my dissociation of how his paternalism both drew and disturbed me. For instance, a year or so after I had begun analytic training, he said, in that off-hand macho manner he liked to affect, "Theory? That's for the geniuses. You and me, we're mechanics, we stick to technique." You will not be surprised to hear that I was struck dumb by his misrecognition of my interests, as well as by his splitting of theory and clinical work. Could he have missed my passion for theory manifest in my graduate anthropology career? Perhaps I had been indirect, or maybe the theorist in me did not show very well (and in all likelihood theories of cultural evolution did not interest him). Nor is it a secret that, even after 8 or 12 years of treatment, patients can still surprise us with unsuspected traits and interests.

You might count this as a grossly botched pre-Oedipal paternal countertransference (Benjamin, 1988), but I think we were in the Oedipal bramble as well (Cooper, 2003). Dr. O's ignorance of a central aspect of my intelligence dashed my hopes for the meeting of minds that never took place with my father. Certainly his creation of a hierarchy between the intellectual and clinical practices of psychoanalysis—his splitting—put me in a bind. Pulled toward the "us" he made of him and me, and away from the "them" he proposed we were not, I found no space clear of shame. To have accepted his characterization of "our" interest in technique meant to gain mutuality with him but disown what I valued in myself (the theory part), which was a loss akin to the shame of deficiency (Stein, 1997). But to have claimed the theory side at that precise moment would have been to claim genius, risk the shame of excess (Stein, 1997), and lose him. Thrilled to be among the honest elect, if also humbled and embarrassed to join the laborers (my class mobility was not irrelevant to this treatment), I elected neither to interrupt his inverse snobbery nor to damage his pride: I declined to observe what I unknowingly apprehended—how his narcissism disguised his intellectual self-doubts.

Dr. O took no interest whatsoever in analyzing the Oedipal transference/countertransference, only in enacting it. From time to time towards the end of my treatment, I would complain: "But we've never really talked about my father." No response. I dreamt of a man in a Speedo with a mesh crotch. This reference to barely veiled male genitalia would surely, I thought, lead us to my father, sexuality, and, I see now, the erased enactment, not to mention Dr. O's other narcissistic self-display. Nothing. I did not know how to push it further. All I recall is a later, rather mad prediction he made as if in reply: "One day, you'll dream about a desirable man, maybe at a conference, and he will be your desire."

II. Desire and the incest taboo

However much Dr. O might have helped me (re)start my fire, he often stood in its light. Invigorated, perhaps, by the patriarchal dialectic animating us, he rarely left me alone-while-being-held to discover my desire's vicissitudes. Instead, in a mutually exciting way, he inserted himself into my lack (Lacan, 1966/1977; Bernstein, 2006). Clotting my desire with his, he generated a holding pattern—a psychological incest—in which we hung in a sort of suspended animation for far too long. It is futile, if irresistible, to wish he had done things differently. Still the longing for what might have been can inspire a search for what could be. In what follows, I will assess Dr. O's Oedipal failure. Although he and I did not—could not—talk about it then, now I can delve into that atmosphere thick with longing, frustration, and shame by using some new ideas about desire, Oedipus, and incest.

Dumbshows of desire

Desire is about longing, not having. It may be sweet or poignant or terrible. But without it, one is as without appetite. And its preservation is accomplished, at least in part, by the prohibition on incest. Desire entails several paradoxes, and it seems useful to lay them out here because they manifested so oddly and silently in my treatment with

Dr. O. Chief among these is desire's ambiguous location both between and within those who feel it. Claude Lévi-Strauss (1949/1969, p. 12) mines the irony: desire, he aphorizes, is our "only instinct requiring the stimulation of another person." The relational version might be that desire emerges in relationship but, belonging to the child alone, survives only if lightly held, even benignly neglected, by the authorized caretaker(s).[2]

Eluding the neat binary between one-person and two-person psychologies, desire centers a tricky debate that one must enter, if perhaps, as Levenson (1994) writes, with trepidation. In one-person terms, desire seems to spring full-blown in intrapsychic process, almost a species characteristic. In the linguistically based Lacanian view, it emerges as a consequence of the failure of speech, of the gap between the Imaginary and the Symbolic. From a two-person vantage point, however, desire turns out to be oddly intersubjective. Lacan (1966/1977), in turn, mindful of Lévi-Strauss's assessment of desire's doubleness, situates its origin in a relation that is, all the same, not quite a relationship: as the yearning to be the object of the (m)other's desire, it emerges in pre-Oedipal (maternal) intimacy, a nexus situated, however, in the presymbolic Imaginary. Levenson (1994) would have it both ways, insisting that "desire requires another person" (p. 692) while stressing the "peculiar paradox built into this wish to find one's completion in the regard of the Other" (p. 693).

Betwixt and between, desire tends toward the cryptic, a quality attended to in several psychoanalytic traditions (with which I wish Dr. O had been more familiar). Winnicott (1971) and Khan (1974) place it in a private self that, to one's pleasure and regret, no one else can access. Laplanche (1976), in turn, deems it an enigma. Beamed from the maternal (or, as one might now emend it, *parental*) unconscious—always already sexual (Kristeva, 1983)—desire registers in the infant's psychic reality as an "enigmatic message" that, in its muteness (Stein, 1998), eludes the promised clarity of the talking cure.

Desire's wordlessness often reduces us to bumbling idiots. Yet (or therefore), analysts need to create a way at least to talk about this "alien internal entity" (Laplanche, 1976), whether or not it manifests as explicitly sexual or not. That desire is mutually experienced and meaningful (Fairbairn, 1954; Mitchell, 2000; Davies, 1994) is certain.

That shared speech—intersubjective understanding—can decipher its meaning is, however, less clear. What analysts can do, which perhaps the parent cannot and certainly Dr. O did not, and which patients like children need to hear, is to acknowledge and articulate this unspeakability.

If Dr. O's *lapsus linguae* showed rather than told, I gave as good as I got, or maybe better (this story is not without my own aggression). Some years later I put on a dumbshow. Dr. O's Danish modern couch was oddly positioned: its foot abutted the wall and its head protruded into the room. His chair, four or five feet away, was angled at about 45 degrees to the head of the couch, thus affording him a full-length view of his reclining patient. When I sat down on the couch or rose from it, I faced him. But one day, at session's end, I reversed my action. Instead of facing him as I stood up, I impulsively swung my legs over the couch's far side. Feeling an obscure frustration devoid of any accompanying thought, I knew I was protesting, but had no idea what. Nor do I recall our discussing this pantomime at all (which doesn't mean we didn't).

His gratifying look of surprise, which greeted my good-bye, was nothing compared to what happened another time, when, having risen on the usual side, I turned away from him and began lifting the couch along its length in order to flip it. As I was doing so, I glanced back to see his eyebrows practically somersaulting. But he only said, "Watch your purse, it's going to fall." Setting my bag on the floor, I turned the couch over. I am pretty sure, though, that, before I left, I righted it and replaced the pillow that had landed on the ground.

At that early date, Dr. O could not have read Little's (1990) later account of smashing Winnicott's vase. Still, let us congratulate him for having survived this disruption of his office, and for having stayed his anger at my attempted parricide (Loewald, 1979). Let us sympathize with him too. In the face of a patient's act, who is light on their feet? By definition, Lacan (1973/1980) insists, the Real leaves most of us speechless most of the time. It is only after the fact, upon reflection—usually with someone else—that we can begin to name, with varying degrees of success, that which refuses symbolization. Myself, not having had the chance to talk this over with my analyst, I am going to talk it over with you, with the community that, as I will relate, I chose in Dr. O's stead.

Looking back, I want, first, to read my very modest temper tantrum literally: What was I trying to upend, halfway through my treatment, by turning the couch upside down? Something about the consulting room? Or *his* consulting room? Psychoanalysis? The couch itself? Was there an old order I was trying to overthrow in those days when cultural revolution and political protest were either in the air or recent memories? Maybe by making the medium my message, I was pointing out (a gesture in itself) that he was doing something too. Perhaps I hoped my mime would make silence speak. It is hard not to infer that his dumbness, his not-speaking, was my target.

But, in writing, I am also drawn to the symptom's specificity. If incest was in the air, Oedipus was not far away either. It is worth noting that I did not remove from the wall the line drawing of the prone naked woman hanging above the foot of the couch. Half-aware of the unsettling fantasies and wishes it excited as I gazed at it three days a week, I might have wanted at least to protest that this décor sexualized the room or, rather, that Dr. O had eroticized his office with it. Instead, I wrote a poem about it, but never told him. Did I fear he would retaliate, invalidating my complaint by deeming it a projection of my desire? Or having penned the verse only 14 months after Dr. O's lapse, was I reluctant to disturb sleeping dogs?

Here, I suppose, was an iatrogenic repetition compulsion. Or shall we call it collusion? Enactment? If I wanted to turn my back on the treatment's rot, maybe I also wanted to keep it hot. Doubtless, I wanted Dr. O to want to look at me all day too. But, I see now, I would have felt so stupid had I shouted: "You think she is more beautiful than me and I hate that and I hate you for making me feel jealous and ugly by hanging this drawing where I know you gaze upon it too!" Jealous of an image? How immature is that? I needed help with this triangle but got none.

This silence—mine, Dr. O's, ours—about what his décor meant to me entailed an unanalyzed Oedipal repetition. It prevented reflection on the fact that, for me, sexual crudeness, disrespect, and love came in the same paternal package. Consider my fascinated horror in the face of my father's sadistic lewdness. For example, his jest at a family Thanksgiving—"Are we having sliced breast of Marilyn Monroe?"— could register and be assessed only in my second analysis. Who knows what primal scene fantasies Dr. O and I might have come upon had we scrutinized my response to his aesthetics? Instead, I just felt sick, sensing but unable to speak my gloriously self-abnegating desire to slice and dice myself so as to win a patriarch.

Typically transforming anxiety and shame into thought, I now recall noting that, like me, the artist's model was lying down. At the time, I failed to connect the dots. In contrast to me, for example, she was physically naked but a psychic cipher. I, on the other hand, was trying to undress for the doctor in hopes he would heal my torment. From my second session onward, I believed that, if I told the whole and especially the most shameful truths to this man who knew better, I would get better. And maybe, I may have gradually come to hope, he would love me more than her.

No, when I got up, I flipped the couch instead. I do not think I was exactly trying to show that I disliked that couch or its weird positioning. Perhaps I was defying his injunction at the beginning of treatment: "You can do whatever you want except spit on the floor or break up the place." Except I did, as I noted, clean up after my fit. Perhaps, then, I was flipping the bird at the whole set-up. Consider this: even if the viewer saw the model as though from the foot of the artist's divan and me from the side of Dr. O's couch, still Dr. O, from his rather more in-charge position, commanded a view of both of us, differently naked, lying on our backs, the object of his gaze. At ease in his slightly reclining chair, not hidden behind analytic neutrality but, rather, clothed in his power to disclose whatever he pleased about himself (or not), even as I was obeying the command to reveal all (Foucault, 1976/1980)—he could contemplate not only her pulchritude but my young embodied self, which was, I now understand, far more attractive than I knew or could handle. (Although tempted, I will refrain from speculating about his fantasies of two prone, bare women in his visual field.)

To put it starkly, the room's layout made him its subject and the analysand—in this case, me—his object. That he seemed in charge of his desire was made more exciting by his charge of me. Dr. O's masterful vantage on me (and the image) was pleasing, titillating, and deeply distressing. Once, I seem to recall, he voiced pleasure in my stockinged legs; it may have been when, six months into treatment, I was considering the couch. If I can still picture his smile, I recall only nonsense: he liked (women) patients to lie down, he said, because "I get to look at their legs." I was, I see now, both delighted and dismayed that he shamelessly acknowledged exploiting the couch, not to mention the patient, for his own pleasure. I was also jealous of these other patients, as well as unsettled by his mentioning them. Decoded in hindsight, his remark unconsciously introduced, without analyzing, the Oedipal dynamics already at play. But at the time, my mind grasping at nothing, I found only the shamed suspicion that, as the cliché goes, he said that to all the girls, a fairish bet because he was really talking about no one but himself.

In fact, I have a hunch that central to his self-image was being a man who made no bones about his enjoyment of women, who, he believed, enjoyed his desire. Yes, I can imagine that, working in emotionally corrective mode, he thought his compliments would heal my fractured and frightened sexual narcissism: perhaps, at least momentarily, believing in the omniscience with which I endowed him, he may have thought that I could take his (hetero)sexual appreciation of me as the truth about myself. Yet, even within such a sad and harmful delusion, had he inquired how I might feel about his admiration, he might at least have helped me to my own language, desire, and mind. Given a moment to name my shamed pleasure in being only (*only!*) the object of his desire, I might also have been able to claim the more tacit wish to sit not on his lap (a desire he once attributed to me in a fit of ill-timing) but in his chair, to command a view not so much of the patient as of myself.

Dr. O should have kept the noise of his desire to himself. I do not fault him for having it; I fault him for not making room for mine. Sex may encompass both relatedness and enigma, but that it remains a site of selfishness (see Stein, 2005) makes it dangerous—if also by that token exciting. It is good to remember Freud's (1908) original insight about the amorality of desire. This ruthlessness may show up in mind as well as actions, in incest of the heart as well as of the body. Indeed, for Dr. O and his professional kin, perhaps being the object of patients' (unregistered) unrequited love/lust is as gratifying as sexual intercourse itself.

Intersubjectivizing Oedipus

So maybe civilization begins when parents (not, *pace* Freud [1913], the siblings) recant their incestuous desire. By tradition, the incest taboo is read through the Oedipal drama, which stars a unique subject of desire, a child who must single-handedly manage triangulated love and hate (Freud, 1913, 1924). To be sure, the father has a supporting role, for he disrupts the (incestuous) mother-son merger so as to redirect the boy's desire away from his mother (and father) toward a future mate.[3] But, in this classical account, the parental objects otherwise lack subjectivity. Postclassical revision, in contrast, thickens the Oedipal plot, recognizing that insofar as the play is only internal, it tells but part of the story. Fairbairn (1954) and, to a lesser extent, Kohut (1977) cue the dyad: the child is not onstage alone. Front and center are the parents as subjects; their pleasure, inhering as it does in object-relation, influencing if not generating the child's.

Erasing sexuality from the equation, however, this quiet revolution overcorrected a problem remedied by later relational revisions, especially Davies (1994, 1998, 2003) and Cooper (2003). Not only do these new narratives resexualize the Oedipal child, they also recognize that parental sexual desire circulates in the family field altogether. The classical model has the Oedipal parent (i.e., the father) aiming to preserve his conjugal rights (which reads as a power move as well). But, according to this construction, the father does not reciprocate: he does not surrender his desire for his son as his son forsakes his desire for the parents. Postclassical models, in contrast, redraft the Oedipal story by construing both desire and its renunciation as intersubjective. Together, Oedipal adult and child forswear their mutual sexual desire, with the former facilitating the latter's renunciation.

Costarring in these emergent Oedipal narratives, therefore, are the parents and their sexual desire, whose underexplored and possibly even buried psychoanalytic history (Balmary, 1979/1982; Krüll, 1979/1986; Masson, 1984) contains a puzzle or two. Some archeological work being in order, I wonder whether some light might be shed if, heuristically, we were to divide the Oedipus from the incest taboo, using them as twin lenses through which we could view the same drama? If, that is, we consider the Oedipus as speaking to children, could we construe the incest taboo as addressing adults, even while we view both processes as concurrent and interpenetrating? This stereoscopic view might amend a lacuna in the new narratives, whose perhaps necessary tendency to occlude a triad in favor of a dyad two-dimensionalizes a three-dimensional process.

As I see it, the Oedipus, a developmental crucible, infuses a nascent psyche with a particular genre of desire in a triangular space. At the same time, the ban on incest embargoes the materialization of adults' desire in dyadic relation to their children (and, in the background, to the other parent). Possibly delivering a developmental torque of its own, the incest prohibition addresses substantially formed beings, the adults in charge who, adept at personal and intersubjective multitasking, can hold the other(s) in mind without erasing the self; tend relationships (dyadic, triadic, multiple) without the self-sacrifice from which children need protection; and, in fact, find this juggling act self-enhancing (a partial job description for analyst and parent alike; Cooper, 2003; Davies, 1998, 2003).

These twin injunctions on desire's realization are interimplicated; their accomplishment is interdependent. The Oedipal fiat demands that one abjure the fantasy of sexual and personal completion with one's parent(s). But one cannot achieve this loss without the parental willingness to endure the complementary loss (Davies, 1998, 2003), that is, to tolerate and grow from the suffering caused by the ban on materializing one's sexual desire for one's child (a submission implicit in Loewald, 1979). This intersubjective context, in which adults can reap the bittersweet power and pleasure of helping children toward their own sexuality, resonates in the analytic dyad, where it requires reflection as well as (in)action.

The analyst's refusal and the patient's desire

As goes Oedipal resolution, so goes the adult incest taboo: neither is ever fully accepted or resolved. The relation is likely causal: to the degree that adults' own Oedipal closure is always only partial (Meltzer, 1973/ 1979) and precarious (Freud, 1924), their observation of the prohibition becomes as difficult as it is necessary. Lingering Oedipal regrets, stirred in adult fantasies of revitalized fulfillment, haunt analysts too (Gabbard, 2008; Twemlow & Gabbard, 1989), even Dr. O. However intersubjectively carried are such ecstatic fantasies of repair, still their disposition belongs finally to the person in charge—parent, analyst— who must register their presence but forego their realization. Achieving this surrender—tolerating the permanence of sexual melancholy—is no small task (Davies, 1998, 2003). It requires support from various sources, what Benjamin (2006) calls the moral Third but also all that is denoted by *le nom du père* in its protective as well as disciplinary sense—community, culture, morality, the Law. This accomplishment is crucial: the negotiation of desire that constitutes one's life flourishes when tended by another's restraint.[4]

Dr. O's refusal to examine Oedipal dynamics inhabited an intellectual and clinical void. He did not employ the classical one-person model; and a two-person model of sexual desire, in which adult desire may serve as a technical consideration is, as I have noted, still in the making. At the same time, other factors were at work. Framing that void were not only flaws in his training and gaps in psychoanalytic knowledge, and the enduring power dynamics of authority and of gender, but, I am sorry to say, basic character faults too. Woulda, coulda, shoulda. Yet I cannot help but wonder what might have happened had psychoanalysis offered a theory of adult incestuousness as a partner to its theory of Oedipal longing. Might all the Dr. Os out there, including my own, have been able to keep their desire to themselves and leave room for their patients?

What I wanted was a paradoxical—and reparative—relation in which "me first" happily puts itself second. What I got instead was a "me first" on parade, its glow magnified in and by my delight. To be sure, he did opine on my identificatory wish to be the center of my universe. Still, the sort of reflection I required was rather more mutual than Oedipal, a sort of dyadic version of the triad, what we can now call the pre-Oedipal homoerotic transference/countertransference (Benjamin, 1988). I needed to hear more about us, less about him. I have no idea whether, beyond (I suspect) reductively deeming his passion for me "natural," he mulled what he did and felt. He should have. But then, given that he had materialized his phallic desire, I needed him to show his analytic desire too, to make some version of his private musings public between us, so that together we could process what was going on for me, what his actions and feelings had to do with mine.

As is well known, if perhaps infrequently articulated, analysts' ability to contain their own desire with self-awareness equates to parents' observance of the incest prohibition. Such self-conscious containment creates and protects a gap in which the patient's subjectivity can come into its own (Bernstein, 2006). Bound to the mast of professionalism and care, analysts, like Odysseus (Wilner, 1998), ought to hear but not dance to the music of patients' desire. Their holding back depends on their cultivated capacity to recognize and contemplate their own desire (hence the required training analysis).

Recursively, in fact, the two abilities, to reflect on desire and to contain it, enhance each other. One may read Odysseus's mast as phallic (*le nom du père*) (Schein, 2009). Or, with Benjamin (1998), one may theorize the labor of holding and reflecting as a (traditionally) maternal practice: revising the active/passive binary, she argues that passivity is not just activity's opposite, but also signifies containment. Others (e.g., Davies, 1998; Cooper, 2003) style this work as an analytic capacity, technique, and obligation. They argue that, by detecting and analyzing adult sexuality, analysts can decode and manage sexual countertransference.

Conceived thus, the taboo on adult incest causes a rupture—the parent says "no"—that allows one to know one's own desire. By making room for child or, *mutatis mutandis,* the patient, the two-person materialization of the incest prohibition cultures a one-person experience. The ban, observed, opens a space (in Lacan, a lack; Mitchell & Rose, 1982) that is at once full and empty (which might be as good a description as any to capture the feeling of desire). This opening is replete with potential: the option of sex between parent and child or analyst and patient, ruled out, transmutes into the child's/patient's potency and fantasy (see Samuels, 1996, p. 310). The parent/doctor who slips desire's leash leaves the child/patient at once famished and over-full. By contrast, analysts who contemplate their passion for their patients can exchange stolen pleasure for the sense of a job well done. They can savor a subtle, privileged view of dependents becoming what they need and will: autonomous (Cooper, 2003). Or, to be more realistic, analysts may get to survive the equally delicate pain of watching patients make their own errors and discover that they no longer want what they once (thought they) did—which may, indeed, be one way to capsule the Oedipal resolution.[5]

In revising the psychoanalysis of incestuous desire, it is important to render desire as neither wholly discharge-driven nor solely object-seeking. What matters is that, insofar as the ban on incest is observed, childhood's bolus of longing and loss, of disappointment, shame, and anger, is part of growing up. Parents cannot save their children from it, just as analysts cannot save patients. Indeed, they foster it and, with it, an interior space for imagination, wish, and fantasy. One of those predictable life wounds that Freud warns about, the suffering of unrequited love, is also key to a certain freedom: having endured it, one both gains oneself and is spared the unbelievable confusion attendant on one's desires being granted by the very other from whose desires one is trying to free oneself. One is granted the room to create oneself as if one were autonomous. I am here varying Benjamin's (1988) paradox of separation. If independence requires separation from the (m)other on whom one depends, so claiming one's desire, in all its impossibility and ambiguity, rests on having it separately and, in effect, differently from those with whom it birthed and still lives—and who understand the pain they inflict.

Hence my wish that Dr. O, the man who listened as well as talked, would have helped me utter the dilemma of our real relationship: getting what I wanted—emotional and corporeal incest—kept me from realizing my need, that is, a validation of the legitimacy of my complaints. If you can reflect on it, unrequited love permits you to sense your desire *as distinct* from, other to, the desire of the other who matters to you as much as your own life. But you need someone else to help you do it. This growth takes place via the experience—or maybe even a fantasy—of being held by a parent or analyst or teacher or author or, I suppose, even an idea. Symbolizing the previously unsymbolized, the abjection (Kristeva, 1982) that survived results from such restrained containment, and constitutes a painful, profoundly personal corner for self-knowledge and self-containment (perhaps Eigen's [1981] "area of faith"). You need to be able to experience your desire, abject and soaring, with your parent who is feeling this too and knows it and is intentionally not acting but is instead bearing the poignant sight of your passion as it bursts into flame, you with whom your parent has identified, whom she or he identifies as her or his own, and whom she or he is allowing to live.

When, instead, that noisy "confusion of tongues" (Ferenczi, 1933) clogs the space that ought to have been full of nothing but piercing possibility, longing dries up. A dream I told Dr. O: "There was a man named Sussman, I think we knew him in the country. Out of his lower bicep, which had somehow been pierced, drained a liquid, a mixture of sugar, vinegar, and water." Dr. O did not opt to interpret "Suss" as referring to the contemporaneous idiom for discovery: "to suss something out." Nor did I. Instead he chose the bucolic reading: "*Süssman, sweet man, aren't you talking about your feelings for me?*" He ignored the vinegar (semen is only sometimes sweet) and, in an unconscious, sublimely self-immolating blow-job, I let him do it by acting as though his omission (emission?) had not taken place. In this narcissistic evasion of the bittersweet, he resembled my father, who, unable to bear criticism or imagine himself as hurtful, appeared to ignore love's ambivalence.

You need, as I say, someone to help you. And although an adult love relation may offer this help, it is fairly unlikely. I have often wondered about women I treat, as well as those in my acquaintance, who pine for lovers they cannot have. My sense, speaking from my own experience too, is that those suffering this particular variety of unrequited love—especially the heterosexual subjects of *Women Who Love Too Much* (Norwood, 1985)—want someone they cannot have because they want not an object but a boundary. (This may also be true of some men.) Unavailability symbolizes the limit they long for, the incest prohibition observed in heart and/or body. They aim to redo a vital if bungled childhood process, not to self-destroy.

They seek their own desire. They want *not* to be able to have their parent(s), despite a mutual longing (Samuels, 1985, p. 168), so as to be left with nothing *but* their own private desire in all its differentiating, lonely pain and hope. Unfortunately, if, as an adult, you try this "do-over" with lovers whose self-restraint in service of your growth neither can nor ought to be expected, you may waste a lot of time. You are better off in therapy. Even so, the repair is hard—Freud (1937) sometimes thought it impossible—and to have it reinflicted by that selfsame professional is a terrible betrayal of psychoanalysis's promise. Apropos my marital problems, Dr. O once quoted *Othello,* who says of himself (after he has been apprehended for killing his wife): "one that lov'd not wisely but too well." Why didn't he apply that to us?

Splitting the difference

If, when I was in treatment with Dr. O, he was big and I was little, now our positions are reversed: in the analyst's chair (literally and figuratively), I can observe and assess him from a position of authority.

That my work with him made this reversal possible is ironic. Curiously, it was in the very (academic) year of the initial transgression that I began to consider becoming an analyst. It has taken me a long time, and the writing of this article, to understand what will have been immediately obvious to the reader: becoming an analyst was one gigantic save. I had placed all my faith and trust in this man. In our first five years, I mourned my mother with him. During the fourth, I endured a year-long walking breakdown, in the latter part of which my father died. So when, 18 months after that death, Dr. O's lapse revealed his untrustworthiness, I had nowhere to go. My real father gone, I had only his disappointing stand-in. I could not bear the pain, which I could begin to register only after I ended my 30-year silence. In retrospect, I see that I was stuck: I lacked the internal structure to engage full-on the heartbreak, anger, and disillusionment that would have rushed in had I relinquished whatever guilty pleasure keeping that incestuous secret had bestowed.

So I leapt. I split the difference—choosing to change jobs, I left Dr. O without leaving him. Call it my own private Oedipal resolution. Finessing the gendered snares faced by a girl working her way out of the Oedipal funhouse, I chose to take him at his word and reach for the phallus myself. I was going to do what he did. But I was also going to do what *I* did. I was going to be an analyst, like him, and I was also going to continue what I was already doing, which is writing and speaking about what mattered to me. Indeed, even though I did not publish my first clinical article until about 15 years after I'd begun training (Dimen, 1991), my literary life gathered steam as new ideas, topics, and genres found their way to me.

This radical shift had a rational context: by this time, I was becoming disenchanted with my first profession. Although my awe for anthropology endures, by 1973 my zeal to share its wonders with students was waning. At the same time, psychoanalysis was working its transformational magic. Early in college, it had flashed on me, while reading Durkheim (1930), that life's jumble could be decrypted. Just so, as a patient, I quickly saw, with poignant clarity, that the mind's mishmash held meaning too. Add to that an excitingly systematic way to think about women and desire—despite the feminist anti-Freudianism of the time, it was plain to me that psychoanalysis was just what the doctor ordered (Dimen, 2003)—and I was hooked.

Did my embrace of psychoanalysis permit me to identify with, differentiate from, and (even) exceed Dr. O? Yes, but that's not the whole story. As my analysis heated up, Dr. O's support was helping me become more intellectually confident and active. Inspired by his favorite image, Prometheus's theft of fire, and willing to incur its risks (striving for the phallus always fails), I deployed my gains not only in the academy. Even as I lay on the couch, I had climbed onto the barricades; weirdly enough, I entered psychoanalysis in the same year as I joined my first consciousness-raising group. Throughout my treatment, women's liberation, as I have hinted, served as a parallel home. So as, in Dr. O's office, I was both kindling and damping my own speech, my voice was already shifting into new registers in the study groups, protest politics, and (academic) thinking that have marked second-wave feminism. Sisterhood's righteous and unstinting, if also sometimes rivalrous (Buhle, 1998), encouragement empowered me to speak out even as Dr. O's office rang with the sounds of silence.

For me, psychoanalysis and feminism were not either/or. I needed both. It would be banal to say that feminism was the protective mother intervening in paternal incestuousness. Movements such as psychoanalysis and feminism do not work like that. Furthermore, each of these, even if historical antagonists, carried similar hopes for the self and for change (Dimen, 2003; Mitchell, 1974). But, as it turned out, psychoanalysis recapitulated the hierarchy from whose domination I was seeking release and, paradoxically, both enlivenment and authorization. Feminism, less attuned to (though preservative of) interior life, created a temporary utopia in which women were authorizing themselves outside patriarchal limits. Dr. O helped me to a new self (albeit in certain ways a false one that required repair by later treatment), but I could not have cultured that self without the nurture of feminism.

That life transformation, like this writing, constituted my personal compromise formation. If I could not save the actual relationship, I could fix it by proxy; if Dr. O wasn't going to help me, I was going to help myself. It was as though I transferred my attachment from him to a set of intellectual and clinical practices that meant a great deal to me, to him, to the damaged us. Coming closer to him while keeping my distance, I was going to make good on his promise. That this operation bootstrap entailed calling in the cops—the Third that Dr. O seems not to or could not have known—was not in my mind at the time. Now it looks like an unconscious wish: I am asking the psychoanalytic community to bear witness to one of its recurrent mistakes.

I have also beaten Dr. O at his own game. Theory is only for the geniuses? Maybe not. Or maybe it remains to be seen who the genius is. I do hope that this critique of my incestuous analysis with him advances a bit our grasp of a crucial intersubjective process in a way that sheds some clinical light. (Unlike him, I am not so willing to split theory and technique.) I am no longer ashamed, as I once was, of having taken inspiration from the man who hurt me. If I was identifying with the aggressor, perhaps I was also competing, aiming to do what he did but to do it well, better, right. Women too inhabit the Symbolic.

It is true as well that, by historical accident if nothing else, I am now on top. In the era when Dr. O and I worked together, psychoanalysis was starting to take a beating for its interpersonal and ethical transgressions, an attack that has only intensified. Being around when therapy was being deidealized and democratized was not the only way I had history on my side. I entered the field at a time when women's increasing prominence began contributing to the profession's long-deferred but intensifying recognition of its sexism and homophobia. That psychoanalysis could not continue to demean or erase the feminist critique surely helped me to achieve my own voice, standing, and recognition for integrity and moral authority.

So, having the upper hand by virtue of the reversal of fortune between analyst and patient, as well as by my own, post-Dr. O achievements, I no longer had, when I began drafting this article six years ago, to look him in the eye. Perhaps, instead, I looked down on him, secure in the knowledge that I could afford to dismiss him and thereby not have to confront him. For these reasons, this writing may be retaliatory and unfair to Dr. O, who, now dead, cannot reply. I cannot help that. If I cannot quite forgive him the damage he did, and even if no speech on this topic is pure (Harris, 2010), including my own, still I hope my reflections on the strange mutuality of our never-analyzed enactment, on my gains as well as my losses, will serve as sufficient mourning.

I had two terminations with Dr. O. The first occurred after a decade of treatment; I do not recall its impetus. But, a year later, I returned for two more years, attending sessions only weekly, sitting up. I took notes after each session because, as I saw it, I was trying to understand something that had eluded me. Those notes seem to have vanished in the course of a domestic renovation or two. But I don't need them anymore.

III. Conclusion: the problem that won't go away

When I began this article, Dr. O was, as far as I knew, alive. Were he still alive when I finished it, two things are certain: news of it would have reached him, and personal honor would have demanded I confront him. As it turns out, his death has spared but also deprived me. Without a doubt, had I arranged to see him, I would have managed my terror, anger, and shame by bringing a colleague for support during what I expect would have been an unpleasant 50 minutes. I cannot imagine Dr. O welcoming my accusation, nor do I see him taking a long-awaited opportunity to reflect with me. You never know, of course. He might have surprised me: as I write, I imagine his apology and my eyes well up. I feel obliged to say that, either way, the confrontation would likely have been salutary. Still, whenever I think of having missed it, I usually feel more relief than regret.

You may be wondering why I did not go to him before. Here is the paradox: had I not written this article, I could not have found "the words to say it" (Cardinale, 1975/1983). Not only, now that I think about it, did my slow comprehension require his absence to find life. It required someone else's presence. Only while writing for an audience I expected would listen could I recover the meanings in what otherwise was rote reporting. It took, one might say, a village, a relational process: I fashioned a repair for myself by noticing, at a moment when I could imagine someone open to me and when a suitable speaking invitation came my way, that I was, to my surprise, ready to tell (Dimen, 2005a). (The context for my seizing the day was of course thick: a third treatment relationship, other major life events, and the like. But that is another story.)

As meaning returned, shame receded. Before writing this article, I dwelled somewhere on that continuum from seduction through exploitation to abuse—neither thought nor sense, only a wish echoing in a paradoxically shame-filled vacuum: "this isn't happening." Performatively, shame intensifies itself: you are ashamed, therefore you feel you deserve shame. Abjection (Kristeva, 1982) solidifies, and you prefer to go on as though nothing has happened. As I spoke out, however, my shame, which marred those silent decades and even the first couple of tellings of this story, gradually subsided, even if it resurges now and again. I have been fortified by the praise and, yes, the criticism called forth by these tellings: speaking despite my own and others' (willful and unconscious) efforts to stop me, I have dined so well at the banquet of respect that shame no longer persecutes me. Rather, it has become interesting.

On not naming Dr. O

I would like to say that my shame, having dissipated, no longer demands vengeance. When I began this project, *Schadenfreude* beckoned: I did indeed fantasize the malicious triumph of naming Dr. O. I cannot imagine doing so now. No, at this moment, I rue the whole damn thing: if I have emerged from this enigmatic treatment intact, I am also scarred. Not only that: some of this grief may, sad to say, contain traces of that self-sacrificial love that recoiled from injuring the one I loved and the relationship I treasured, the loyalty that prevented me from connecting the dots during that three decades' silence.

At the same time, though, my discretion is pragmatic. Although it would be dignified and ethical to say I want to protect his family and colleagues, I am not so noble. Were I to name him, attention would flock to his character and devolve into gossip. I have needed to tell this story for personal reasons, but in the course of doing so have come upon matters vital to psychoanalytic work, and I want the focus to be on them. This story bares complications that trouble us in daily clinical life, as well as mysteries in how we think about mind, relationship, and treatment.

Consider my appellation for him. "O" situates our working relationship in psychoanalytic tradition. It conjures the putative inventor of the cure we use and puts that praxis into question. "O" honors Bertha Pappenheim's determination in treatment, and her independence and originality in the rest of her life. This sobriquet also summons the sexual transference/countertransference on which Anna O's analysis with Josef Breuer foundered. It asks: If sexual acting out, or enactment, is so venerable as to be inevitable, what becomes of us? How do we ensure that analysts stand by those whom they have harmed?

By dubbing him Dr. O, I also wish to evoke the protagonist of *The Story of O* (Declos [Réage], 1965/1973), the gendered power dynamics the novel depicts, the thralldom of sexuality, and the novel's place in contemporary sexual and feminist history. Perhaps by reversal— naming him after her—I am attempting to turn the tables, which, as you saw in Part II, I literally tried to do one day. But I also mean to ponder the conundrum of one's own contribution to one's own suffering. *The Story of O* has two endings, in one of which the protagonist, O, seeks her master's permission to kill herself. At this moral and clinical juncture, feminist and psychoanalytic interests meet. How, asks feminist thought (e.g., Benjamin, 1988; Butler, 1990), are women complicit in their own subordination? *Mutatis mutandis,* psychoanalysis is equally fascinated: how do people play into their own tragedies? In this personal article with theoretical implications, I have struggled to maintain this moral tension: on the one hand, I call both of us to account; on the other, I call a spade a spade: the guy hurt me.

Psychoanalysis on the spot

In the most classic way, an analyst hurts the person he's supposed to help and he won't even talk about it. And it's not even a patient who's complaining. Or, rather, the complainant is indeed a patient but is also an analyst who has ideas about the ins and outs of mistakes, their rectification, and their erasure; who knows something about our profession's sexually addled history; and whose authority merits attention. If it were just a patient crying foul, we could sympathize but also protect ourselves by splitting: us against her, analysts against patient, good against bad. Perhaps the analyst was doing a bad job; because good psychoanalysis does not include this sort of mistreatment, it is therefore, properly speaking, not implicated. Or maybe the analyst was a rotten apple; throw him out and we are safe. Or, if worse comes to worst, the patient is a bad egg. Too bad. But *we* are fine.

But we—a collectivity to which I belong—know better: the problem of sexual infraction is endemic. We have not, as yet, made it go away, and therefore we feel a shared, often mute helplessness that renders us anxious and ashamed. Anxiety and shame may be occupational hazards. Arising for many reasons, they evaporate fairly quickly in the case of run-of-the-mill mistakes—bungling an interpretation—or even "delinquencies" (Slochower, 2003)—e.g., making a note about something personal—and, of course, neglecting to inquire about the impact of any of these errors. Many a time, Dr. O slipped up in this way. So have I. So have you. As Ken Corbett (2009, p. 187) put it,

> Luckily analyses rarely, if ever, turn on such micro-moments; rather they are held and built in a different experience of time— a web of contingent associations and an ever expansive relay of construction/reconstruction that moves unhindered through past, present, and future; such that [for example] an intervention can drop a stitch and pick it back up in the next thought/association.

Some infractions, however, are less micro than others. Insoluble, unmetabolizable, they block vision and thought, and create a shared dilemma. In their shadow grows not only shame but stigma or, as Erving Goffman (1986) defined it, "spoiled identity." Such violations, sullying the whole, taint each of us. To the extent that professional identity is also personal (as it tends to be in the professional-managerial class; Ehrenreich, 1989), the offender's shame rubs off on everyone else, including the victim.

Nowhere is this truer than at the spot where psychoanalysis planted its flag; not even tax evasion bears such a stigma. It was psychoanalysis that named sexuality the site where pleasure and danger combust, each serving as the other's fuel. Yet this is the place where psychoanalysis keeps shaming itself, or being shamed. Plainly, the sexual anxiety that plagues civilians bedevils analysts too. Psychoanalysts have extraordinarily important ideas about sex. But we also have our unique sexual madness, nor do we escape the maddening sexual hierarchies and disciplinary practices that, both culturally instituted and personally meaningful, inform our desire.

Mix all that with indigestible regrets about the inevitable flaws in the very means by which we learn our trade and you get, on occasion, something toxic. Analysis does not fix everything, not even for analysts, and a fall from grace that can produce stubborn idealizations. Indeed, as Masud Khan (1974)—no slouch in matters of abuse, sexual and otherwise—opined, this shortfall may propel some into the profession: "those [...] content to live with their problems seek treatment" (p. 117), whereas those who seek training are those who, in their delusion, hope for cure. That he was wrong—civilians want cure too—is not the point.

Analysts live with the discomfort of incomplete Oedipal resolutions, lingering incestuousness, and unrenounced attachment needs. Transference, home to extraordinary transformation and unspeakable pain, is never completely resolved. Angry and disappointed by our own, our analysts' and, yes, psychoanalysis's limitations, and somehow shamed by all this imperfection, we are stigmatized by the analyst who commits a crime and then by the patient who blows the whistle. Our ambivalence riding high, we want to be rid of the disturbance they create, as do the exploited patient and exploiting analyst themselves.

A psychoanalytic transvestite

My tale unsettles a discourse that nests the analytic relationship, what cultural historian Raymond Williams (1961) calls a "structure of feeling." Consider what happened when, in response to another conference invitation, I proposed a paper assessing collegial responses to the first iteration of this article (Dimen, 2005a). At first, the committee moved to disinvite me: they deemed me unethical towards Dr. O, who, bound by confidentiality, could not defend himself against my charges (for a similar predicament, see Cornell, 2009). I protested and, upon assuring them that Dr. O was deceased and would go unnamed, they reinstated their invitation and I gave the lecture (Dimen, 2006).

My injury and anger having yielded to curiosity, I found myself wondering what panic would impel analysts to concoct the nutty idea that patients are subject to an ethical code. I imagined, to put the best face on their rescission, that the committee must have felt torn between competing loyalties. Impelled to protect both damaged patient and impugned colleague, alarmed as (even) psychoanalysts tend to be by sexual impropriety, they didn't know which way to turn. So they compromised by inverting the usual binary. Not the analyst but the patient was in power; not the patient but the analyst needed protection. The analyst was no longer shamed by his sexual infraction; rather the patient was shamed by her ethical breach.

Perhaps my having presented myself as both analyst and patient had created a "category crisis," a moment when the familiar arrangement of things was put up for grabs. Literary theorist Marjorie Garber (1991) coined this term to account for the presence and function of transvestites "in texts as various as *Peter Pan*, *As You Like It*, and *Yentl,* in figures as enigmatic and compelling as d'Eon and Elvis Presley, George Sand, and Boy George." A category crisis has, she argues, a "resultant 'transvestite effect'" that, in confounding the usual discrete categories of male and female, focuses "cultural anxiety, and challenge[s] vested interests" (p. 17). As both analyst and patient, I became a sort of analytic transvestite, panicking the authorities who moved to regulate my speech (Foucault, 1976/1980).

Not everyone with a story like mine could have had a hearing. Nowadays a patient would no longer be dismissed out of hand, as she most certainly would have been in Dr. O's era, but her legitimacy probably would not be as solid as that of a professional analyst. In contrast, my professional privilege to speak as an analyst gives me a leg up so that I can be heard; that I have written substantially about sexuality makes such a hearing even more likely. Yet the very reason we are willing to attend to a respected colleague who unveils an experience of sexual malfeasance puts us at risk: authorized as a knower (Foucault, 1976/1980), she is privy to the family secrets that everyone agrees not to talk about.

Written from both perspectives, then, my account puts the profound and reassuring binary into question, which the alarmed committee tried to recoup by maintaining the dichotomy between analyst and patient, but switching their attributes. This mad swap hints at a panic of the sort that ensues when, as anthropologist Mary Douglas (1966) proposes in *Purity and Danger*, culturally constructed polarities are breached. Cultural symbolism, she explains, often lines things up in pairs. Whatever falls outside such conventional dualities creates disorder, thereby becoming dirty and dangerous. My psychoanalytic transvestite story is just one of those disorderly things. There exists in psychoanalysis a deep structure that aligns analyst and patient in two separate columns: knower/known, wise/ignorant, powerful/needy, and so on. My tale mixes categories. Like other marginal creatures and things, "unborn children and pubertal initiands in some tribal cultures, or ex-prisoners and mental patients in our own," as Garber's (1991, p. 7) explication of Douglas puts it, I and my story enter or generate a state of "'contagion' and 'pollution,'" both endangered and endangering.

Not only does my effort to hold myself in mind as both seasoned analyst and naïve patient merge opposites. It also challenges the implicit hierarchy behind the seemingly coeval pairs: analyst the greater being on top, patient the lesser on bottom.[6] Sullivan's (1953) two-person model tried to heal this binary inequality between analyst and patient by relativizing the pair: the former as comparatively well, the latter as comparatively ill. Relational psychoanalysis continues this equalizing deconstruction by both validating patients' wisdom and acknowledging analysts' influence and participation in enactment, not to mention iatrogenesis (Boesky, 1989; Mitchell, 1997; Renik, 1998).

I add another step. I would like to undo the dissociation and hierarchy that structure the internal categories, the "self-states" (or "subject positions") of analyst and patient. Each analyst has had at least one analyst, each has therefore been a patient, each of us is, therefore, both top and bottom, empowered and abjected. Yet even though we know that much of what we learn about treatment comes from our own treatment(s), we find it strange to imagine that there are, in effect, two self-states alive in us at once, each with different knowledges. Instead, a no-person's land seems needed, because of the analyst-patient hierarchy and its toxic traffic in power and shame.

Can we inhabit the space between (Bromberg, 1996)? If analysts can hold themselves as wise and ignorant, powerful and weak, can they also imagine themselves as both self-contained and abject, and continue working? What state of mind would that balancing act entail? Some combination of the depressive position and skepticism? I speak at once as both recognized, dignified clinician and desperate, mute patient who has found her voice. I am an insider who has trained and studied and written, entered second and third treatments, and wants to confer with her colleagues about a personal dilemma in terms of the complications marking our field. And I am outsider, perhaps standing in for all the patients whom we have all damaged in lesser or greater ways and who insist on recognition and empathy.

More than one colleague, crumbling under the weight of this demand, has resorted to rationalization. Often, for example, I have been congratulated for my courage in telling this story. One time, I dared look a gift horse in the mouth and asked why I was being praised. "Because," my colleague replied, "you put yourself in a bad light." Talk about regulatory practice. In her view, telling this story made me look bad because, when the sexual transgression happened, I was an adult, 31 years old, not a virgin, married. I had entered psychoanalytic treatment of my own free will. Which, of course, was true.

Except, of course, it also wasn't. What my friends couldn't entertain was a not uncommon paradox: like other free agents driven by suffering to our offices, I too was desperate, a shameful thing to admit among civilians and, it may be, even among professionals. And (or but) as we know, desperate patients cannot be asked to be responsible in the way analysts are. A central feature of "professional [analytic] responsibility," writes Mitchell (2000, pp. 51–52), assessing Loewald, is to bridge the patient's organized and disorganized mental states. This bridge helps the patient, now relieved of that mature psychic labor, to enjoy "freedom from conventional accountability" in which states of "unintegration" may be productively mined.

I do not think I am alone in forgetting, on a day-to-day basis, how at risk patients feel, how frightening it is to denude oneself of the defenses that protect but also construct and constrain, to be the unhappily ill one longing for the state of grace embodied by the happily cured analyst, the gosling worshipping the god. Might we see writ large, in my history with Dr. O, the mundane hazard of being a patient? When your doctor breaks the faith, your own faith trembles. And when you are, as I was, psychoanalytically uninformed, greatly distressed, and much regressed, you cannot afford to lose your faith in the process. So you don't notice, and you don't notice that you don't notice, and you don't bring it up, because you fear he will either disavow or acknowledge his role: if he's bad and denies it, then you're crazy, and if he's good and cops, then you have no right to be angry and your anger makes you bad and so it's your fault and, *voilà,* you've no right to speak at all. And you don't tell anyone else because you don't want them to tell you to leave the analyst whom you need beyond reason.

Primal crime

That the hardships and humiliations of being a patient linger, unremarked, amidst the gratifications (Smith, 2000) of being an analyst creates a certain personal difficulty, if not also a professional opportunity, that has been insufficiently addressed. Maybe the moral hierarchy between analyst and patient, the us/them dynamic, issues from the shame and stigma of being a patient in the first place, the enormous comforts of treatment to the contrary notwithstanding. Maybe this explosive combination of power and shame in the analyst/patient hierarchy has something to do with why sexual betrayal of patients by analysts is a systemic hazard: it has nowhere to go but up and out. Analysts suffering the dissociated, unforgettable abjection of having been patients may indeed find themselves inducing that very feeling in their own patients, in order to cleanse themselves and, thus cleansed, to become pure and strong. Hence, perhaps, the draw of that "subtle continuum" of gratification, which, as identified by Twemlow and Gabbard (1989, p. 72), "reminds us that the potential for exploitation of patients exists in all of us."

That the analyst knows indicates another subtle dilemma: professional shame. The analyst, knowing, knows that there's something wrong, something to be ashamed of. But the act we least want to be caught in is the act of self-shaming. We do not want colleagues to transgress, and, by identification, are shamed by such sexual misconduct. More poignantly, the condition we dread being found in is self-shame. We do not want anyone to know that we are ashamed, because being ashamed, as is familiar from childhood, means *we know we are doing something wrong but cannot—even do not want to—stop ourselves.* As analysts, we are aware of our common problem (Celenza & Gabbard, 2003), a primal crime that we have not yet solved. We do not, however, want this crime and our knowledge of it to be public, either among ourselves or the laity, lest we risk the shame that shames. No wonder that, for all our contemporary acceptance of analysts' fallibility and even selfishness, when it comes to the primal crime of nearly every analytic institute—that is, sexual exploitation—not curiosity but preemptive, regulatory silence carries the day.

Let's not kid ourselves: the problem is not going away, any more than incest is about to disappear. But perhaps there is a way to keep the impulses toward it in mind, fantasy, and speech, to ensure that, when countertransference infractions happen, the analyst knows how to discuss them. To do that, analysts need to be able locate sex in relational context. For a long time, sexuality had dropped off the psychoanalytic radar. We can be relieved that it is once again in our sights (Green, 1996 1997; McDougall, 1995; Bach, 1995; Kernberg, 1995; Lesser &

Domenici, 1995; Dimen, 1995; Davies, 1994, 1998, 2003; Stein, 1998; Widlocher, 2001; Fonagy, 2008; Blechner, 2009), for we may thereby find a language in which to address our recalcitrant difficulty.

Many reasons have been offered for this temporary if protracted eclipse: the repudiation of reductionist orthodoxy; the runaway success of ego psychology, attachment theory, and the two-person psychologies; classical theory's incapacity to incorporate insights about sex and gender from the humanities and feminism; and so on. Perhaps yet another culprit is our collective impotence in the face of our family transgression: unable to solve this refractory problem, psychoanalysis just decided not to think about sex anymore. Or, more kindly, maybe we merely took a little break; like artists, we looked away from our work to get a little perspective.

Psychoanalysis has, fortunately, now returned to the port from which it set sail.[7] Much of the revived thinking about psychosexuality focuses on reconstruing sexual phenomenology, identity, and development. In my view, this renewal is also a first-rate opportunity to fine-tune our decryption of erotic countertransference, so as to make sexual infraction grist for the analytic mill before it happens. Until now, our way of forestalling sexual transgression has taken what we might call a superego form: "Don't." As with all top-down injunctions, however, this one probably intensifies the problem it aims to solve by inciting guilt and shame, which oddly impel us to mime the perpetrator and act without thinking. To help engage sexual countertransference, it would be useful, in both clinical and supervisory settings, to have some ideas, to think about how desires that actually feel forbidden routinely emerge in treatment and how they inhere in subjective and intersubjective process. Lichtenberg (2008, pp. 9–15) suggests one might employ what I (Dimen, 2005b) have called "the Eew factor": if you feel this mix of excitement, alarm, and disgust in response to a patient's sexual or other material, you might twig sexual countertransference and self-reflect accordingly.

The development of those ideas exceeds this article's needs and the reader's patience, so I will suggest only some key requirements: (1) locating sexual infraction and its refusal in a two-person psychology so that it can be part of clinical conversation between analyst and patient; (2) a relational theory of the subject as psychosexual, to help analysts keep sexuality systematically in mind as they work with their patients—and themselves; and (3) a three-dimensional relational theory of the incest prohibition that, as I have already begun to indicate in Part II, encompasses both children's desire for parents and adults' desire for children. A clinically pertinent theory would also show why analysts, like parents and other caretakers, might want to sacrifice the inevitable urge to enact the forbidden. Analysts have called on each other to behave like (good) parents, to abstain from sexual action. But better than exhortation would be, in my view, a redefinition of abstinence as the pleasure one takes in another's desire, which would afford a way to appreciate the conflicts analysts inevitably undergo relative to patients'—and their own—desire.

Dr. O's lapse was a perfect storm, a disastrous meeting of technical error, intellectual vacuum, and moral failure. I hoped to tell of it without singing a song of victimization in the key of good and bad, and using my shame to tarnish him and burnish myself. I sought a voice to speak the unsayable, words that would help me think through the unthinkable. Now I see the problem inhabits an additional register: psychoanalysis deserves to be construed beyond idealization and demonization, a task to which a judicious skepticism (Harris, 1996) is well suited. Let us acknowledge our collective lapse: psychoanalysis did not protect me, and it has not protected others, from an all too common betrayal, and this failure is very sad. In grieving, of course, I am also claiming psychoanalysis can do better. There *is* a worst, there *is* a best, and then there is the mundane middle, in which, despite our shame about our personal and collective errors and failings, we can and should maintain our self-critical stance and keep on thinking.

Notes

1 I have tried, first during my treatment with Dr. O and then years later, to get the hospital records. But St. Joseph's Hospital of Far Rockaway, having been closed down twice by the New York State Department of Health, went out of business for good sometime in the 1970s, its records buried in the caverns beneath Great Neck's North Shore Hospital—imagine the final, ironic scene of *Raiders of the Lost Ark*.

2 As Freud (1913) already knew, it is vital to locate the incest taboo in culture. Outside psychoanalysis, the incest prohibition has been variously

theorized. Evolutionary biology deems it an adaptive mechanism, because genetic inbreeding generally endangers species survival. With marriage and kinship as subtext, anthropology argues that the taboo, by sanctioning particular sexual and procreative relations, forces families to intermarry, thereby, in Lévi-Strauss's (1949) view, weaving the bonds of society itself or, from other angles, at least darning them. Thus, transmitting and/or maintaining the incest prohibition becomes a social function that might be dubbed a sexual third.

3 I remain uneasy with the classical implication that mothers, or women, cannot self-regulate. The notion of father as principal moral guardian is troubling. Although I understand that Freud and Lacan claim to describe and account for the intrapsychic process by which the turbulent triangular space is traversed, I cannot help being distracted by the sociology: the prevalence of father/daughter incest, which is the most common sort of intergenerational intrafamilial sex (Turner, 1996). So if the paternal principle is deemed to interrupt the Imaginary in which mothers' and children's unboundaried incestuous desire flourishes, nevertheless the relative frequency of paternal incest suggests that fathers might have a bit more difficulty actually regulating their own incestuous acts. Likewise, even if one accepts a woman's place in the psychic interior as a signifier for absence, women still have a subjective life. By definition, then, mothers are capable of self-reflection and hence self-regulation (Benjamin, 1988; Ruddick, 1980). And, if the lesser frequency of maternal incest is any indication, their capacity for self-awareness and self-management might very well mean that their need for the regulating father has been exaggerated, thank you very much. Perhaps it is only my experience with Dr. O that makes me want to consider incestuous desire at once unconsciously motivated, subjectively experienced, and intersubjectively (and socially) lived. But I do not think that is the only reason I would prefer a narrative that allows for both interiority and intersubjectivity, dyads as well as triads, and for parental self-regulation in relation to the incest taboo, itself seen as a Third (Benjamin, 2006) that both contextualizes parent-child relations and permeates adult psychic process.

4 At least within the culture I know, for I am too much of an anthropologist to make this a universal claim.

5 Can tantrums signify the ineluctable, fatal twinning of parental failure and unrequited love? If so, then, when recurring in transference, they need interpretation. In my case, they required countertransference analysis as well. I am guessing that, if Dr. O had mulled his desire and its object-relational context, then maybe, rather than flinging things around (albeit

in slow motion), I could have identified my tangled sexual, filial, and romantic longings. Instead, my tantrums fed on a mess of unregistered desire, disappointment, shame, and anger. In the relational view, such a vortex may be a developmental certainty. Or so my reading of Fairbairn's (1954, p. 113, n. 1) revision of psychosexual theory suggests. As he sees it, (sexual) frustration registers as rejection. It is true, he writes, that "frustration" might accurately describe the classical Freudian construal of drive denied its outlet. But if, as he proposes, libido seeks and enjoys connection, then frustration means that a desired attachment with another has failed. To the extent that such failure registers as lost love, the object's dis/regard will in turn seem repudiating. Taking this further, I would add that rejection morphs into humiliation insofar as the child, sparing the beloved and needed object by faulting the self (Winnicott 1975; Guntrip 1973), comes to feel like a fool. Finally, shame snarls with (more) unwelcome anger and, *voilà,* a tantrum.

6 That the analyst has less power than the patient both structurally (as the patient's employee; Dimen, 1994) and dynamically (as, for example, the patient's transitional object; Winnicott, 1953) is of course true but not my point here.

7 It has been moved to do so, I would assert but cannot here argue, by the multiperspectivalism of the contemporary cultural climate as informed by feminism, gay politics, queer activism, and thought; the discovery of the ubiquity of child abuse (Rush, 1980; Masson, 1984); investigations into sexual transgressions in professional relationships; and a new psychoanalytic generosity toward other bodies of thought.

References

Alexander, F., French, T. M., and others (1946), *Psychoanalytic Therapy: Principles and Application.* New York: Ronald Press.

Aron, L. (1996), *A Meeting of Minds: Mutuality in Psychoanalysis.* Hillsdale, NJ: Analytic Press.

Bach, S. (1995), *The Language of Perversion and the Language of Love.* Northvale, NJ: Aronson.

Balmary, M. (1979/1982), *Psychoanalyzing Psychoanalysis: Freud and the Hidden Fault of the Father,* trans. N. Luckacher. Baltimore, MD: Johns Hopkins University Press.

Benjamin, J. (1988), *The Bonds of Love.* New York: Pantheon.

Benjamin, J. (1998), Keynote address. Division 39, April, Boston.

Benjamin, J. (2006), Two-way streets: Recognition of difference and the intersubjective third. *differences,* 171:116–146

Bernstein, J. W. (2006), Love, desire, *jouissance:* Two out of three ain't bad. *Psychoanalytic Dialogues,* 16:711–724.

Bion, W. (1962/1967), A theory of thinking. In: *Second Thoughts: Selected Papers on Psychoanalysis.* London: Karnac, pp. 111–119.

Blechner, M. (2009), *Sex Changes: Transformations in Society and Psychoanalysis.* New York: Taylor & Francis.

Boesky, D. (1989), The questions and curiosity of the psychoanalyst. *Journal of the American Psychoanalytic Association,* 37:579–603.

Boston Change Process Study Group (2008), Forms of relational meaning: Issues in the relations between the implicit and reflective-verbal domains. *Psychoanalytic Dialogues,* 18:125–148.

Bowlby, J. (1982), *Attachment and Loss.* New York: Basic Books.

Brenner, C. (1979), Working alliance, therapeutic alliance, and transference. *Journal of the American Psychoanalytic Association,* 27(suppl.):137–157.

Brigandt, I. (2005), The instinct concept of the early Konrad Lorenz. *Journal of the History of Biology,* 38(3):571–608.

Bromberg, P. (1996), *Standing in the Spaces: Essays on Clinical Process, Trauma, and Dissociation.* Hillsdale, NJ: Analytic Press.

Buhle, M. J. (1998), *Feminism and Its Discontents: A Century of Struggle with Psychoanalysis.* Cambridge, MA: Harvard University Press.

Butler, J. (1990), *Gender Trouble.* New York: Routledge.

Cardinale, M. (1975/1983), *The Words to Say It.* Cambridge, MA: Van Vactor & Goodheart.

Celenza, A., & Gabbard, G. O. (2003), Analysts who commit sexual boundary violations: A lost cause? *Journal of the American Psychoanalytic Association,* 51:617–636.

Chodorow, N. (1996), Reflections on the authority of the past in psychoanalytic thinking. *Psychoanalytic Quarterly,* 65:32–51.

Coles, R. (1998), Psychoanalysis: The American experience. In: *Conflict and Culture,* ed. M. Roth. New York: Knopf, pp. 140–150.

Cooper, S. H. (2003), You say Oedipal, I say postOedipal. *Psychoanalytic Dialogues,* 13: 41–63.

Corbett, K. (1993), The mystery of homosexuality. *Psychoanalytic Psychology,* 10:345–58.

Corbett, K. (2009), *Boyhoods.* New Haven, CT: Yale University Press.

Cornell, W. (2009), Loves and losses: Enactments in the disavowal of intimate desires. In: *The Past in the Present: Therapy Enactments and the Return of Trauma,* ed. D. Mann & V. Cunningham. New York: Routledge, pp. 82–101.

Davies, J. M. (1994), Love in the afternoon: A relational reconsideration of desire and dread in the countertransference. *Psychoanalytic Dialogues,* 4:153–170.

Davies, J. M. (1998), Between the disclosure and foreclosure of erotic transference-countertransference: Can psychoanalysis find a place for adult sexuality? *Psychoanalytic Dialogues,* 8:747–766.

Davies, J. M. (2003), Falling in love with love. *Psychoanalytic Dialogues,* 13:1–27.

Declos, A. [Réage, P.] (1965/1973), *The Story of O,* trans. S. d'Estrée. New York: Ballantine.

Dimen, M. (1991), Deconstructing difference: Gender, splitting, and transitional space. *Psychoanalytic Dialogues,* 1(3):337–354.

Dimen, M. (1994), Money, love and hate: Contradiction and paradox in psychoanalysis. *Psychoanalytic Dialogues,* 4(1):69–100.

Dimen, M., ed. (1995), Sexuality/sexualities [Special issue]. *Psychoanalytic Dialogues,* 5(2).

Dimen, M. (2003), *Sexuality, Intimacy, Power.* Hillsdale, NJ: Analytic Press.

Dimen, M. (2005a), The hug and the hard-on: Fidelity and psychoanalysis. PEP Conference, "Impediments to loving," New York, February 25.

Dimen, M. (2005b), Sexuality and suffering, or the Eew! factor. *Studies in Gender and Sexuality,* 6:1–18.

Dimen, M. (2006), A tale of two kisses, Division 39, Spring meeting, Philadelphia, April.

Dimen-Schein, M. (1977), *The Anthropological Imagination.* New York: McGraw-Hill.

Douglas, M. (1966), *Purity and Danger.* New York: Praeger.

Durkheim, E. (1930), *The Rules of Sociological Method,* ed. G.E.G. Catlin, trans. S. A. Solovay & J. H. Mueller. Glencoe, IL: Free Press.

Ehrenreich, B. (1989), *Fear of Falling: The Inner Life of the Middle Class.* New York: Pantheon.

Eigen, M. (1981), The area of faith in Winnicott, Lacan and Bion. *International Journal of Psychoanalysis,* 62:413–433.

Fairbairn, W. R. D. (1954), Observations on the nature of hysterical states. *British Journal of Medical Psychology,* 27:105–125.

Ferenczi, S. (1933), The confusion of tongues between adults and children. *Contemporary Psychoanalysis,* 24:196–206.

Fonagy, P. (2008), A truly developmental theory of sexual enjoyment and its implications for psychoanalytic technique. *Journal of the American Psychoanalytic Association,* 56:8–34.

Fonagy, P., with G. Gergely, E. Jurist, & M. Target. (2002), *Affect Regulation, Mentalization, and the Development of the Self.* New York: Other Press.

Foucault, M. (1976/1980), *The History of Sexuality,* Vol. I, trans. R. Hurley. New York: Vintage.

Freud, S. (1908), "Civilized" sexual morality and modern nervous illness, *Standard Edition of the Complete Psychological Works of Sigmund Freud* (vol. 94). London: Hogarth Press, pp. 177–20.

Freud, S. (1913), Totem and taboo, *Standard Edition of the Complete Psychological Works of Sigmund Freud* (vol 13). London: Hogarth Press, pp. 1–155.

Freud, S. (1924), The dissolution of the Oedipus complex. *Standard Edition of the Complete Psychological Works of Sigmund Freud* (vol 19). London: Hogarth Press, pp. 173–181.

Freud, S. (1937), Analysis terminable and interminable. *Standard Edition of the Complete Psychological Works of Sigmund Freud* (vol 23), London: Hogarth Press, pp. 216–253.

Frosh, S. (1993), The seeds of masculine sexuality. In: *Psychological Perspectives on Sexual Problems,* ed. J. M. Ussher & C. D. Baker. New York: Routledge, pp. 41–55.

Gabbard, G. (2008), *Into a Bigger Darkness.* Unpublished manuscript.

Gabbard, G., & Pope, K. (1989), Sexual intimacies after termination: Clinical, ethical, and legal aspects. In: *Sexual Exploitation in Professional Relationships,* ed. G. Gabbard. Washington, DC: American Psychiatric Press, pp. 115–128.

Garber, M. (1991), *Vested Interests.* New York: Routledge.

Glare, P. (1982), *Oxford Latin Dictionary.* Oxford: Oxford University Press.

Goffman, E. (1986), *Stigma: Notes on the Management of Spoiled Identity.* New York: Simon & Schuster.

Goldner, V. (2003), Ironic gender/authentic sex, *Studies in Gender and Sexuality,* 4:113–139.

Green, A. (1996), Has sexuality anything to do with psychoanalysis? *International Journal of Psychoanalysis,* 76:871–883.

Green, A. (1997), Opening remarks to a discussion of sexuality. *International Journal of Psychoanalysis,* 77:345–350.

Guntrip, H. (1973), *Psychoanalytic Theory, Therapy, and the Self.* New York: Basic Books.

Harris, A. (2005), *Gender as Soft Assembly.* Hillsdale, NJ: Analytic Press.

Harris, A. (1996), The anxiety in ambiguity: Reply to Brenneis, Crews, and Stern. *Psychoanalytic Dialogues,* 6:267–279

Harris, A. (2010), Personal communication, August 11.

Kernberg, O. (1995), *Love Relations: Normality and Pathology.* New Haven, CT: Yale University Press.

Khan, M. (1974), *The Privacy of the Self.* London: Hogarth Press.

Kohut, H. (1977), *The Restoration of the Self.* New York: International Universities Press.

Kristeva, J. (1982), *Powers of Horror*, trans. L. Roudiez. New York: Columbia University Press.

Kristeva, J. (1983), *Tales of Love*, trans. L. S. Roudiez. New York: Columbia University Press.

Krüll, M. (1979/1986), *Freud and His Father*, trans. A. J. Pomerans. New York: Norton.

Lacan, J. (1966/1977), *Écrits*, trans. A. Sheridan. New York: Norton.

Lacan, J. (1973/1980), *The Four Fundamental Concepts of Psychoanalysis*, ed. J-A. Miller, trans. A. Sheridan. New York: Norton.

Laplanche, J. (1976), *Life and Death in Psychoanalysis*, trans. J. Mehlman. Annapolis, MD: Johns Hopkins University Press.

Leary, K. (1994), Psychoanalytic "problems" and postmodern "solutions". *Psychoanalytic Quarterly*, 63:433–465.

Lesser, R. & Domenici, T., ed. (1995), *Disorienting Sexuality*. New York: Routledge.

Levenson, E. (1982), Follow the fox: An inquiry into the vicissitudes of psychoanalytic supervision. *Contemporary Psychoanalysis*, 18:1–15.

Levenson, E. (1983), *The Ambiguity of Change*. New York: Basic Books.

Levenson, E. (1994), Beyond countertransference. *Contemporary Psychoanalysis*, 30:691–707.

Lévi-Strauss, C. (1949/1969), *The Elementary Structures of Kinship*. New York: Eyre & Spottiswode.

Lichtenberg, J. (2008), *Sensuality and Sexuality across the Divide of Shame*. New York: Analytic Press.

Little, M. I. (1990), *Psychotic Anxieties and Containment: A Personal Record of an Analysis with Winnicott*. Northvale, NJ: Jason Aronson.

Loewald, H. W. (1979), The waning of the Oedipus Complex. *Journal of the American Psychoanalytic Association*, 27:751–775.

McDougall, J. (1995), *The Many Faces of Eros*. New York: Norton.

Masson, J. (1984), *The Assault on Truth: Freud's Suppression of the Seduction Theory*. New York: Farrar, Straus & Giroux.

Meltzer, D. (1973/1979), *Sexual States of Mind*. Glen Lyon: Clunie.

Mitchell, J. (1974), *Psychoanalysis and Feminism: A Radical Reassessment of Freudian Psychoanalysis*. New York: Basic Books.

Mitchell, J. & Rose, J., eds. (1982), *Feminine Sexuality: Jacques Lacan and l'École Freudienne*, trans. J. Rose. New York: Pantheon.

Mitchell, S. A. (1997), *Influence and Autonomy in Psychoanalysis*. Hillsdale, NJ: Analytic Press.

Mitchell, S. A. (2000), *Relationality*. Hillsdale, NJ: Analytic Press.

Norwood, R. (1985), *Women Who Love Too Much: When You Keep Wishing and Hoping He'll Change*. New York: Pocket Books.

Ogden, T. (1994), *Subjects of Analysis.* Northvale, NJ: Aronson.

Renik, O. (1998), The analyst's subjectivity and the analyst's objectivity. *International Journal of Psychoanalysis,* 79:487–497.

Rivera, M. (1989), Linking the psychological and the social: Feminism, post-structuralism, and multiple personality. *Dissociation,* 2:24–31.

Ruddick, S. (1980), Maternal thinking. *Feminist Studies,* 6:342–367.

Rush, F. (1980), *The Best Kept Secret: Sexual Abuse of Children.* Englewood Cliffs, NJ: Prentice Hall.

Samuels, A. (1985), Symbolic dimensions of Eros in transference-countertransference. *International Review of Psychoanalysis,* 12:199–214.

Samuels, A. (1996), From sexual misconduct to social justice. *Psychoanalytic Dialogues,* 6:295–321.

Schein, S. L. (2009), Personal communication, August 2.

Schein, S. L. (2010), Personal communication, July 10.

Slochower, J. (2003), The analyst's secret delinquencies. *Psychoanalytic Dialogues,* 13:451–469.

Smith, H. F. (2000), Countertransference, conflictual listening, and the analytic object relationship. *Journal of the American Psychoanalytic Association,* 48:95–128.

Stein, M. (1981), The unobjectionable part of the transference. *Journal of the American Psychoanalytic Association,* 29:869–892.

Stein, R. (1997), The shame experiences of the analyst. *Progress in Self Psychology,* 13:109–123.

Stein, R. (1998), The poignant, the excessive and the enigmatic in sexuality. *International Journal of Psychoanalysis,* 79:253–268.

Stein, R. (2005), Skimming the milk, cajoling the soul: Embodiment and obscenity in sexuality. *Studies in Gender and Sexuality,* 6:19–31.

Stern, D. (1997), *Courting Surprise.* Hillsdale, NJ: Analytic Press.

Strachey, J. (1901/1960), Editor's introduction. In: S. Freud, *The Psychopathology of Everyday Life: Standard Edition,* S. Freud. London: Hogarth Press, pp. ix–xiv.

Sullivan, H. S. (1953), *The Interpersonal Theory of Psychiatry.* New York: Norton.

Turner, J. S. (1996), *Encyclopedia of Relationships across the Lifespan.* Santa Barbara, CA: Greenwood.

Twemlow, S. W. & Gabbard, G. (1989), The lovesick therapist. In: *Sexual Exploitation in Professional Relationships,* ed. G. Gabbard. Washington, DC: American Psychiatric Press, pp. 71–88.

Widlocher, D., ed. (2001), *Infantile Sexuality and Attachment,* trans. S. Fairfield. New York: Other Press.

Wilner, W. (1998), *Interorientation panel on sexuality, relational collo-quium series, post-doctoral program in psychotherapy and psychoanalysis*, New York University, March 6.

Williams, R. (1961), *The Long Revolution.* London: Chatto & Windus.

Winnicott, D. W. (1953), Transitional objects and transitional phenom-ena: A study of the first not-me possession. *International Journal of Psychoanalysis,* 34:89–97.

Winnicott, D. W. (1971), *Playing and Reality.* New York: Penguin.

Winnicott, D. W. (1975), *Collected Papers: Through Paediatrics to Psychoanalysis.* New York: International Universities Press.

Part 2

Boundary trouble in the psychoanalytic process

Chapter 3

Shadows that corrupt

Present absences in the psychoanalytic process

Andrea Celenza

The history of psychoanalytic theorizing might be characterized as a series of erasures. As in all psychically forced erasures, there survives a ghostly evanescence, a void that emanates an aura-like force field. The memory traces and longings contained within this very real "present absence" must be contended with. No psychic or relational erasure goes gently into that good night.

Before countertransference came into focus in the 1960s, the studied erasure of the analyst's participation (and presence) contorted the shape of the analytic interaction to fit the scientism of the Enlightenment era. The so-called one-person psychology of the first half of the twentieth century has now been thoroughly deconstructed and we are well on our way toward its correction through a kind of re-inscription of the analyst's presence, whose boundaries are continually negotiated and re-negotiated. (Note the literature on disclosure, for example. What is implicitly disclosed in the analyst's presence as well as through direct interpretations?) Within the analytic dyad, decontextualized for our purposes only, we now have two persons existing, however, in a temporal and spatial vacuum. This vacuum is essentially the professional community in the sense that it constitutes what we now call a "third." In that context, we could say that the previous erasure of the analyst was a denial of the "second." Now we are more likely to turn our attention to the context of the analytic dyad—that is, the first and second in the context of the third, in its temporal and spatial dimensions, thus making explicit the nature and experience of the setting on the individual psyches and the intersubjective process.

I would venture to say that the erasure of the "second" in one-person theorizing allowed for a kind of scotoma regarding the analyst's behavior—anything that happened was understood as emanating from the patient and if something bad happened, it was due to the patient's pathology.[1] How many sexual boundary transgressions were ignored or went unseen because the analyst was not in our focus? Similarly, there was an accepted erasure of the analyst's countertransference—it just didn't make it onto the slide that was placed under the microscope. Then we have the unfortunate coincidence that the field of psychoanalysis was attractive to those who were comfortable behind a blank screen, those who tend not to examine their own contribution to a relational engagement. We had, for some time, a match from hell.

Erasures of the containing third

Perhaps the context might be viewed as an absence or invisible third. I refer to the various ways in which the psychoanalytic context, constituting a plurality of thirds, has been erased. We know how the denial of time and space can create an impenetrable "hyperconfidential treatment bubble" detached from these inescapable reality constraints (Celenza, 2007). Another kind of third is represented in our psychoanalytic theories. I am often asked whether there is a difference in the prevalence of sexual boundary transgressions according to theoretical orientation. There is, I often sense, a hidden, subtle, almost delicious anticipation in the question, as if to say, "Please tell me the relational analysts are the bad actors and are single-handedly bringing down the profession"—there is a kind of perverse relish in this subtle expression of internecine psychoanalytic politics. Their disappointment is almost palpable when I reply, "No, actually, there is no difference in theoretical orientation." However, that's not the end of the story.

Our theories (and theories of technique derived from them) all fail us, but in different ways. So there may actually be some differentiations to be made, in types of sexual boundary transgression and profiles correlated with theoretical orientation, but not in quantity or frequency of occurrence. These distinctions highlight different aspects of our beloved theories and their fallibilities, including the different types of pressures on the analyst to maintain the "appropriate stance," especially over time. How our theories are embodied and, may I say, caricatured, can teach us much about the implications of certain theoretical stances and what is needed for us to live them out in humane (for our patients) and salutary (for both patient and analyst) ways.

We are all drawn to this infinitely interesting and compelling profession for very personal, characterological reasons. In an earlier paper on the analyst's needs and desires (Celenza, 2010a), I made the point that most of us have unconscious needs to heal ourselves and we identify with our patients to address these. So, in a general way, we are all here to find the quasi good/bad mother/father we have been searching out all our lives. To be the good/bad mother/father for our patients is to find salvation for ourselves. These motivations drive us to certain theories and repel us from others, finding us situated and perhaps entrenched in a way of performing our craft that is inextricably tied to what we ourselves need and want.

Some of us have a concordant relationship to our theoretical persuasion in that we identify with the (usually idealized) preferred stance of the analyst of that particular orientation because it is consistent with our personality tendencies. It is easy to see how the attuned, naturally empathic, and emotionally expressive analyst, perhaps a bit less loved than she might have needed, would be drawn to the relational tradition to make good use of her empathic skills and propensities.

Others have a compensatory relationship to their preferred theoretical persuasion in that the associated analytic stance gives them cover, something that they need but do not readily have in their armamentarium. We could say this group has a complementary relationship to their theory of choice. The classical analytic stance as a blank screen can serve as protection for the more schizoid and inhibited among us. I'm not saying this is true for all, but that it can function this way. You may think that the latter example is much worse for our patients than the former; however, both fail us in great measure.

For the relational analyst, the problem lies in the idealization of love and its healing power. While, of course, the emphasis on the mutuality and humanness of the analytic relationship has been a much needed corrective to the wooden, inaccessible classical caricature, the emphasis on mutuality to the exclusion of disciplined, asymmetric restraint is an undeniable problem, especially as this imbalance evokes omnipotent rescue fantasies. This is one profile of sexual boundary transgression where the subjectivity of the analyst is impassioned to a level of grandiosity that knows few limits. Here, it is likely that a relational analyst has a concordant relationship with her theories—a way in which theory is used to impel a tenuously restrained potential waiting in the wings to take off, so to speak. What has been hidden is a denied grandiosity that is now rationalized as mutuality to the exclusion of asymmetry. It is the inherent authority and structured power imbalance in the analyst's role that poses a vexed and contested theoretical and technical challenge.

On the other hand, the problem with the idealization of anonymity and the supposed mental freedom it affords is that this stance fails to guide our more schizoid, narcissistically impaired analysts when things heat up. Like a boat in a storm without a mooring, intense erotic transferences can overwhelm the more schizoid, inhibited analyst who has only a one-person epistemology—a mandate to "act like you're not there"—to rely upon (see Mayer, 2001). To emphasize the asymmetry in the analytic relationship to the exclusion of mutual and authentic interchange can be interpreted as permission to shyly withdraw from the analysand. A masochistic surrendering to the patient's intensely driven demands is more likely to derail this kind of limited analyst whose subjectivity finds safety under cover of the mysterious shroud of anonymity.

Most sexual boundary transgressions are a composite of the two: one compensating where the other falls short at one time, the other colluding when rationalizations are needed. This is a special fallibility in these pluralistic times. Omnipotent love can shore up a flagging armamentarium and incite inhibited longings. And we shouldn't think this only happens to the young and unseasoned. Our fantasies of seniority feed our omnipotence too in ways that blind us to the most basic limitations, especially at a time of life when fears of mortality loom. Here, denied grandiosity beckons in the embraced authority of the analyst's role to compensate for subjectively experienced insecurities and fragilities.

The evaporation of a heretofore beloved analytic stance might be termed the erasure of the containing third where the analyst's theories fail to hold, guide, or find a containing place for the analyst's desires and needs. But these theories do not exert their effects on their own. Our theories may be employed, co-opted, and embodied by us in a form that blurs the boundaries between them and us; through narcissistic identification with our deeply cherished theories, we may imagine that we have *become* the authority that in reality we can only strive imperfectly to represent.

Our theories, then, can become actors in the drama through the ways in which we try to embody them and the ways our theories are used, how they transmit and embody us (so to speak). Inevitably, they will fail us and this, consequently, can become a breeding ground for hostility. For example, we may resent the limiting or restraining potential of one theory while rationalizing the use of a more permissive alternative. Or we may erase the guiding presence of all theories, containing thirds representing the presence of others in our professional community, to create a hyper-confidential dyadic bubble (Celenza, 2007) unhinged from temporal-spatial and professional constraints. (Included in this erasure can be the otherwise present, limit-setting function of a spouse, as well.) Or we may develop resentment over time for the constant decentering and gradual depletion associated with our psychoanalytic role regardless of theoretical persuasion. We can hold our theories responsible for our own inadequate self-care.

The present absence of institutionalized power

It is no news that the problem of sexual boundary transgressions revolves around power, one's relationship to power, and the authority inherent in our professional role. Conflicted relations to power or authority are always evident in one's way of embodying the professional stance, our relationship to certain theories and in the ways our lives are lived out as psychoanalysts. There is no hard and fast boundary between the way we live through our profession, the way we live our lives, and who we are. In the numerous consultations I have conducted about sexual boundary transgressions, it cannot escape notice that problematic relations to power and authority are part of the picture and can be exposed in the way treatment is conducted, in the analyst's relationship to his or her institute, and in the analyst's personal life. All of these relations tend to fit a pattern of one sort or another and represent another present absence that exerts its insidious effect.

Aside from the issues associated with theoretical persuasion (discussed above), the power imbalances inherent in the treatment relationship are often repetitions of, or complimented by, power imbalances in the analyst's marital relationship. This I have repeatedly noticed in my clinical consultations with sexual boundary transgressors. There may be a tendency toward masochistic surrender to the (subjectively experienced) powerful other, i.e., the patient (regardless of the structured power imbalance inherent in the psychoanalytic role which, in large part, is structured in the opposite direction). It is not uncommon to hear a transgressing analyst state, "I didn't have any power. She had all the power." This is usually mirrored by a patterned repetition of a power imbalance in the marital relationship where the transgressing analyst is engaged in a similar masochistic tie to his spouse.

In a more general way, researchers in this area have noted long-standing problems with authority as a characteristic of sexual boundary transgressions (Gabbard, 1994; Celenza, 2007). While I am not arguing for a simple, one-to-one causation, the problematic relationship to the psychoanalytic institute or overseeing professional organization occurs often enough to raise a question of intergenerational transmission as at least one factor in the problem of sexual boundary transgressions.

What leads some therapists to engage in sexual relations with a patient? Is it the intensity of the feelings, an unusual and specific affective state itself, something inherent in a particular dyad or special vulnerabilities in the therapist? Inevitably, we also find hostility toward the institute or overseeing professional organization as a fundamental motivator. Many have written about the shaming culture, the hypocrisy, pretentiousness, and elitism that pervade the experience of candidates and junior faculty members in their respective psychoanalytic institutes (see, for example, Lippmann, 2013). I need only remember my experience teaching Theory V to fifth-year candidates, a seminar made up of guest visitors from among our most revered and senior Training Analysts. Many of these guest speakers would regale the class with horror stories about their own experiences as a candidate or young faculty member of humiliating experiences on their way to the top. The pernicious effects of the training analyst system and its monarchical hierarchy have been sufficiently exposed as "authoritarian" and "elitist," inevitably resulting in rebelliousness by the oppressed (see, for example, Kernberg, 2004; Kirsner, 2009; Renik, 2003; Levin, 2014a; in press). This is a kind of power that continues to be systematically erased as the nefarious force it is. Not to expound further on these studies, however, my aim here is to hone in on the more personal level of its destructive effects as they are lived out and reacted to by those who end up committing sexual boundary transgressions.

Our increasing appreciation of and sensitization to the insidious effects of power and authority, especially those forces inherent in the analytic setting, render our ethical obligation and responsibility to maintain the boundaries of the setting all the more important. Added to the endowed authority of the analytic setting is the fragility of our patients as they seek help from an often idealized other. We should never underestimate a person's craving for authority (Schafer, 1983) and our patients' frustration with our unwillingness to "tell them what to do" exemplifies this urge. History, politics, and culture abound with examples of individuals participating in their own subjugation. "People do not want freedom and truth which only cause deprivation and suffering; they want miracle, mystery, and authority. The pain that accompanies compliance is preferable to the pain that attends freedom" (Benjamin, 1988, p. 5). This paraphrase of Dostoevsky (1880/1976) by Jessica Benjamin seeks to reveal the elusive part of the psyche that is drawn to domination, that *willingly submits*.

Erasures of the patient

Thus, the psychoanalytic situation can be likened to a drama in which certain parts are pre-cast: the role of the analyst is pre-emptively endowed with a measure of authority and power while the role of the analysand is collusively cast as an idealizing patient all too ready to comply.[2] When psychoanalysis is the stage on which this drama is set, we have a scenario of potential erasures, depending upon the particular dynamics of the persons involved. The essential question is, "Who or what is being erased or degraded?" I have discovered two kinds of scenario in this regard: whether the drama is *direct* (erasing the dangerous subjectivity of the other) or whether it is a *displaced* scenario where a third object is degraded (and thereby erased) in the mind of the transgressor.

The direct perverse scenario is an example of a classic perversion where the perverse act is focused directly upon the other. In classic perverse fantasies, there is usually an attempt to degrade the other in order to manage, control, and reduce (that is, objectify or erase) the other's potentially dangerous subjectivity. This is essentially an unconscious scenario where the drama revolves around the other who is objectified, thereby reduced from a separate subject to an object, and then sado-masochistically controlled. Most sexual boundary transgressions have this "one-person" fantasy structure.[3] These include merger fantasies, as seen in many female/female sexual boundary transgressions.

Other sexual boundary transgressions, especially the most notorious, predatory type, make use of a displacement object and are thus more accurately formulated as a *displaced perverse scenario*. In these cases, the effort to degrade is often not primarily directed at the other but is directed at the profession, the body or figure that, in fantasy, oversees the dyad. Hence the frequent use of the symbol of the couch, the icon of psychoanalysis, as a place to enact this scenario.[4] In this sense, the couch is the third[5] and symbolically represents psychoanalysis. *The patient is a displacement object*, a stand-in, so to speak, for an aspect of the setting or context. In displaced perverse scenarios, the primary motivation is the erasure or degradation of the third.

Displaced perverse scenarios

The question of who is being degraded and whether the unconscious drama is essentially direct or displaced depends on the type of sexual boundary violation. As I have written elsewhere (Celenza, 2007), it is possible to broadly categorize the different types of sexual boundary transgressions into two types (Gabbard and Lester, 1995; Celenza and Gabbard, 2003; Gabbard, 2016). One includes the egregious, notorious cases that have attracted statewide and sometimes national attention. These usually involve a therapist or analyst who is a psychopathic predator and who has sexually exploited multiple patients numerous times over many years. Though this is probably the best-known type, largely due to the extensive media attention such cases typically attract, these are not the most prevalent type of sexual boundary transgressions.

For the psychopathic predator, the unconscious drama that is being played out is best characterized as a *displaced degradation*. It is largely the profession that is being degraded, though of course, the patient, in the way he or she is used, objectified, and even minimized in dynamic importance, is degraded along the way. In the main, however, patients play a relatively small role in the unconscious psychic drama of the transgressor. By this I do not mean to downplay the traumatic effects such an experience can have on them, but rather to point out that, in the mind of the transgressor, patients are usually replaceable by multiple others who may or may not be involved contemporaneously. The externalization of the drama extends as well to the staging and props, including here, perhaps especially so, the couch.[6]

So, in this way, the perversion of the psychoanalytic process—largely aimed at corrupting the profession itself—is brought about by using the very means of healing in order to exploit and harm rather than help, and to do so in a sometimes flagrant manner. We all know the cases that have involved Chairs of Ethics Committees, the most trusted "analysts of analysts," or the couple's therapist who, while treating the couple, is having sex with one of them between sessions. These are, invariably, displaced perverse scenarios and, even when these psychodynamics are understood, it is difficult to put ourselves in the transgressor's shoes. The perverse nature of these sexual boundary transgressions is inherent in the means/end reversal (see Celenza, 2014).

Direct perverse scenarios

The most prevalent type of sexual boundary violation involves a heterosexual male analyst or therapist who becomes sexually involved with only one of his patients. Gabbard (1994) refers to this type of offender as lovesick; I have called him narcissistically needy (Celenza, 2007). The analyst or therapist of this type is usually mid-career, isolated in his practice, and is treating a difficult patient at a highly stressful time in his life. The "love" relationship that ensues is an intensely absorbing love affair (psychically unhealthy as it revolves around the structured power imbalance of the setting). It may last for several years and the couple may feel that they have found "true love," at least initially. Sometimes the therapy relationship is terminated while the sexual relationship continues. If the relationship is brought to an end by the therapist, this is the time when a complaint is most likely to be filed by the patient.

This type of sexual boundary violation usually occurs because the analyst experiences an unconscious danger. From the analyst's perspective, something is threatening and it has to be managed. More than love, or even sexual attraction, this type of sexual boundary violation happens when a narcissistically fragile analyst or therapist feels that the treatment process is undermining his own delicate narcissistic equilibrium. He feels overwhelmed by the patient, by the instability of the treatment, and is in a subjectively helpless, desperate state. A related point, it is important to note, is that acute suicidality in the patient is a major factor in over half of these cases (Celenza, 2007; Celenza and Gabbard, 2003). This is not an intersubjective engagement, as in subject/subject, but one better characterized as subject/object or doer/done to (Benjamin, 2004).

Here, I believe, the degradation, though unconscious, is primarily aimed at the patient (as opposed to a third object). It is a sadomasochistic relation, focused on the other who is objectified, reduced from subject to object, and in that sense erased. This is an example of a classic perverse scenario where the dangerous subjectivity of the other is controlled and reduced through objectification. I say this because in this type of sexual boundary violation, the seduction occurs when the therapist believes that the therapy is at an impasse: it is a time of threat, acute suicidality, or some other type of critical juncture (Celenza, 2007). The sexualization serves to shift the process from one of enormous frustration and challenge to one of seduction and sexual gratification. It also manages to transform the patient's emerging negative transference to a positive idealizing transference, a much more comfortable mode of relating for such a narcissistically fragile analyst or therapist.

Another type of boundary violation that can be characterized as a direct perverse scenario is the type often seen in female/female dyads. In past studies, female therapists have accounted for only 3 percent of the prevalence rate; however, it is my clinical impression that the incidences of female transgression are on the rise, perhaps due to the overall dominance of females in the profession. The great majority of these transgressions are with female patients and, interestingly, some preliminary data suggest that female therapists who engage in sexual boundary transgressions with female patients are not necessarily self-identified as homosexual prior to their involvement with their patient. The underlying dynamics with female transgressors, however, are different from heterosexual dyads. While the one-time male transgressor uses seduction to manage and transform the patient's negative transference and his own countertransference, the female transgressor engages in an over-identification with her female patient, sometimes involving an unconscious merger fantasy. One therapist said to me, "She was the child I was. I couldn't stand the pain she was in." Here the other's subjectivity is psychically erased by its manic appropriation.

Other shadows

Erasures cast shadows that belie the presence of unknown forces exerting their influence on the psychoanalytic process. Other kinds of shadows are cast by theoretical ambiguity that can be capitalized upon for defensive purposes. Such is the case with certain views of transference and the question of whether it is, in essence "real love." Under the sway of intense passionate feeling, the analyst can rationalize, "This is not transference, this is real love." Or the analyst can perform another sleight-of-hand by deeming "the transference" as only in operation inside the office, while outside the office a "real love affair" can blossom. Other theoretical ambiguities revolve around the question of what is the nature of the betrayal associated with sexual boundary transgressions. Is it the sexual exploitation, the appropriation of power, or something else? In the brief discussion that follows, I aim to address these areas of theoretical ambiguity. For the interested reader, a more detailed discussion of these ambiguities and others can be found in Celenza (2017).

Erasing the realness of transference

First we consider the question of transference love (and its corollary, countertransference love) and whether or not it is "real love." Freud himself displayed a lack of clarity regarding the status of transference love in his paper, "Observations on transference love" (1915). Though the concept of transference permeates almost all of Freud's writings, in this paper he sets out the ambiguities with which we struggle today in their most accessible form. As Morris (2012) recently observed, this paper is structured around *the polarity of transference as real or unreal.* In Freud's resolution to this vexing question, he straddles both sides: "[The analyst] *must keep firm hold of the transference love, but treat it as something unreal...*" (p. 166, italics added). To the question of whether or not it is real, Freud seems to be on both sides of the fence.

Underlying the derivation of the concept of transference, and perhaps causing the schism between real and unreal dichotomous conceptions of it, is the axis of time and the phenomenal experience of temporality. Transference itself is a concept that telescopes time[7]—it is a description of the process whereby the past lives in the present, in contrast to a sequential, linear, chronological view of time. The idea that what is past is past flies in the face of the work transference endeavors to perform.

With these conceptual clarifications in mind, we understand the real/unreal polarity to be a false dichotomy. Transference (as in the history of our relationships and, in particular, those that remain unresolved) is the lens through which we ascribe meaning to the present. In this way, *transference defines what is real.* It is the eye that sees (Schafer, 1983). Transference viewed through this lens is a shaping, a structuring that signifies, rather than a static phenomenon that might be deemed real or unreal.

Erasing the authentic feeling of love

Psychoanalysis invites dreams of love.[8] The dreams that emerge in the analytic setting are responses to the seduction of the setting, a seduction parallel to the primal seduction of the mother (Laplanche, 1997) because the analyst *promises to maintain the boundary* between analysis and external life. The modes of thinking and being in analysis are also seductions to more raw, unprocessed, and "real" (in the sense of undefended) ways of being. We could say that the analytic process is more truthful and, in that sense, edges closer to "real" feelings than the typical evasions that characterize polite social dialogue. Most importantly, *were this promise not made or trusted to be kept, these forms of desire would not emerge.*

For these reasons, we can definitively say that *transference love in analysis is more real than in ordinary life.* Why, then, is it so difficult for the patient-victim to feel the analyst's love? There is always a profound inner doubt that lingers in the mind of the patient-victim. This raises the question of what exactly the nature of the betrayal in sexual boundary transgressions is. Is it the sexual exploitation? Is it indeed the sex? I suggest that the fundamental violation, and the most painful disillusionment, is *the lie*, stated sometimes explicitly, "This is for you." It is an unsustaining love because it is rooted in a broken covenant and thereby has sown the seeds of mistrust.

Erasing the multiplicity of experience

Just as transference captures the phenomenology of temporal reality (the telescoping, synchronic experience of past, present, and future temporality), so do we embody multiple relations with our patients that have both temporal and spatial dimensions. We are not one thing to our patients and many of these modes of relating contradict each other despite the synchronicity of their emergence (see Celenza, 2010b, 2014 for clinical depictions of this multiplicity, including several case studies). For example, we are, at once, a *person* to our patients (reflecting a level of ordinary reality), simultaneously a *woman* (or man), an *analyst* (with attendant expectations of role), and (perhaps) a *parental figure* (depending on the patient's unconscious experience). These identities and associated modes of relating are undergirded by transferences that may or may not conflict with each other. In addition, they correspond to different levels of reality (Modell, 1990) that represent multiple lenses through which we can sort out the complex layering of relational engagement at any one time.

A frequent erasure is the emphasis of one particular relational modality to the exclusion of other modes of relating, as if they were discontinuous with other self-experiences. For example, to speak to the baby while discounting, ignoring, or otherwise neglecting the adult can be regressive and humiliating.

Most often, the erasure in sexual boundary violations is that of the analyst as analyst in order to foreground the man/woman mode of relating. Given that the analyst embodies multiple self-states in relation to the patient, the associated multiplicity of roles can collapse under the pressure of undue desire or need. The perplexity we often feel when a previously competent, even revered psychoanalyst comes to describe his role in relation to his patient in an oversimplified, justifying manner is shocking both in its distortion of the process and especially for its *unidimensionality*.

Conclusion

If psychoanalysis is about nothing else, it is about deepening the capacity to experience one's life in all its complexity and wholeness. The theme of this paper has revolved around various erasures, ways in which psychic experience is truncated, limited, and constricted, representing the very opposite of a psychoanalytic intent. I have considered erasures from an epistemological point of view (nineteenth-century scientism), the so-called "third" of the professional community, erasures of theoretical orientation, institutionalized power, personal power, different perverse scenarios (direct or displaced), erasures of realness in transference, authenticity, and, finally, erasures in the multiplicity of experience. My hope is that this discussion has shed light on the impact of sexual boundary transgressions and the various ways in which they remain the profession's most limiting, constricting, harmful, and perverse phenomena.

Notes

1 One colleague recalled a common quip from that era: "Say whatever comes to mind and everything can and will be held against you" (Gerry Stechler, personal communication, 2001).
2 See Celenza (2007, 2011) for a more detailed analysis of the inherent power imbalances in the analytic setting. In the example of a male/female dyad, this structure is consistent with the power differential inherent in patriarchal societies and conventional definitions of gender roles in heterosexual romantic relationships. This may explain the high prevalence of sexual boundary violations before the feminist movement took hold and the frequency of marriages that culminated from them.
3 See *Erotic Revelations: Clinical Applications and Perverse Scenarios* (Celenza, 2014) for a more detailed elaboration of a variety of perverse scenarios as unconscious fantasied creations of a one-person universe.
4 For one clergy transgressor, the iconic symbol of his profession was the altar whereupon he was able to "fuck God and fuck the church at the same time" (Celenza, 2007, p. 44).

5 The term, third object, as used here, is differentiated from some of the ways in which the concept of the third is used in contemporary theory (see Benjamin, 2004; Britton, 2004; Hanly, 2004 for helpful reviews). In the present discussion, the use of the third object is to be rigorously distinguished from the intersubjective third or symbolic third in that there is no recognition of a separate subjectivity in the mind of the transgressor. Rather, the third is used as in Benjamin's (2004) 'negative third' in complementarity or doer/done to relations, as Ogden's subjugating third (1994), or the way in which Aron (1999), Greenberg (1999) and Spezzano (1998) use the concept, as representative of the analytic community.

6 Dimen's (2011) felicitous overturning of the couch is a case in point.

7 See many authors' (Freud, 1907; Laplanche, 1989, 1997; Civitarese, 2008; Harris, 2009) discussions of *nachträglickeit*.

8 For illustration and discussion of a variety of erotic transferences, see Celenza (2014).

References

Aron, L. (1999). Clinical choices and the relational matrix. *Psychoanalytic Dialogues*, 9, 1–30.

Benjamin, J. (1988). *The Bonds of Love: Psychoanalysis, Feminism, and the Problem of Domination.* New York: Basic Books.

Benjamin, J. (2004). Beyond doer and done-to: An intersubjective view of thirdness. *Psychoanalytic Quarterly*, 73, 5–46.

Britton, R. (2004). Subjectivity, objectivity, and triangular space. *Psychoanalytic Quarterly*, 73, 47–61.

Celenza, A. (2007). *Sexual Boundary Violations: Therapeutic, Supervisory, and Academic Contexts.* New York: Jason Aronson.

Celenza, A. (2010a). The analyst's needs and desires. *Psychoanalytic Dialogues*, 20, 60–69.

Celenza, A. (2010b). The guilty pleasure of erotic countertransference: Searching for radial true. *Studies in Gender and Sexuality*, 11(4), 175–184.

Celenza, A. (2011). Teaching boundaries, experiencing boundaries. In *Sexual Boundary Violations: Therapeutic, Supervisory, and Academic Contexts* (revised paperback edition). New York: Jason Aronson.

Celenza, A. (2014). *Erotic Revelations: Clinical Applications and Perverse Scenarios.* New York: Routledge.

Celenza, A. (2017). Lessons learned on or about the couch: What sexual boundary transgressions can teach us about everyday practice. *Psychoanalytic Psychology*, 34(2): 157–162.

Celenza, A. and Gabbard, G.O. (2003). Analysts who commit sexual boundary violations: A lost cause? *Journal American Psychoanalytic Association*, 51(2), 617–636.

Civitarese, G. (2008). *The Intimate Room: Theory and Technique of the Analytic Field.* London: Institute of Psychoanalysis.

Dimen, M. (2011). *Lapsus linguae*, or a slip of the tongue? A sexual violation in an analytic treatment and its personal and theoretical aftermath. *Contemporary Psychoanalysis*, 47, 35–79.

Dostoevsky, F. (1880/1976). *The Brothers Karamazov*, trans. C. Garnett, rev. R.E. Matlaw. New York: Norton Critical Editions.

Freud, S. (1907). Letter from Sigmund Freud to Karl Abraham, July 7, 1907. *The Complete Correspondence of Sigmund Freud and Karl Abraham 1907–1925*, 1–4.

Freud, S. (1915). Observations on transference love. *Standard Edition of the Complete Psychological Works of Sigmund Freud* (vol 12, pp. 157–171). London: Hogarth Press.

Gabbard, G.O. (1994). Psychotherapists who transgress sexual boundaries with patients. *Bulletin of Menninger Clinic*, 58(1), 124–135.

Gabbard, G.O. and Lester, E. (1995). *Boundaries and Boundary Violations in Psychoanalysis.* New York: Basic Books.

Gabbard, G.O. (2016). Boundaries and boundary violations in psychoanalysis (second edition). Arlington, VA: American Psychiatric Association Publishing.

Greenberg, J. (1999). Analytic authority and analytic restraint. *Contemporary Psychoanalysis*, 35, 25–41.

Hanly, C.M.T. (2004). The third: A brief historical analysis of an idea. *Psychoanalytic Quarterly*, 73, 267–290.

Harris, A. (2009). "You Must Remember This". *Psychoanalytic Dialogues*, 19, 2–21.

Kernberg, O.F. (2004). Discussion: "Problems of power in psychoanalytic institutions". *Psychoanalytic Inquiry*, 24, 106–121.

Kirsner, D. (2009). *Unfree Associations: Inside Psychoanalytic Institutes.* Updated edition. New York: Jason Aronson.

Laplanche, J. (1989). *New Foundations for Psychoanalysis.* London: Blackwell.

Laplanche, J. (1997). The theory of seduction and the problem of the other. *International Journal of Psychoanalysis,* 78, 653–666.

Levin, C. (2014a). Trauma as a way of life in a psychoanalytic institute. In *Traumatic Ruptures*, ed. R. Deutsch. London and New York: Routledge.

Levin, C. (in press). Boundary trouble in the psychoanalytic republic: Reflections on Muriel Dimen's concept of the primal crime. In *Social*

Aspects of Sexual Boundary Trouble in Psychoanalysis: Responses to the Work of Muriel Dimen, ed. C. Levin. London and New York: Routledge.

Lippmann, P. (2013). *The "scandalous" patient: Outrage, titillation and compassion*. Paper presented at the William Alanson White Institute U3 (Unknowable, Unspeakable, Unsprung) Conference, Fall, New York, NY.

Mayer, E.L. (2001). *Sexual abuse of patients and problems in our psychotherapeutic theory of technique*. Paper presented at the Boston Psychoanalytic Society and Institute, Spring, Boston, MA.

Modell, A. (1990). Transference and levels of reality. In *Other Times, Other Realities* (pp. 44–59), Cambridge, MA: Harvard Universities Press.

Morris, H. (2012). *Constituting the ethics of psychoanalysis: Observations on "Observations on Transference Love," the story*. Paper presented on Panel on Ethics, Boston Psychoanalytic Society and Institute, May, Boston, MA.

Ogden, T. (1994). *Subjects of Analysis*. Northvale, NJ: Jason Aronson.

Renik, O. (2003). Standards and standardization. *Journal of the American Psychoanalytic Association*, 51, 43–55.

Schafer, R. (1983). *The Analytic Attitude*. New York: Basic Books.

Skorczewski, D. (2012). *An Accident of Hope: The Therapy Tapes of Ann Sexton*. New York: Routledge.

Spezzano, C. (1998). The triangle of clinical judgment. *Journal of American Psychoanalytic Association*, 46, 365–388.

Chapter 4

Sex and ethics

Protecting an enchanted space

Orna Guralnik

Why not sex?

What is wrong with having sex with a patient? A supersonic boom seems to accompany this question, yet no clear way to arrive at an answer presents itself, no "chain of significance" (see Dimen, 2011, p. 37, and Chapter 2 in this volume, describing how Dr. O.'s kiss and hard-on resisted becoming an object of knowledge). Is this blanched out no-thought a marker of repression, or the manifestation of a social order that has come to feel like "bedrock" (Freud, 1937)? What should have guided Dr. O. before asking Dr. Dimen for a real kiss—before positioning his hard-on as a sex toy rather than as an analytic object?

Transgression

On the face of it, a sexual relationship between two consenting adults does not sound alarming or inherently wrong. One obvious problem that is not unique to the psychoanalytic pair is the power differential and its challenge to the idea of "consent". This is compounded by the fact that, by virtue of being a patient, one has handed over the judgment of what is good for oneself to the doctor. Yet we seem to be dealing with a more disturbing, ruinous kind of transgression here, one that has tipped participants into suicide, destroyed professional careers, and mobilized communities to completely ostracize the transgressors. Sexual relations become transgressive when they violate a social contract. In the case of psychoanalysis, the social contract is a web of partly explicit arrangements between the analyst and his/her patient, the training institute, legal codes of conduct, and ethics that define the psychoanalytic profession, and thus by extension the fiduciary relationship between the psychoanalytic profession and the public. In all of this, a deeper contract is implied: the analyst's intrapsychic contract with their role (their personal version of the Hippocratic Oath). Thus, every seemingly private instance of the analyst's violation is actually a cultural and social action that reverberates throughout the contractual web, corroding the ethical specificity of psychoanalysis as a discipline that in its pure form is about suspending rather than enacting normative assumptions about relations of power.

The analyst's role and ethics

Although it is not always explicit in our theories, psychoanalysis is an ethical moral practice based on the awareness that vulnerability is at the center of the human condition (Freud's *Hilflösigkeit*; Freud, 1927; Butler, 2006). The role of a psychoanalyst carries obligations, responsibilities, and opportunities for virtue, centered on responsibility to the vulnerable. Upholding "the Frame", the way we perform our social contract with our patients, is the way we express our commitment to the patient's vulnerability. The entirety of our personhood is called upon to perform this role; it is not like a business suit we can put on and remove at the end of the day or when it doesn't fit; our "private" inner experiences (fantasies, reveries, desires, fears) all fall under the jurisdiction of this role.

When we think of sexual transgressions in analysis, we often conjure the incest taboo and speak about "Oedipal failures"—the failure to abstain from incestuous desires (child's and parent's). Why? It is certainly not assumed in other professional relationships. Our theories of therapeutic action call for the analytic relationship to evoke, replicate, and correct a parental scene and its prohibitions. The analyst commits to a unidirectional, asymmetrical orientation of "responsibility" for the well-being of the patient. Certain aspects of the adult relationship are disavowed and the transference becomes a portal to earlier configurations of experience. This is a state of enchantment that has implicit references to the deep family structure and syntax of the parent-child relationship. It thus taps into states of passion and seduction that may precede Oedipal arrangements, during which ambiguous and polymorphous potentialities (from the overinclusiveness of gender fluidity to the polymorphous, or what Freud termed bisexuality of the pre-Oedipal) become constituted into life-defining structures (see below). By inviting the patient into this scene, the analyst assumes an obligation to not confuse the tongues of childhood and adult seduction (Ferenczi, 1949).

As-if

The analytic scene depends on the creation of a kind of dissociative spell. The analyst must continuously hail the patient into a certain ambiguous relationship to reality; both must live in an "as-if" environment that allows for a new kind of meaning making. The psychoanalytic frame is what inflates this analytic space. The frame and its prohibitions are the discursive parameters that define how the participants are to understand what is going on, and thus how to feel and behave. The frame defines the language game the patient and analyst share, to borrow Wittgenstein's term for how we give things their specialized meaning.[1] The Barangers (1961–1962/2008) called it the essential ambiguity of the analytic situation, stating: "it is essential for the analytic procedure that each thing or event in the field be at the same time something else" (p. 799). In other words, what defines the scene as psychoanalytic, the cardinal rule of the game, is that the manifest can always potentially be a stand-in for latent, unconscious meaning. We want patients to enter such an enchanted state in order to reduce the grip of their habitual ways of being and thinking. It is related to the function of dreaming (Bion, Bromberg), or the pretend mode, in which reality is suspended enough to become less fixed, allowing deep structures to loosen and change. Emde et al. (1997) found that by the age of 2 infants have two different kinds of psychic reality: one formed by the representation of everyday reality and the other a "pretend" reality formed by the imagination. Target and Fonagy (1996; Fonagy & Target 2000) described the unique state of mind that is the pretend mode. In it, the child is in a way "a head taller than himself" and has a much greater understanding of mental states as representations, as well as increased access to processes and knowledge otherwise not consciously available. Parsons (1999) similarly put forward the idea that the work of psychoanalysis is made possible by sustaining a continuous state of play, by which he means a "logic of the underlying situation", a paradoxical reality (Winnicott, 1968), where things may be real and not real at the same time. Parsons pays special attention to the rule-bound quality of the "game" of psychoanalysis, rules that may block more exploratory kinds of play, but that are absolutely necessary for play, for analysis to feel safe enough.[2]

In this transitional state, the patient may be able to resume processes that were traumatically interrupted at some earlier point and have become defensively rigidified. Obviously, to surrender into it requires that the patient extend a profound level of trust in the psychoanalytic project (the frame) and in the analyst. It is the analyst's task to maintain, nurture, and protect the frame against challenges from the patient and the analyst's own impulses. To do so, the analyst must assume this very particular role, mentioned above, and its corresponding mindset. This role includes an unwavering ontological stance according to which everything that occurs in an analysis also has the status of a stand-in for something else. The analyst relates to all that is said or done with the peculiar quality of a riddle. Whether it be words uttered upon entering the office, a dream, the death of a loved one, or the seductiveness of a patient, the analyst refrains from fixing concrete meanings, but continues to listen in the way one reads poetry. The scene is uniquely psychoanalytic by virtue of being a "theater".

Transference

Transference is sustained by a frame within which a statement like "I am experiencing you as my father" is both true and known not to be true. Past and present, truth and illusion are inextricably mingled in the transference. The analyst, as the guardian of this specialized state, knows to continuously experience countertransferential reactions as marked by the same ambiguous (true and illusive) qualities. What follows is that when sexual tension mounts between patient and analyst, we assume it bears reference to earlier childhood scenes of passion and seduction (of both participants) and to the more general constellation of these scenes as they continue to exist unconsciously.[3]

Breaking the spell with passion

It is often said that the prohibition against sexual relations is the most important supporting wall of the analytic structure. The Barangers see the taboo against physical contact as essential to the as-if spell, as a method of disconnecting from the need to act, so that a different and unknown body can emerge in relation to a different kind of space and time. Indeed, the prohibition may require the most powerful expression of the analyst's role and orientation towards the patient. When passion floods the field, the nature of the psychoanalytic scene and its ambiguous relationship to reality is tested. Freud (1915) equated the eruption of an "outbreak of a passionate demand for love" to the screams provoked by the outbreak of fire in a theatre (p. 162), a fire that over the development of psychoanalytic theory has morphed from material reality threatening the treatment to the flaring up of transference, thus placing transference love smack in the midst of the framework of the cure. Passion poses a profound question about how the analyst understands and performs (Butler, 1988) the nature of the relationship between external and internal reality.

Erotic transferences evoke much concern in both patient and analyst for the future of the analytic relationship; the patient may become overwhelmed with the concreteness of the relationship, but the deepest anxiety is that the analyst will abandon the role of protecting the analytic space and thus render the entire project fraudulent. The analytic spell threatens to immediately and completely collapse in the moment of sexual transgression. It is potentially catastrophic for the analytic scene to lose its ambiguous quality through the analyst's failure to register desire oneirically, as a stand-in for something else (for example, as an expression of the unconscious world informed by prior unresolved Oedipal seductions). How terrifying: a promise betrayed. Play space turns Real; the jungle gym is a spaceship.[4] A confusion of tongues.

An analyst in love

A while ago I concluded a long work-week with a visit to a crowded yoga studio. My mat was right next to a "hot dude", the proximity of whose shirtless, sweaty body turned the class into, let's say, an exciting experience. The next Monday I was shocked to learn that the "dude" was a long-term patient of mine. He was amused by the fact that I "didn't notice" him (ha!). We could think of this little moment as an expression of my dissociative capacity, or of the ways the body can become split off in the treatment room, at times perhaps in a defensive way that dilutes the treatment (I had not until then noticed my patient's body in the same way as I would doing yoga beside a capable moving body).

Yet there is something else here that I am trying to articulate. Notice how, like the example in note 1 of the woman wearing only a bra, the "neural network" activates differently in response to the description "hot dude at a yoga class" versus "my patient". We do not orient towards the imagined/external other in the same way at all. There is a collective, discursive background that mediates our perception. It informs our gaze differently in each of these contexts. This mediating discursive filter also determines who becomes our object of desire.

How does the analyst preserve the analytic field's imaginary quality? Analytic love is different from many other kinds of adult love in being marked through and through with awareness of why the patient is in treatment and our responsibility to them. Mary Gail Frawley-O'Dea's analyst (Frawley-O'Dea, 2011) "eventually acknowledged that had we met under other circumstances, he could imagine wanting to know me (read biblically) in ways that were excluded by our analytic work". Or, in my yoga vignette, "if I saw you on a yoga mat and didn't know you were my patient, I'd find you attractive". This is a fundamentally different statement than "I have desires for you but am constrained by my role".

Our patients are not ours to have

I am trying to speak to an idea of love, an orientation, that does not separate passion from ideation, affect from context, desire from role, or mind from body. From a certain developmental moment, once Oedipal renunciation has occurred, desire for someone requires an assumption that they are the "good object" to have. In other words, feeling desire implies the belief that the other is potentially yours to have.[5] Part of what Oedipal structuralization implies is that previous love objects fall out of that category for good; they do not need to be renounced over and over (Guralnik, 2014).

The deep knowledge that our patients are not ours to have supposedly informs every aspect of how we relate to them. It is woven into our very role as psychoanalysts and is an expression of how truly we identify with being a psychoanalyst. When we are fully identified with our role (rather than it being a pretense), our patients register to us differently than other people. As embodied objects, they are of the world but only visitors to our theater, which is "not of this world". We are often alarmed when patients treat analysis as a substitute for real life; it is a failure to use the scene analytically, as a transitional space. When a trained and experienced analyst is not clear about this, I believe it is a sign of something disruptive at work, even if desires are not acted upon and even if discussed. In the following section I will propose a developmental context for this way of formulating desire.

Post-Oedipal desire

We do not desire and love blindly. Our preferences become established through a long and mysterious process. One of the more enigmatic concepts Loewald (1979) used to describe the resolution of the Oedipal crisis, letting go of the primary incestuous love object, is desexualization: lawless and polymorphous desires succumb to diacritic language and societal structure; desire is transmuted (bewitched) into "good" libidinal strivings. The super ego can emerge only "after the distinction between ego and objects, and ... between heterosexual and homosexual objects, is ... established" (Loewald, 1962, p. 496). From the wild state of pre-Oedipal mutual excitement, parents and child come out of the black box of Oedipal time transformed: now there are boys and there are girls, and there are good and bad desires. Magic! Banished are incestuous love objects and polymorphous desires; in comes heteronormative genital love. Once interpellated into one's place in the social order, the ideology of the good family becomes embedded in us, all the way into our unconscious and our personality structure, in the form of procedural knowledge. Ceremonies, rings, bridesmaids, and other accoutrements function to reproduce our induction into the right hypnotic state (Guralnik, 2014).[6]

Once you've been through the Oedipal black box, your desires are never raw or naked; you are, in a Lacanian sense, alienated. By the time desire reaches psychic registration, it has been interpellated over many times. In this we see that desire is constituted by various discourses, including their ethical and moral codes: to speak of sexuality as separate or in opposition to culture would be to introduce a false division. The limits on desire, the "no" that is at the heart of internalization, mobilizes the powerful recollecting of libido back into the ego and thus the structuring of the personality—as per Freud's original language and Loewald's elaboration. The limits on desire have a profound impact on our body-mind (psychesoma) and inflect who turns us on, not only how we are to manage being turned on. I do not believe in maintaining a distinction between unconscious desire and culture. The Oedipal process is an expression of the way culture shapes unconscious desire and fantasy.

The analyst's desire

What does it mean to truly internalize the "prohibitions", or guidelines, for creating an analytic space that will invite our patients to take the risk and enter the as-if dimension? We internalize limits and make them our own rather than wearing them like a mask, or an unintegrated super-ego introject. Instead of accepting what I consider a false split between desire and regulation, I propose that we understand the analyst's desires as interpellated and constituted by their relationship to their role. There is an anachronistic tendency in the psychoanalytic literature to assume a kind of natural-desire-before-culture. Yes, there is excess in sexuality, and a promise of less familiar secrets that nest within it. Indeed, the press of desire, the way one experiences one's body-mind, often exceeds one's capacity to signify. However, when romanticizing sexual excitement as the seat of the enigmatic creative unconscious, it is easy to delude ourselves that sexuality is prior to, or blind to, culture and its social order. This way of thinking resorts to the old binary sexuality-conformism, and allows one to interpret the motivation for boundary violations as lodged in some romantic, untamable, true-to-self kind of desire, which is simply a variation on the cultural trope of the natural-gendered-body, that then must be so.[7] Since it has become fashionable for the contemporary relational literature to focus on the dimension of deadness-aliveness, it is easy to equate sexual excitement with the sign of health.

My position here is that when the analyst becomes overwhelmed with actual desire towards the patient, it betrays their intra-psychic relationship to the analytic role and is a sign of a fundamental fracture, a dissociation from responsibility towards the patient. As described earlier, after oedipal development the limit/prohibition constitutes and shapes the urge, rather than continues to impose an external restriction on a pre-existing essential desire. Once we've internalized the symbolic grid that constitutes us as subjects and shapes our desires, our ethics and desires are inter-woven. From this perspective, one never experiences desire towards someone that is unrelated to who that someone is to the subject. We desire someone because of who they are, not despite who they are. Similarly, an analyst desiring their patient is not independent of who the patient is to the analyst. Their desire does not operate before, on the side, or independently of the exact role and relationship they have. What does it mean to desire someone who is forbidden to us? It is a response to the other's forbidden-ness. It expresses the analyst's intrapsychic relationship to their role and the various issues that are embedded in it: power, dependency, vulnerability, and omnipotence. Thus we interpret boundary violations as an attack on psychoanalysis.

Notes

1 To provide a simple example: a woman *wearing only a bra* will be understood entirely differently depending upon whether she is seen in the context of a sexual scene at home (sexy), marching in a gay pride parade (a feminist political act of protest), marching the same street but not in a gay pride parade (insanity), or on the beach (compliant with gender norms). The seen body actually registers differently—the rules of the game change how one perceives and registers objects. My thesis is that such language games call for corresponding hypnoid states of mind, suspending disbelief and realities that conflict or shatter any particular spell.

2 Parsons gives as an example of this paradox the scene between master teacher and students in karate training. Knowing that they were not engaged in a real fight allowed the trainees to make attacks with full seriousness and commitment, to make them as real as they possibly could. When the trainees failed to make use of the framework of the class in that way, there was no reality at all and the instructor dismissed them. If, on the other hand, they had lost touch with the pretense, and started really trying to hurt their opponents, they would have broken the frame in the opposite way and, again, the training situation would have ceased to exist. The activity has to be accepted as real. But this is only possible if we know that it is not real.

3 In this chapter I will not be able to address how these scenes also exist within a much wider cultural context that gives them their particular discursive

meanings—be they gender, sexuality, power, class, age, race, and the place the psychoanalytic discipline has within its community.

4 From this perspective, Dr. Dimen and Dr. O *had* to split off what happened if they were to try to hang on to the hope for an analytic space. Muriel's wish for the kiss and hard-on to become an analytic object of thought would have required a very complicated labor of morphing their world back into the magical land of *not quite the thing itself*. One is not always capable of flipping the couch *and* restoring it back to its original place...

5 Patriarchy is an example of such a collective spell that interpellates us all into a pseudo-lawful social order that declares women "good objects" of the man's pursuit—a spell stronger than other laws (rape being an extreme example). In the case of Dr. O, this cultural spell clearly trumped his identification with his professional role.

6 What is *othered* by dominant narratives has the option of remaining alive in dissociative enclaves. Dissociative enclaves can operate "off the grid", so that the person functions in an alternative psychic zone which seems untethered, lawless, and unsupported by clearly organizing principles and ethical codes (Guralnik, 2010, 2014).

7 Such arguments bolster the transgressing analyst's plea for the Trueness of their love.

References

Baranger, M. & Baranger, W. (1961–1962/2008). The analytic situation as a dynamic field. *International Journal of Psychoanalysis*, 89: 795–826

Butler, J. (1988). Performative acts and gender constitution: An essay in phenomenology and feminist theory, *Theatre Journal*, 40: 519–531.

Butler, J. (2006). *Precarious life: The powers of mourning and violence.* New York: Verso.

Dimen, M. (2011). *Lapsus linguae*, or a slip of the tongue? A sexual violation in an analytic treatment and its personal and theoretical aftermath. *Contemporary Psychoanalysis*, 47: 35–79.

Emde, R., Kubicek, L., & Oppenheim, D. (1997). Imaginative reality observed during early language development. *International Journal of Psychoanalysis*, 78: 115–133.

Ferenczi, S. (1949). Confusion of the tongues between the adults and the child—(The language of tenderness and of passion). *International Journal of Psychoanalysis*, 30: 225–230.

Fonagy, P. & Target, M. (2000). Playing with reality: III. The persistence of dual psychic reality in borderline patients, *International Journal of Psychoanalysis*, 81: 853–873.

Frawley-O'Dea, M. G. (2011). More thoughts. *IARPP Colloquium 18: Muriel Dimen's "Lapsus Linguae, or a Slip of the Tongue?"*. May 9–22. K. Gentile and E. Rozmarin (Moderators).

Freud, S. (1915). Observations on transference-love (Further recommendations on the technique of psycho-analysis III). In J. Strachey (Ed. & Trans.), *The standard edition of the complete psychological works of Sigmund Freud* (vol. 12, pp. 157–171). London: Hogarth Press.

Freud, S. (1927). The Future of an illusion. In J. Strachey (Ed. & Trans.), *The standard edition of the complete psychological works of Sigmund Freud* (vol. 21, pp. 1–56). London: Hogarth Press.

Freud, S. (1937). Analysis terminable and interminable. *International Journal of Psychoanalysis*, 18: 373–405

Guralnik, O. (2014). *The Sphynx's spell*. Paper given at the Psychology of the Other conference, Boston, MA, and at the annual Division 39 conference, New York.

Guralnik, O. & Simeon, D. (2010). Depersonalization: Standing in the spaces between recognition and interpellation, *Psychoanalytic Dialogues*, 20: 400–416.

Loewald, H. W. (1962). Internalization, separation, mourning, and the super-ego. *Psychoanalytic Quarterly*, 31: 483–504.

Loewald, H. W. (1979). The waning of the Oedipus complex. *Journal of the American Psychoanalytic Association*, 27: 751–775.

Parsons, M. (1999). The logic of play in psychoanalysis. *International Journal of Psychoanalysis*, 80: 871–884.

Target, M. & Fonagy, P. (1996). Playing with reality: II. The development of psychic reality. *International Journal of Psychoanalysis*, 77: 459–479.

Winnicott, D. W. (1968). Playing: Its theoretical status in the clinical situation. *International Journal of Psychoanalysis*, 49: 591–599.

Chapter 5

The analyst's narcissism and the denial of limits

James P. Frosch

In a recent paper (Frosch, 2014) building on the contributions of many others (Freud, 1915; Ogden, 2002; Kris, 1977; Steiner, 2005), I focused on one of the many aspects of narcissism: the relationship between narcissistic defenses and the inability to mourn. In order to avoid the experience of unbearable loss, human beings utilize defenses of grandiosity, devaluation, and idealization. They attempt to negate the painful existential realities of death, separateness, and vulnerability to loss by means of fantasies of the omnipotent self and/or the omnipotent object. States of uncompleted mourning, upon analysis, reveal underlying narcissistic fantasies that impede the grieving process necessary for emotional growth and the development of whatever contentment is possible under the conditions of life as we know it. Similarly, narcissistic states, upon analysis, reveal a motive to deny an experience of overwhelming loss, especially the loss of a fantasy of an ideal self and/ or an ideal other. The affect that mediates experiencing the distance between the real self and the ideal self is shame (Morrison, 1989). At times, all of us use others in ways that help us avoid feelings of shame and humiliation. Some do this more often than others.

The analytic literature on patients' narcissism is voluminous. Contributions about the analyst's narcissism and its effect on the analytic process are comparatively sparse, although this asymmetry is decreasing. Chused's (2012) article is one of the most honest and specific yet. A few others before her paved the way (Finnell, 1985; Coen, 2007; Kris, 2005; Wilson, 2003; Smith, 2004). The recent emphasis on intersubjectivity and the bi-personal field (Baranger and Baranger, 2008; Brown, 2011) has no doubt facilitated this continuing development. In this chapter I will discuss the interplay between the narcissistic desires of the analyst and those of the patient. In particular, I will examine the tendency for the patient and analyst to enact a mutual idealization, so as to ultimately avoid facing limits in each of themselves, in their relationship, and in reality.

In the analyst, the wish to be idealized is gratified by the patient's natural tendency, in the transference, to idealize. For the analyst as well, the patient can become an ideal object who promises to heal the pain in the analyst of experiencing the gap between the real self and the ideal self. If recognized, this enactment can be analyzed and both participants can face the necessary grieving of a lost ideal reality. Muriel Dimen's (2011) paper (also Chapter 2 in this volume) movingly illustrates these themes, especially how the powerful interplay of narcissistic desires clouded the capacity of an analyst to help his patient, and to recognize his patient's communication of her need for help. I will also recount two moments from my own practice in which these issues were very much in play.

People become analysts for many reasons. A fascination with the mind, identifications with important teachers, and deeper needs to rescue ill parents of childhood are all common motivations. Analysts, like everybody else, have narcissistic needs. They are trying to find ways of feeling good about themselves, and do not always succeed. They wish to feel important, to be admired, and to have an impact on other people, including their patients. Like parents, teachers, ministers, and bosses of all kinds, they have power over their patients. The power is based on both the actual dependency of the patient, who has come for help, and the transference, which regressively amplifies this power from its association with the profound dependency for survival of the child on his/her parents. One good and quick way to judge health or pathology in the narcissistic sphere is to observe how people treat those they have power over: children, pets, students, patients, and subordinates at work.

Among the common motivations to become a psychoanalyst is the opportunity to feel idealized by our patients. Though our patients' feeling for us is partly based on the reality of our helpfulness, the most powerful loves and hatreds that come our way are not earned, but rather directed toward us because we are there in the analytic situation taking an analytic stance. This creates a bubble that often promotes idealization. The idealization can be a reaction formation to envious hatred, and/or it can be the reappearance of developmentally thwarted aspirations that need to be integrated into the mature personality. There are many technical controversies about whether and when to actively confront idealizations as opposed to waiting for the inevitable and hopefully optimal disillusionments. It is clear, however, that the analyst's wish to be idealized and the patient's need to idealize can lead to mischief. It can even lead to the displacement of critical and hostile feelings onto others. Finnell (1985) and Greenacre (1966) both pointed out the many opportunities to do this through Institute politics. And, at times, in the bubble of the consulting room, analyst and patient can engage in a mutual idealization and together create a mythic utopian reality more gratifying than the reality of other parts of their lives. Impossible love is the stuff of romantic poetry and myth for a reason: it has great draw, no doubt partly based on the impossible wishes of children to love and be loved in all ways at once, to be both children and adults at the same time, both daughter and wife, son and husband, to take the example of the positive Oedipus complex. In development and in the analytic process it is a tricky balance. Many examples of boundary violation of the non-predatory type, the "love sick," as Gabbard and Lester (1995) called them, occur in this bubble of mutual idealization. It is rare and perhaps impossible that such a relationship can make the transition to real life in an enduring way.

Sexual boundary violations are the most extreme and dramatic example of the misuse of patients by analysts for their own narcissistic purposes, whether to restore lost self-esteem, find needed affirmation, reclaim lost youth, or, in a grandiose and death defying fashion, to live on the edge of danger, and eventually over it. The more subtle expressions of the analyst's narcissism occur often and in every analysis. The analyst may want to feel smart, or giving, or tough, or wise, or whatever, and the patient often complies in order to obtain what they want from the relationship. Analysts generally want to feel emotionally connected to the patient. When they don't, they can feel thwarted, frustrated, and rejected. If analysts are not familiar with such reactions in themselves, or even if they are, they then experience shame and anger at the patient and sometimes retaliate with subtle expressions of contempt toward the patient. Or there can be a mutual admiration society between analyst and patient. The analysis feels wonderful to both; meanwhile the patient's marriage or other significant partnership gets worse and worse and the patient's difficult sides do not find expression in the transference, where they might challenge the analyst and reveal the analyst's limitations. In a good and deep analysis, inevitable collisions occur between the patient's narcissism and the analyst's. They may occur around the fee, or they may occur around the patient's experience of limitations in the analyst's character and capacity to analyze, which are always present. Then patient and analyst both have to face the experience of loss of the ideal. Shame, guilt, and hostility are released, like inevitable by-products of a volatile chemical reaction. Sometimes they rule the day, and the crunch crunches the treatment to a halt. This is a tragic ending. Other times there may be, in the Aristotelian and Shakespearean sense, a comic ending with both patient and analyst stretching and growing and developing better capacity to bear separateness and difference, and becoming more accepting of the pragmatic limits of magical thinking. The acceptance of such loss can provide immeasurable gains. What sometimes stands in the way of such constructive resolution is the inability of the analyst to mourn, to bear a loss of an ideal self-connected to an ideal other living in an ideal reality.

Recently, a colleague in another state called to ask if I would see a patient of his in consultation. He had seen her in weekly psychotherapy for about two years and had then moved to another city. She insisted on continuing with him on the telephone and he agreed to do this, though with considerable reluctance. Now he thought the two of them were stuck and that perhaps it would be best if she worked with someone in the city where she lived. I said I was willing to do a consultation and that I would prefer to see the patient first and then, with her permission, would speak with him further about his perspective on their work together. Soon afterwards, the patient called and made an appointment to see me. When she appeared in my office she was extremely upset, alternating between overwhelming anxiety, self-loathing, and rage. Gradually she told me her story. She was 54, unmarried, and had worked in the same job as a middle manager for many years. Within the last two years both parents had died and her brother in law had developed cancer. She had first consulted her therapist around ten years before and she vividly remembered seeing him for the first time. "I knew I shouldn't work with him," she told me, "because I liked him too much." I asked what it was that gave her that feeling, but it was difficult for her to say. Thinking of what might be immediately apparent I asked, "Was it the way he looked, or his voice, or something else about his manner?" "It was all of those things," she replied. She told me that she loved his hands, his expression, everything. "I should have walked out of his office right then," she said more than once. She then wept and attacked herself for being a fool. She understood, she told me, the way therapy worked. She knew she was just a patient, and that Dr. X did not love her. When she said, "just a patient," it sounded like she was referring to some sub-human species. She didn't know what to do. She didn't think the therapy was helping her but could not bear the idea of leaving it. At times she seemed paranoid, like when she said that no doubt Dr. X and I would enjoy discussing the pathetic state she was in. She especially couldn't bear the idea that she would not have children, and, in her own mind, was unlikely to marry.

As I listened to Ms Y, I felt an intense sadness. Her situation seemed so poignant, and I thought to myself that some people, rather than being helped by therapy, are consumed by it. Over the years I have been consulted regarding a number of people who were struggling with an unmanageable transference, and I knew how painful the process was going to be, no matter what I recommended or what Ms. Y decided. Ms. Y went on to say that a few months earlier she had attended a conference in the city where Dr. X now lived, and he had suggested they meet four times over the course of the week in order to get some better understanding and resolution of her situation, but that did not seem to help. I said to Ms. Y that in psychotherapy we worked with powerful and sometimes uncontrollable feelings. It was a little like working with radioactive material. Much good could come of it, but one needed to respect the power and potential destructiveness of the feelings that were released in the process.

Ms. Y reported no inappropriate behavior on Dr. X's part. With the wisdom of hindsight, some might not have agreed to continue the therapy by telephone. But, in those early years, there was some progress, mainly a reduction in Ms. Y's anxiety and a new-found ability to speak in public. There was no change in Ms. Y's inability to find and sustain a relationship with a man. Perhaps Dr. X should have sought consultation earlier; he might also have underestimated a certain, almost psychotic tendency in his patient, who had a schizophrenic brother and had always felt like an oddball herself. However, my feeling was that the enactments that took place in the dyad were within the bounds of common practice, and were of the sort that can arise in a particular match. I remembered Dr. X as a handsome, soft-spoken, and gentle man. It might be said that he was subtly seductive in a certain way, but again, well within the bounds of usual and accepted therapeutic practice. For this patient, however, his appearance and style had caused an instant and intense reaction. Perhaps this was so because of Ms. Y's history of idealizing her powerful and handsome father, a connection Dr. X tried to make with no success, and because of Ms. Y's tendency to live in fantasy, rather than to experience the disappointments of reality and her own intense anxiety about sexual intimacy.

A much more prosaic moment occurred with a patient of mine. Mr. A came to see me about six months after his father died, saying that he had always intended to seek therapy, and that this was the right moment. His father, a charismatic and gregarious man, had been a psychotherapist. The father had developed cancer at the age of 60 and within a year he was dead. Mr. A was an extremely appealing golden boy. Tall, dark, and handsome, he had been successful at everything he ever did. He was happily married and the father of a toddler boy. He was having some anxiety about moving up the ladder in his career, fearing that promotions would compel him to increase his already long hours. And he missed his father greatly. They had spoken nearly every day when his father was alive. A predominant countertransference feeling was that I felt like a version of his father, and he felt to me like a golden boy of a therapy patient: hard working, appreciative, and emotionally engaged. In short, everything I could have hoped for in a son. No doubt this feeling was determined both by Mr. A's past and inner world and by my own particular response to it (having been the son of a father and the father of two sons in my personal life).

Mr. A and I had been talking a great deal about moments when he would get panicky at work. This would occur when the work would pile up and when there were many people counting on him to perform: unreasonable clients who wanted things to be less complicated than they were and bosses who wanted those clients to be happy. Mr. A would begin to panic: There was too much to do. What if he made a mistake? People would be angry and disappointed. While there was no doubt about the real time pressures of the present, the quality of Mr. A's anxiety could make these concerns feel like life or death. In that respect they had the quality of childhood danger situations and their attendant unconscious fantasies. If he made a mistake he would be abandoned, unloved, and castrated, and he would fail to live up to his ideal self.

One time he had a close call. In going over documents he discovered that he had made an error, which, if it had gone uncorrected, would have caused a serious problem. At first he couldn't think of a solution and panicked. After a while he was able to calm himself down and he did discover a way to address the situation. Eventually, after listening to his account, I said that the emotion he was describing seemed to me to have the power of the feeling a child has when he feels he has done something bad. He immediately remembered one time in grade school when he felt that way. He had been ill and missed school for a few days. There was a math test, but he was confident he could take it without studying and still do well, as he always did. In the event he got a D on the test—punishment, he felt, for being too cocky. For days he couldn't bear to tell his parents because of his feelings of fear and shame. While he was speaking about this, I vividly and uncomfortably recalled a time in eighth grade when I got a D on a math test. I was devastated, since much of my self-esteem was based on superior academic performance, and, in my mind, the love and regard of my parents was based on it as well. I went to the teacher to tell him that I was not a D student, and to ask whether there was anything else I could do to perform better in the course. I started to cry as I spoke to him, and then felt a double shame about the D and about the tears. This teacher had the reputation of being mean and unsympathetic, but this time he was supportive and said that everybody's lowest test grade would be dropped and there would be many future tests.

So far, so good; I was empathically resonating with my patient, attuned to his anxiety and to the internal psychic stakes. Then I noticed a powerful urge to tell him of my memory, to say to him something like, "Those childhood experiences are so powerful and painful and they can return in full force and take over the present. Your story reminded me of the time..." So I started thinking, "Why do I want to tell him? What's to be gained?" I suppose I wanted to join him in what Crastnopol (2007) has called "uneasy intimacy," a feeling of closeness that went beyond the empathic resonance of separate individuals and blurred into some feeling of sameness and mutual knowledge.

Thinking later on about the powerful urge I had felt to relate my memory, I wondered whether it was also part of a mutual collusion to avoid the negative transference, for instance the feeling Mr. A might have had that he needed to perform for me too, by being a "good patient" in order to get my fatherly love. Furthermore, though he had loved his father dearly, his father could be annoying and self-centered. He was not always a good listener, but would sometimes launch into stories about himself. Was my urge to launch into a story about myself part of an unconscious, mutually determined reenactment in which these less pleasant parts of the paternal relationship were to be replayed?

Ms. Y came to her first meeting with Dr. X with a readiness to establish uneasy intimacy. For her, the therapy situation and her therapist's style evoked the illusion of love. She felt this love not to be transference love, but rather that she knew him and loved the person he was. For her, therapy felt like a seduction, and the romance in her head served to distract her from deep anxieties and powerful griefs and grievances. My moment with Mr. A is a more everyday occurrence, a more subtle, mutually determined interaction where both patient and therapist feel the pull toward uneasy intimacy. The key to uneasy intimacy, as Crastnopol defines it, is that it is a relationship that leads to an "emotional exploitation in which one or both participants can neither leave nor thrive within the relationship" (Crastnopol, 2007, p. 69). She describes how two individuals "become privy to each other's inner world to an excessive degree and at an artificially heightened rate ... that ... fails to take into account other features of the two individuals' roles vis-à-vis each other ... like age discrepancy, role asymmetry, conflicting ties, value differences etc." (Crastnopol, 2007, pp. 67–68). She contrasts this kind of illusory intimacy with a mature relationship between two differentiated individuals who appreciate and acknowledge the subjectivity of the other person, and who respect and take care of each other.

In psychoanalytic theory we are constantly making definitional distinctions and then demonstrating how these distinctions blur and reform in shifting and ambiguous ways. Transference and real relationship, reality and resistance, conflict and deficit, intrapsychic and interpersonal, are but a few examples of these complicated dialectics. Freud himself was a master at creating definitional distinctions and then convincingly demonstrating how they break down upon closer examination. So too is the case with Crastnopol's concept of uneasy intimacy and its more legitimate cousin, mature love. She is correct in making a distinction, and it is a distinction with a difference. And yet, upon reflection the plot inevitably thickens. Her own earlier paper, "The rub" (Crastnopol, 2006) helps us to understand why. In that paper she suggests that there are biologically separate motivational systems responsible for lust, pair bonding or companionate love, and romantic love. These building blocks of *eros* sometimes join in temporary bliss, but as often fragment back into parts. This is not so different from Freud's notion of mature sexuality arising from the union of developmentally earlier phases to form an unstable mature sexuality.

At the extremes, we all know the difference between exploitative attachments that inhibit growth and benign attachments that promote growth, just as we know the difference between art and pornography. But, as with that distinction, there is a lot of gray in between the black and white. And, as complicated as it is in real life, it starts to get really complicated in psychotherapy. To begin with, we psychoanalysts invite the patient to develop a kind of uneasy intimacy with us, the transference. While it is generally not as instantaneous and extreme as Ms. X's instant love, it always has powerful elements of the desire to seduce and be seduced. Most of our patients can handle it, and most analysts are able to interpret and analyze rather than exploit, though in subtler ways analysts struggle with their own desire to gain narcissistic gratification from the patient, in whatever form they seek it. And then there is the countertransference. Analysts, like their patients, are seducible and seductive. The tendency to seek uneasy intimacy is universal. It may dominate in the psychological make-up of some people and be much less prominent in others, but it is always there. Its motivational core is not lustful, but narcissistic. In other words, it arises from the universal desire to be perfect and to find perfection through connection to a perfect other, and, in so doing, to enter an alternate, Edenesque reality governed by the pleasure principle. The fantasy is that the individual can triumph over limits and never has to experience loss, whether loss of an ideal self, loss of another person, loss of self-esteem, or the prospect of loss of the self itself through death. Relationships of uneasy intimacy are characterized by idealization. Sometimes the idealization is mutual, while sometimes it is unidirectional. It is a question worth pondering whether the urge for uneasy intimacy is necessarily pathological, or whether, like other urges, it can be pathological or healthy when transformed. Kohut felt that narcissistic desire, while it could take perverse and destructive forms, was also the necessary fuel for ambition and the formation of ideals. I would say that such healthy transformation can only occur if an individual develops the capacity to mourn, which involves acknowledging and bearing the reality of loss. Such a capacity does not exist unless an individual is able to understand and endure the separateness of objects and the consequent limits on the fantasy of omnipotent control.

Though one of the cases described above came to grief and one did not, neither is an example of the analyst's narcissism running amuck. In contrast, Muriel Dimen's painful account of her first analysis confronts us squarely with the radioactive nature of unanalyzed idealization in the analytic process. In her story we read about an analyst who by both character and time of life was vulnerable to the (for him) irresistible pull of being admired by a younger woman headed into the prime of her life while his was soon to be in decline. It is a story of the analyst's unresolved narcissism culminating in an action that could not then be contained and metabolized, presumably because of his shame. It is a common enough dynamic between an older man with status and power and a younger woman. Many accounts of sexual abuse and misuse in the analytic situation involve a male analyst in late mid-life and a younger woman. However, on occasion, I have seen such a pattern when the patient is an older man and the analyst a younger woman. Even though the power differential is different in that instance, the pull between a vulnerable older man and a younger woman with her own unresolved Oedipal issues can be strong enough to result in boundary crossing. In the confusion of tongues, to borrow Ferenczi's phrase, the primary mover inside Dimen's analyst was not only lust, but that which occurs in the area of overlap between lust and narcissism. In that nether land, it is easy for the analyst to mistake the patient's admiration for sexual excitement. As Ferenczi was one of the first to point out, there are always two aspects to a traumatic event: the event itself and the lack of available help to contain, metabolize, and symbolize the event. In this instance the silence was deafening.

In this case, many cards were stacked against a healthy outcome. The analyst liked to pontificate and play the role of the wise father, and preferred talking to listening. It was a period in the history of psychoanalysis when psychoanalysts had prestige and power in the culture, perhaps attracting narcisists and reinforcing narcissism. It is so easy for the analyst to forget that the love and admiration of the patient is in some measure due to her transference regression, especially if her own father did not appreciate her. Dimen (2011, p. 36; this volume, p. 26) writes that the analyst "regarded the patient as responsible, an adult like the analyst." While it is essential to recognize this part of the relationship as being that between an adult patient and an adult analyst, and to respect the patient as an adult with choices, it is equally important not to underestimate the asymmetry of power and regressive pull in the analytic relationship. For both analyst and patient mutual admiration can feel wonderful, but it can serve to avoid aggression and counter-aggression. All the bad objects and bad selves are then outside of the room.

The pull toward uneasy intimacy is a ubiquitous pressure in both analyst and analysand even in the best analytic work. It is a constant feature of analytic life, and, like so many universal urges, the best one can hope for is that the acceptance of the existence of such narcissistic desire can pave the way for an understanding of the enactments it creates. The Reality Principle can have it's way only if the power of the Pleasure Principle is acknowledged.

References

Baranger, M, & Baranger, W. (2008). The analytic situation as a dynamic field. *International Journal of Psychoanalysis,* 89: 795–826.

Brown, L.J. (2011). *Intersubjective process and the unconscious.* London: Routledge.

Chused, J.F. (2012). The analyst's narcissism. *Journal of the American Psychoanalytic Association,* 60: 899–915.

Coen, S. (2007). Narcissism and boundary crossing. *Journal of the American Psychoanalytic Association.* 55: 1169–1190.

Crastnopol, M. (2006). The rub: Sexual interplay as a nexus of lust, romantic love, and emotional attachment. *Psychoanalytic Dialogues,* 16: 687–709

Crastnopol, M. (2007) Uneasy intimacy, a siren's call. In M. Suchet, A. Harris, & L. Aron (Eds.) *Relational psychoanalysis, Vol 3.* Hillsdale, NJ: Analytic Press, pp. 33–91.

Dimen, M. (2011). *Lapsus linguae,* or a slip of the tongue? A sexual violation in an analytic treatment and its personal and theoretical aftermath. *Contemporary Psychoanalysis,* 47: 35–79.

Finnell, J. (1985). Narcissistic problems in analysts. *International Journal of Psychoanalysis*, 66: 433–445.

Freud, S. (1915). Mourning and melancholia. In J. Strachey (Ed. & Trans.) *The standard edition of the complete psychological works of Sigmund Freud* (vol. 14). London: Hogarth Press, pp. 237–258.

Frosch, J.P. (2014). From grievance to grief: Narcissism and the inability to mourn. *Canadian Journal of Psychoanalysis/Revue canadienne de psychanalyse*, 22 (2): 259–275.

Gabbard, G.O. & Lester, E.P. (1995). *Boundaries and boundary violations in psychoanalysis*. New York: Basic Books.

Greenacre, P. (1966). Problems of overidealization of the analyst and of analysis—Their manifestations in the transference and countertransference relationships. *Psychoanalytic Study of the Child*, 21: 193–212.

Kris, A. (1977). On wanting too much: The exceptions revisited. *International Journal of Psychoanalysis*, 57: 85–95.

Kris, A. (2005). The Lure of hypocrisy. *Journal of the American Psychoanalytic Association*, 53: 7–22.

Morrison, A.P. (1989). *Shame: The underside of narcissism*. Hillsdale, NJ: Analytic Press.

Ogden, T.A. (2002). A new reading of the origins of object relations theory. *International Journal of Psychoanalysis*, 83: 767–782.

Smith, H. (2004). The analyst's fantasy of the ideal patient. *Psychoanalytic Quarterly*, 73: 627–658.

Steiner, J. (2005). The conflict between mourning and melancholia. *Psychoanalytic Quarterly*, 74: 83–104.

Wilson, M. (2003). The analyst's desire and narcissistic resistances. *Journal of the American Psychoanalytic Association*, 51: 71–100.

Chapter 6

Unraveling

Betrayal and the loss of goodness in the analytic relationship[1]

Dianne Elise

In this essay, I will be addressing the situation of patients who have had an experience of traumatic betrayal by a clinician whom they had previously trusted. The nature of the betrayal can range along a continuum from overt boundary violations—with the patient, or as revealed to have occurred with another patient—to various ethical lapses and to more ambiguous clinical errors that contribute to impasses and to broken off treatments. Regardless of the particular aspects of any given betrayal, a unifying factor for these patients is the traumatic disruption to their sense of trust in a good object. My focus will be on the *subjective experience of the patient*, not on an attempt to delineate the specific nature of the betrayal.

I will be writing from the perspective of the subsequent analyst sought out in the wake of a betrayal and a disrupted termination. This next analyst encounters a situation with particular implications for the transference-countertransference matrix. The analyst is challenged to assist the patient with a task that is exceedingly complex *for them both*. This analyst is charged, as witness to the loss of a clinical relationship between two others, to aid the patient in her or his confusion over the disappearance of a good object. The analyst must help the patient to look back, to sort out experiences of good and bad, and to "dream" a goodbye.

In the film *Imagining Argentina* (Hampton, 2003), the protagonist Carlos has prescient, waking dreams about the fates of lost loved ones who have "disappeared" and with whom no goodbyes have been possible. As person after person comes to Carlos with their painful query about their missing person, he dreams a response. There is actual death in these disappearances, but also symbolic death through tyranny and betrayal, as most of the missing have been taken away by corrupt political powers whose function ought to have been to protect them. Instead, loved ones have been abducted, likely murdered, maybe imprisoned, leaving only a desperate hope that they are in hiding and will at some point return.

In providing a context in which to say goodbye, Carlos's dreams offer a process of closure to those who cannot move forward until they have looked back and found the truth of what has occurred—that their loved one will not be returning. Though painful, this process stands in stark contrast to the fate of the bereaved left in limbo. Without a third person standing outside of, but deeply concerned with, the fate of the original relationship between two others, a process of grieving is obstructed.

The role of waking dreaming by a third in facilitating the mourning of one person for another has its parallel in the analytic situation: "The past cannot become memory without a dream-work furnished by the analyst" (Botella & Botella, 2005, p. 32). Ogden (2005) describes the analyst as "participating in dreaming the patient's undreamt and interrupted dreams" (p. 2; see also Ogden, 2000, 2004). When confronted with the symbolic loss of one's former analyst due to a betrayal, one needs to be able to look back, to make the past the past, and one needs help in order to accomplish this painful task.

As evocatively depicted in the film, when loved ones are abducted by corrupt political powers, a separation between good and bad can be maintained. Loved ones are gone, but they are still good; badness lies with the abductors. But if one is betrayed *by* a loved one, good and bad come to reside in the same person and one loses not only a loved person in one's life but also a good object in one's mind. In the analytic community—with ethical violations[2] and lapses of integrity that lead to a felt sense of betrayal for a patient—good and bad are inextricably intertwined. This crucial element imposes a complex demand on the process of grieving the loss of this trusted relationship.

Although splitting is, at least for a time (often a long time), a possible and likely defense, the most disturbing element for any patient confronted with this experience of betrayal is the registering of a "lost" good analyst who "turns into" a bad object; loss of the good and intrusion of the bad are occurring within the representation of one object. Neither side of this split is viable, yet it is extremely challenging to integrate the two, to retain for oneself what was good about the treatment relationship with the former analyst, while also being able to trust one's own experience of what was problematic and harmful. Resolving this dilemma takes considerable effort. This task of integration is what is at stake in any subsequent treatment. In looking back over an expanse of thirty years, Dimen (2011; also Chapter 2 in this volume) articulates what this protracted struggle encompassed for her.

In her compelling narrative, Dimen shows us the complexity of the psychic task entailed in the effort to come to terms with a betrayal by a trusted other: one's analyst. Her entire text affirms the crucial need to look back in contending with deception, betrayal and loss. With a vantage point of three decades and a very changed sense of self, Dimen utilizes her considerable scholarship and talents as a writer—most especially her impressive capacity to theorize—to form a retrospective realigning of her views of Dr. O, who "broke his compact and my heart" (p. 39; this volume, p. 29). She pulls into focus what she could see at the time but could not make sense of, grasp emotionally, or be willing to integrate into her conscious understanding of Dr. O and her relationship to him. She shares her journey with us.

Yet for many years—"until I wrote about it and had the exchange afforded by writing and speaking with the psychoanalytic community and others" (p. 37; this volume, p. 27)—Dimen found herself in silence, "attempting to manage this painful flood alone" (p. 37). Without a third engaged as witness and container, "feeling could not be contained ... knowledge ... could not coalesce, nor could there evolve an 'I' to hold the self-shards together" (p. 37): She "lacked the internal structure to engage full-on the heartbreak, anger, and disillusionment that would have rushed in" (p. 62; this volume, p. 53) had she relinquished her still idealized view of her former analyst. What then of patients who have to contend with an immediate, unavoidable dismantling of the relationship with their analyst, and without the resources readily available that Dimen now has at her deft disposal? And what is the fate of patients, *themselves clinicians*, where defensive patterns such as denial and isolation may not be tenable in today's clinical climate, where attempts to remain silent will likely soon crumble?

Although absolutely painful and damaging, silence and dissociation were, as protective strategies, a possibility for Dimen for many years.

As Dimen (2011) underscores, her analysis was occurring at a very particular historical juncture where the analyst's authority and wisdom remained unquestioned. She was also a young adult and not yet in the field, and gendered power dynamics—a woman patient with a male analyst—were at play. One could more easily cling to idealization as a way to blur the analyst's culpability. Today, the intense scrutiny that has now been brought to bear on the psychoanalytic relationship makes it more likely that patients (regardless of age or gender), and clinician-patients *especially*, will register that *something* is wrong, and has been for some time, when confronted with an inappropriate action or problematic stance of the analyst.

An announced ethical violation, occurring with another patient, will certainly trigger an avalanche of pain that is virtually unavoidable for any patient. While momentarily silenced as one is bludgeoned by the impact and reeling with shock, silence is not usually possible for long. The reality and egregious nature of such a violation is even less likely to be occluded when the patient is a clinician.[3] More ambiguous infractions embedded within an analyst's countertransferential stance may also be more readily detected by a clinician-patient who can make use of their training to form an opinion, however shaky, that an impasse is not solely to do with their own difficulties. Regardless of the actual nature of the clinical breakdown across a spectrum, my attention in this essay is particularly directed to clinician-patients as a group, though much of what I will discuss is applicable to any patient who feels betrayed.

As Dimen (2011) looks back, she can clearly identify *many* aspects of her analyst's approach to her that, while un-integrated at the time— "I failed to connect the dots" (p. 54; this volume, p. 45)—she can now, many years later, see as both sexually inappropriate and narcissistically motivated acting out. In addition to imposing the sexual kiss represented in the title of Dimen's paper, her analyst was inappropriate in innumerable ways. Referring to women patients on the couch, he commented to Dimen, "I get to look at their legs" (p. 55). A line drawing of a prone naked woman hung at the foot of the couch. He regularly held forth on pet theories. Using his patient's rapt attention to puff himself up as "Doctor Knows Best," he enacted rather than analyzed the Oedipal dynamic in the transference-countertransference. It is truly lamentable that a patient would be subjected to such improprieties in a treatment and, furthermore, that she would not be able to register at the time that she had the grounds to object.

Yet, despite current increased awareness of clinician fallibility, in certain compromised treatments it can still be difficult to discern any obvious "errors" even with hindsight. In trying to assess what is within the scope of appropriate practice, a patient may get lost in shades of gray. Even when an overt violation by one's analyst with another patient becomes a known fact, this news intrudes into a treatment that might have seemed to be going well (enough). In such a situation, a patient may have had a good experience of their analysis, unaware that anything was amiss on the part of the analyst.

Nonetheless, whether violations occur within or outside of one's own treatment, when betrayal *is* registered, a patient's experience of a felt good object is brutally confronted with information that reveals their analyst to be a bad object. How are these two views able to cohere in one's mind when they come into crushing collision with one another? This colliding of good and bad is particularly difficult to resolve when the new information or realization cannot be linked initially, nor often for a protracted time, with any "aha" moments looking back. What if one can find no "dots" to connect with any certainty? The discrepancy between one's lived history and what is newly revealed is at its most dystonic—a tormenting, cognitive and emotional dissonance. The sense of being deceived by another is profound. Particularly disquieting is the added fear of having deceived oneself, of having been "blind" to a situation one "should" have somehow perceived.

In problematic treatment situations where no explicit ethical violation is evident, perceiving clinical infractions can be a very clouded endeavor for a patient, even a clinician-patient. An analyst's character/countertransference problems are not easy for a patient to identify *with confidence.* Feelings of uncertainty abound: "Did I know something was 'off'—yes, no?" The analyst has not committed a boundary violation in any overt, clearly recognizable sense. Instead, the analyst's narcissistic rigidities and subtle lapses in integrity contribute to a treatment stalemated or broken off, with a patient left traumatized.

Such character difficulties in the clinician can include inappropriate ways of handling a patient that antagonize, humiliate or otherwise undermine the patient's state of mind. An overinvestment in adherence to a particular theoretical model and a wedded technical approach can result in abuses of interpretive power, with interpretations functioning as accusations. Clinician defensiveness can be cleverly disguised by lines of interpretation that, although they may be accurate, obscure an entrenched countertransference stance that persistently does not recognize or admit the clinician's contribution to an impasse. Although patients can and certainly do play their part in impasses, it takes two to *tangle* (see Kantrowitz, 1992; Elkind, 1994; Harris, 2009).

As Levin (2014) underscores, in a "tragic betrayal of the psychoanalytic spirit" (p. 195), narcissistic boundary violations by clinicians contribute heavily to impasses, stalemates and inadequate, even tormented, terminations. Levine (2010) describes narcissistic boundary violations as "nonsexual forms of misuse of the analyst's power and authority" (p. 43). Either willingly or unwittingly, an analyst makes narcissistic use of a patient; such misuse is motivated by "personal self-aggrandizement rather than [by] an appropriate subordination of self-interest" (p. 43) to the analytic task. A patient may not have the self-assurance to differentiate analytic authority in the service of *their growth* from an authoritarian arrogance on the part of the analyst that pulls for submission.

Confronted with these more ambiguous lapses in the clinician's integrity, a patient likely *feels* that something is wrong, even though they have an extremely hard time *seeing* what exactly that might be. This dissonance creates a sense of being "crazy" and/or "just a bad patient" with a negative transference. If a clinician, the patient can easily make use of what they know about developmental theory and personality disorders to pathologize themself. This perspective continuously oscillates with the use of training, mentioned above, to critically assess the analyst. The result is a tortured perseveration between one educated "guess" and the other. Much confusion over who is responsible for an impasse can extend over a considerable period of time, even indefinitely, both within and beyond the treatment, without such a patient receiving significant assistance. Yet that involvement from a third usually requires seeing a new analyst right at the time when faith in a therapeutic process is the most undermined and when the patient is also "paranoid" about being pathologized and blamed by the new analyst. After leaving the damaged treatment, patients are likely to try to struggle forward on their own, as Dimen did, with no one to witness the degree of their loss: that a person is indeed *missing*.

This essay looks at the loss of the analyst, experienced as a good object, when a felt sense of deception and betrayal intrudes on the analytic relationship and dismantles what has gone before. Betrayal by a trusted other sends shockwaves reverberating not only forward into one's future but also *backwards* into one's past. One's personal history is retroactively reconfigured (*Nachtraglichkeit*/*après coup*): What has been becomes undone. Such unraveling of goodness is extremely painful in both the loss of the trusted relationship and in the assault on one's confidence in one's own mind, one's ability to detect deceit and bad faith (Elise, 2012). Without a viable termination, post-termination life is then undermined by a pernicious disintegration of the good internal object, along with a registering of the analysis as degraded. The patient is deprived not only of the treatment in the immediate present, but it is retroactively whisked away as well, and little use can be made of it for the future. There is a loss of goodness in the representation of the object, in the self, and in the relationship between the two.

How does a patient cope with such an assault on their sense of reality, their ability to discern falseness in others? How does healing occur, and what is the role of the next analyst in helping a betrayed and despairing analysand to regain a sense of trust not only in the object world and in the analytic community, but in their own mind? When the analysand is also a clinician, what is the impact on their professional identity and how can a new analytic dyad repair such a multi-layered rupture and provide a time for grieving and integration?

A tear in the fabric of time

When confronted by the actual death of one's analyst (Deutsch, 2011, 2014; Elise, 2011, 2014), the sorrowful task of grieving is certainly demanding. Unfortunately, mourning becomes infinitely more difficult when the analyst has "died" as a good object. However sturdy one might be, mourning is initially overtaken by melancholia.

The absence of a hoped-for termination phase, though a somewhat obscured outcome of an ethical violation or a treatment broken off due to an impasse, is, nonetheless, quite malignant in its impact and reverberations. In these ruptured treatments, usually some, perhaps many, sessions were focused on the need to end prematurely, but that discussion was definitely not a *good* goodbye. Patients are then forced to construct their own termination not from a deceased good object, but from an alive, bad object—a haunting, persecutory presence. The "sudden death" of the former good object must be mourned while contending with the intrusiveness of a "new" bad object that not only has taken over and destroyed the treatment trajectory, but that gets in the way of a symbolic goodbye to the lost good analyst. The egregious outcome of these damaged treatments results in the former analyst becoming a ghost—not at rest, nor in peace—in the mind of the analysand. Clinician-analysands are robbed of a crucial ancestor and may come to feel that *only* ghosts haunt their professional identity. The parental generation collapses; along with it goes the foundation of the analysand's professional, as well as personal, well-being.

When one registers the import of a full termination to an analysis, one can more deeply understand how its absence contributes to the fallout of a breach of clinical integrity (see Burka, 2008). The actual breach understandably draws the focus, shadowing the reality that a true termination is foreclosed (Elise, 2014). One sees complicated bereavement rather than a productive process of mourning— something that *may* hopefully be fashioned by the patient at some *much later* point. In betrayal, mourning may be delayed to a time far into the future—a crucial difference when confronted with the symbolic death of a good object versus the literal death of a good analyst. But that delay is only one aspect of how time figures into betrayal and deception: the vicissitudes of time enter the picture in significant and quite complex ways.

Betrayal introduces a rent in time. A thread is pulled and the fabric of time's linearity starts to unstitch itself, slowly at first and then ever more rapidly. The psychic garment woven together by the clinical couple—both for immediate use and long-term wear—is unraveled. There is a progressive and insidious process of dismantling in which a beloved figure has "disappeared." Where did they go, who took them away, who is at fault, where is the corruption to be located? There is now only a chalk outline where the good analyst used to be. And where did the "me" I know as myself go?

Losing one's past

I want to call further attention to the sense of mental confusion that can result from the recognition of a deception regarding events that have been taking place over time, whether internal or external to one's own treatment. When the treating clinician fails to acknowledge a clinical lapse, upon discovery or realization, one registers as the patient that one has been deceived. One now realizes that one's sense of trust was being maintained in a situation that, unbeknownst to oneself, was compromised. In being deceived for some time, the *lived* reality of one's treatment turns out to *not* be true. One now resides in the realm of betrayal.

Even with a slowly dawning realization, a patient's sense of shock can create a feeling of suddenness and totality: that *everything* is changed "overnight." Seemingly dissolved in seconds, lived truth becomes a fiction, replaced with a bad dream that *is* true. In one stunning moment of registering truth, one recognizes that one has been deceived over a substantial period of time. This devastating knowledge attends the shocking realization of a reality that one had not been aware of, but that is true, as one discovers that one's past is no longer one's past.

This dynamic is most clearly evident when a boundary violation becomes an acknowledged fact, yet it also inheres in undermined clinical situations where a patient finally comes to believe that her analyst has actively worked to deceive her into thinking a proper treatment is in place. One may be finally told the fact of a violation; more subtle is the moment when denial falls away in one's own mind that one's analyst has not been functioning as he or she should.

The fact that clinical lapses of ethics and integrity have usually been occurring undetected for some time leads, upon discovery, to a need to rewrite one's treatment history. As the realization "hits" that one has been betrayed, the rug is pulled out from under the relationship to the good object. In being deceived, one's analysis—something that one has lived—has no longer taken place; how can that be so? This unraveling of history—a retroactive reconfiguring (see Faimberg, 2005a, 2005b; Eickhoff, 2006; Perelberg, 2006, 2008)—is profoundly disturbing to one's sense of reality testing, and often leads to crippling doubt about the ability to determine what is true. This assault on truth (Elise, 2012) can be potentially even more disruptive than the actual violation: one does not solely lose trust in the analyst, but in one's own mind, in one's hold not only on the object, but on reality (see Ferenczi, 1949). This dynamic is all the more powerfully disturbing when it resonates with similar elements in a patient's childhood history.

I see in betrayal a subjective experience of temporality where meaning travels backward and suffuses one's object-relational past, creating a *new history* that is now personally registered (though not "remembered") as immensely painful. A complex analytic literature on the workings of *Nachtraglichkeit* and *après coup* focuses on "tricks with time" at play in, and plaguing, personal subjectivity (see Elise, 2012). The non-linearity of time in psychic life is evident—a bi-directionality such that past meaning can be reconfigured and re-transcribed by retrospective attribution.

With deception, *truth is the trauma.* Discovering the truth reconfigures one's personal history without necessarily referring back to any prior event(s) registered as upsetting at the time they occurred. As discussed above, a patient may have experienced their analysis, when it was in progress, as beneficial—a basically good relationship. This earlier life, innocent of the knowledge that any distressing "event" was taking place, now needs to be completely restructured. By its very nature, *deception forecloses the possibility of registering events as problematic.* Truth then becomes the trauma, in that it refers back to an absence of any earlier event that would have undone the deception. Deception constitutes a non-event—something that *did not occur* in the individual's *experienced* history, an "absent event" —where the revelation of the deception and of the betrayal is the event that is traumatic (Elise, 2012). This agonizing realization of truth, in the immediate moment, sends further anguish flooding back into the past, thus spoiling far more than the present experience and future prospects.

Questions of how to proceed in response to a suspected betrayal generate strong feelings of anxiety and self-doubt. A long-standing stalemate is continually approached by the analyst as evidence of the patient's personal difficulties that brought them into treatment. A clinician-patient hears rumors about their analyst being involved in some wrong-doing. In either situation, a patient wonders if they should try to confront the analyst; how should they go about it? What if the analyst denies any culpability? Determining truth against a series of logical dismissals that may be issued by one's analyst rests on trust in one's "intuition"—an emotional conviction such that one is not dissuaded by persuasive denials or rationalizations.

Yet, the registering of such a truth can feel catastrophic: The "sudden" apprehension of a reality previously unknown and unrecognized creates a sense of reality dissolving as one hovers in an endless moment—a sense of time "standing still." A patient may feel that they are truly losing their mind, their psychic stability, and may fear that they no longer know "which way is up." With a felt sense of being dislocated in time and space, one may temporarily lose hold of the coordinates of one's being. An assault on truth has the capacity to disrupt our minds, our "going on being" (Winnicott, 1958); this experience can be quite destabilizing. Patients going through an experience of betrayal by their analyst can feel severely disrupted for extended periods.

Over a prolonged period of time, an anxious preoccupation compels a need to reconstruct *past* reality. As Dimen (2011) states, one must "recast the past" (p. 39; this volume, p. 29) in order to "restore depth and time" to one's experience (p. 38; this volume, p. 28). Efforts to go back in time often focus on intensive, "fact-finding" searches that are excruciatingly painful, yet that continue to have a sense of vital urgency. A patient finds themself absorbed in researching the evolution of an acknowledged boundary violation by her analyst with another patient, trying to line the transgression up with what was happening in their own treatment at that approximate time period. Another tries to put together an eventual understanding of the analyst's compromised clinical stance with what their experience had been as the treatment was unfolding.

In each situation, a patient cannot go forward until the treatment past is revisited and brought into alignment with what has actually been the case, rather than what was believed at the time. The entire period of time absorbed in this effort is one of great anxiety and mistrust, likely blanketing all object relationships, *including and most especially that with a new analyst*. A patient can feel that they have stepped "off the page" that everyone else is on in order to pursue a quest for which others may not understand the crucial need. Eventual restoration is typically preceded by a grueling period of intrapsychic chaos and interpersonal upheaval. Confidence in one's mind, the normal sequence of time and the reality of one's personal history, can all come into question. It is imperative to regain a grasp on the past, to look back, in order to restore confidence in a personal sense of reality testing and thus to have any hope for the future.

In this process, what may hold fast as a continued source of anxiety and "paranoia" for these patients is a fear of being deceived again due to not being able to discern falseness. This fear of the future, based on a past betrayal, shadows the present. Since a betrayed analysand has likely not suspected the first time that they would be unable to rely on the analyst's integrity, what would or could they rely on to tell them if anything similar were to occur in a subsequent treatment? Undermined trust in one's mind in relationship to one's objects has far-reaching consequences, requiring the exceedingly difficult, complex effort at rebuilding *trust in the self*—specifically, trust in one's mind, one's capacity to differentiate truth from fiction, to detect deceit. Each patient's unique personal history regarding the issue of trusting one's own mind will add to the mix and to the need for further analysis. Can a betrayed analysand risk accepting a new analyst's help in this task of internal restoration and further growth?

Complicated beginnings

Dimen (2011) asks, "under what circumstances can the damage inflicted by such an ethical lapse be transformed?" (p. 35). She identifies that, "It is only after the fact, upon reflection—usually with someone else—that we can begin to name, with varying degrees of success, that which refuses symbolization" (p. 53; this volume, p. 43): "In helping you to re-represent your experience, the [next] analyst offers the means to reclaim and regenerate your own life" (p. 45; this volume, p. 35). This outcome is certainly what we hope for in a subsequent treatment, yet we must also be aware that this endeavor is fraught with difficulty.

As when complicated bereavement leads to melancholy rather than grieving, a "complicated termination" leads to a complicated beginning phase of the next analytic effort, with extensive challenges for both parties of the new dyad. The patient is usually in a state of agitation and deep depression, their equilibrium lost. Personal and professional angst are interwoven in clinician-patients. They lament, "What if I can't *be analyzed?*" This question leads directly to the next for candidates: "What if I can't *be* an analyst; would I be an analyst my patients could trust?" As Levin writes (2014), "How does one go on being an analyst, or becoming one, after the traumatic rupture of one's faith in the profession?" (p. 193). What if being an analyst is *not worth being*? All this is at stake as a patient tries to begin again. It is a daunting task for the next analyst as well to cope with this particular "presenting problem." What shape do the specific transferences/countertransferences take when a patient comes to a new analyst after a traumatic experience with a former clinician?

In treating a number of patients, often clinicians themselves, who have come from variously compromised treatments, I have been struck by what a different cast this past places on a new analysis. It feels crucial for clinicians to think about what is involved before actually starting such a treatment, as I believe the situation requires an analyst to provide a very particular type of container—one that focuses centrally on an intricate, three-person relation that includes the prior clinician for an extended period of time (often years). Unlike more typical clinical understandings of what will unfold in the "beginning phase" of an analysis, this treatment, if it does unfold, will be an embroiled *ménage à trois*. This therapeutic context is quite different from the more dyadic transference/countertransference matrix that might be more familiar when beginning analytic work.

The new analyst must be prepared for this tormented triangle and in no hurry to move into any "cozy," dyadic intimacy as they take on the role of offering themself to a patient who is in the midst of a painful "break-up" with another analyst. Not only is this "other" also a clinician, but the individual's identity, if revealed by the patient as it frequently will be, may be that of a known colleague, and that reality is often recognized by a clinician-patient. Then both the patient and the new analyst will have the very difficult task of initiating their relationship by discussing a third person, known to each of them, but with the exact nature of the "knowing" between the new analyst and the former unclear to the patient.

Decisions over whether or not to reveal the former clinician's identity are in themselves conflicted for a patient and complicated for the next treatment. With an ethical violation widely known within the community, the patient may assume that the new analyst already knows about the problem. In contrast, when the difficulty concerns an impasse or a more ambiguous clinical lapse within the patient's treatment, the patient may feel that they are "telling on" the clinician and be anxious that they alone are potentially ruining the new analyst's perception of their colleague. They may both fear this outcome and wish for it. If guilt is a strong element, having revealed a name may reduce one's freedom to speak. Caution and care must be taken regarding this one aspect alone.

When the identity of the former clinician *is* revealed by the patient, a torrent of questions about the possible relation between the two analysts may lead to further anxiety for the patient: "*How well* do you know each other? Are you friends, respected colleagues, supervisee/supervisor? Do you like my former analyst, or do you see something in them that correlates with my feeling of betrayal?" If the new analyst is perceived to think well of the former, the patient quickly concludes that the new analyst will never believe her tale of woe as reasonable lament, but will blame her and exonerate the former analyst. On the other hand, if the new analyst is envisioned as knowing, but having doubts about the competence of the prior analyst, this view then seems to confirm the badness of that analyst in the patient's mind and to deepen the sense of loss and of being the victim of therapeutic misconduct. This question is a looming presence: Who is "bad", the former clinician, the patient, or *you as well*?

It is most apparent that a patient coming from a traumatic goodbye definitely does *not* want to say hello to a new analyst, though they may be desperately in need of one. The patient is in a heightened state of mistrust about seeking help *from a clinician in a therapy context*. Faith in a "good analyst" is at its lowest. The source of the pain is the former clinician, and the new analyst is another such person (see Celenza, 2007). The degree of ambivalence about entering a new treatment is rarely higher. Further treatment feels hopeless, futile, a painful and dangerous liaison with no good outcome. To begin such a clinical venture feels completely daunting when one is already so traumatized and depleted. These patients seriously doubt that there is any therapeutic ground upon which to rebuild or re-establish their own personal well-being and—if clinicians themselves—their professional identity and sense of integrity.

Approach-avoidant impulses oscillate with stunning frequency and intensity. Some part of the patient recalls having had at one time a faith in therapists, but to be helped by you, the new analyst, they must trust you, and this can feel like setting oneself up to be re-traumatized—a vital danger to be avoided at all costs. It is the force of their need that brings these patients to you, ever so ambivalently, and often distraught. They may be vulnerable, immensely distressed, tearful, unable to sleep, regressed, agitated and aggravated, feeling tremendous conflict in their feelings about the former clinician and in angst over their confusion about how to understand their experience. Often still quite attached to the analyst once trusted, even loved, and desperate to protect that experience—the image of the analyst, the relationship and a sense of themselves as loving and good—each patient is also suffused with grave misgivings: Was the former analyst ever *truly* good? Was that belief a fantasy, a self-deception? Is that analyst actually now "bad," or is it me—a "bad" patient—who has spoiled the analyst with the inability to still see them in a good light? Was it me, the patient, who acted destructively and damaged my analyst? All this torment is brought to the initial encounter with the new analyst, and will be the focus for many months, even years, as the new analysis "begins."

The new analyst needs to be prepared for this intricate endeavor, to be sensitively attuned to the patient's competing anxieties, to contain countertransference pressures, and to hold out hope for a working-through, no matter how complicated and protracted this might prove. The new analyst must be fully available for an unfolding treatment, but not eager for it in a manner that overrides the patient's deep ambivalence about such a prospect. Even proving yourself trustworthy—as we typically hope to do with new patients—is a mixed blessing: You could betray your analysand if her or she trusts you, knowing they cannot sustain any more damage. If the analysand is also a clinician, a second analytic disaster would confirm that they are "crazy" and too disturbed to partake of, let alone practice, their own profession.

Mistrust is not limited to despair in the analysand's personal life, but it can seep deeply into the patient's own professional identity as a clinician. To lose one's faith in one's chosen profession is a very profound loss. Confidence built over years of training and clinical practice becomes undermined, as does any sense of promise for an analytic future as a member of the professional community. This devastating sense of professional disillusionment eats away at one's working life right when absorption in work might be an adaptive effort. Each session in one's practice is an hour in confrontation with one's own former treatment, as well as with the current situation. Where to go? This new treatment is no escape, but a stepping-back into the lions' den.

As the former treatment and image of the good analyst unravels with increasing momentum, the patient needs to be held emotionally in the onslaught of this disequilibrium. Yet the *"holding" of the new treatment will itself be threatening*, contributing as it does by contrast to further crumbling of the idealization of the prior clinician. The concept of a therapeutic alliance takes on an entirely new set of meanings: the relationship is paradoxical from the beginning, "going downhill" even when the work is going well. "Going well" means being in a sharp descent into a deepening realization of the prior treatment as having gone wrong somewhere, somehow, all of which is completely unclear and shrouded in confusion. There is a felt sense of being on a bicycle that is going too fast, and is now headed down a steep hill, careening wildly out of control.

Dismay in the countertransference

For the current analyst, especially when struggling with this predicament for the first time, an array of dismaying affects presents in quick succession. Any expectations of a promising analysis, unfolding in a relatively steady manner with a prospective patient, quickly yield to the recognition that one is witness to a disaster. This next analyst hears something they do not want to be true: a treatment has left a patient feeling seriously damaged. Each of us went into the "helping profession" because we wanted to help; we are identified as individuals who help, not hurt. We are deeply disturbed to hear of this reversal; it is an assault on our own professional ideals and our pride in our efforts over many decades, encompassing years of education, training and clinical practice. Now, up close and personal, we are hearing excruciating details of a treatment gone wrong, badly wrong.

Typically, the patient had respected and trusted the former clinician for many years (often idealization was high and sustained), and now hate likely predominates, but both states of feeling alternate in the wake of a crushing de-idealization. When patients speak to one side of their ambivalence, they fear they have "seduced" you into a biased view, whether to the good or to the bad in "assessing" the former clinician. When they speak of their love, and thus their doubt about the clinician's culpability, they fear you will join with them in whitewashing the actions/role of the former clinician. When they speak of their hate, they fear they will have tainted your view of that clinician, and that in siding with the patient, you will have lost any objective balance that could eventually lead to a genuine working-through.

Such anxieties in the patient create immense pressure in the countertransference. Integration of good and bad regarding the image of the former analyst is difficult for the new analyst as well as for the patient. A certain form of neutrality is necessary, yet it can be perceived as suspicion of the patient. We like to be cautious about reaching for conclusions, but hesitation can be taken as disbelief and may sever any delicate bond that might be forming in the new treatment relation. Empathy is greatly needed, yet it can seem like collusion with the patient. Analysts hope to be empathic, especially with new patients in distress, but empathy can be taken as indictment of the former analyst. If you empathize with the patient's feeling of being betrayed, deceived or wounded, you are further "killing off" the good object. Yet, if you empathize with the patient's love for the lost good object, you can seem to be saying that the patient "made all this up" and that the problems are of their own making. Either way, your slightest expression, tone or comment can be taken as a verdict: you are "the judge." In a catch-22 situation, you are likely, *repeatedly*, to either confirm the loss of goodness in the former analyst or in the patient's sense of self. This situation can feel something like a bad dream repeating/see-sawing in sessions for months. It takes significant time and therapeutic skill just to establish a working alliance that encompasses recognition of *all* that the patient feels toward their prior analyst, rather than leaning to one side or the other.

One might say that the initial transference in this new treatment is an acute form of disordered attachment, a situation not unlike fostering an adolescent who has come from a disrupted home. This new relationship is going to start as a tenuous tie at best, threatening to come apart on a regular basis. For both you and your patient, the former clinician will be in your life, in this new treatment, for a long time. The path forward will be rocky and unstable, and this "other" love will shadow your every moment together. It's dispiriting.

Patience will be imperative. Even when a positive connection starts to build with this new patient, a new countertransference anxiety is generated: transitory transference idealization, which could be developmentally appropriate in an initial phase with another patient, can here feel indistinguishable from "trashing" the prior clinician—a triangulation that would cement one side of the patient's feelings and prevent healing.

As time passes, often two or three years, and a trusting and productive analysis begins to unfold, with wounds starting to heal and the patient feeling re-stabilized, the lingering shadow of the former clinician can still seep in like a fog, chilling the transference/countertransference matrix. It may take the entirety of the second treatment before the first is *fully* worked through. The new analyst must never think that the former clinician is gone "for good"; they will keep on returning, again and again. You are not choreographing a *pas de deux*; that "other" will have to be let on (often center) stage as a regular occurrence. It will never be "just you." One's own disappointment, disillusionment and narcissistic wounding—not feeling "important," trusted, even liked—must all be contained while you wait for this former relationship to heal, with you a seeming bystander, though working hard in efforts crucial to the future of the patient and the analysis.

We know well that patients in analysis (including ourselves) want to be the "only one" for their analyst, and experience jealousy of their analyst's other patients, supervisees, friends and partners. Much of clinical practice has us working on this issue as it surfaces in our patients' transferences. But we tend to take for granted much of the time that we are the "only one" for each of our patients. Often, no other relationship can seem to be able to compete with what we can potentially offer to each patient: *we are the special one.* So it is a jolt to the analyst to regularly hear just how wonderful this past analyst was before the patient felt betrayed. Now *you* are the one to come second to a "competitor." Narcissistic deflation can lead an analyst to join too "empathically" in a patient's critical feelings about the former analyst. Clinicians know the dangers of triangulating against a third person, but in these circumstances a fair bit of balance is required for a considerable amount of time to avoid falling into such an enactment.

Community "disappearances"

Just as a betrayed clinician-patient cannot go to their own therapy practice without ending up knee deep in these issues, neither can the analyst of these patients escape regular confrontation with the experience of betrayal, deception and of having to go back and reconfigure the past. Much of the time, you as the analyst *do* know, or know of, the former analyst, who may even be a member of your own institute. You may now be getting a very different picture of that colleague, one that is certainly more disturbing to hear about the closer you feel to that clinician. You may have to rework your relationship to this person, and yet you can say nothing to that individual or to anyone else about what you have learned about them.

The reality of this isolation is especially palpable when no overt violation has occurred that is openly acknowledged. Many clinical offenses are ambiguous rather than identifiable facts. Your new patient's disclosures may be being made solely to you. If you have had cause to register some doubts about that clinician's capacities, character or ethics, hearing what may be confirming disclosures from your new patient is a disconcerting experience as well. Containment of personal countertransference to such revelations can be a demanding, ongoing effort that calls on clinician integrity in maintaining utmost confidentiality.

Your new patient is expressing the feeling that quite possibly no analyst is a reliable, grounded individual, and you can start to join them in wondering if that might actually be true. There is an assault on one's confidence in and respect for the profession: Are we all disturbed individuals unknowingly inflicting further damage on our patients, one generation to the next?[4] This countertransference of subterranean doubt is profoundly disquieting, especially at the exact point when one is trying to convey to a traumatized patient that hope and trust can be restored, in the patient's sense of self, in you as the analyst, and in the profession.

With confirmed ethical violations, the clinical community as a whole must also contend with "disappearances" of individual analysts. Institutes grieve. Silence must give way to shared lament. Much has been written (see Deutsch, 2014) about this group-level reaction to losses of individual members, and of the piece of the professional tapestry that was in place in this individual's contributions. It is so very painful when an admired, respected, highly contributing colleague is suddenly "disappeared" from institute life. The task of coming to terms with this loss spreads out to include most of the community. Everyone is reworking their relationship to that colleague at the same time, but typically with splitting rendering people at odds with one another (often for lengthy periods of time) in how they are holding their relationship to the erring clinician. Group-level shame, guilt, regret and responsibility all come into play when confronted with a loss of pride in a profession that should garner respect.

What I am identifying here is the way in which an individual analyst will have a unique experience of a community-wide loss when treating a patient who has suffered the loss of this clinician as their own analyst. This new treatment relationship becomes a daily confrontation with something very sad. With a clinician-patient who has suffered a compromised earlier analysis, the next analyst is likely to empathically identify with such a loss in a profound manner; these two individuals form a unique pairing in a very troubled circumstance. Perhaps one of the gifts of working through the loss of a colleague due to an ethical violation in the context of a treatment with an injured patient is that *splitting is not a tenable stance.* As together you both look back, acknowledge a loss, re-find a sense of sequence in time and re-establish trust in the capacities of one's own mind, the shock of betrayal and deception softens into poignant recognition of something hopefully more bearable—the frailty of humanity.

Conclusion

As analysts, we are familiar with certain patients coming to us in a very traumatized state, yet when the focus of that distress is another clinician and a former treatment, we find that the clinical picture changes drastically. My intent here has been to elaborate on a patient's subjective experience of betrayal—the loss of their analyst as a good object—and the undermining of confidence in their own mind to discern the truth. The exact nature of a betrayal is of central significance in working with any given patient who has come for subsequent treatment. Certainly, a pronounced difference exists between an acknowledged ethical violation—often known to an entire community and incontrovertible—and a problematic clinical stance. Narcissistic violations tend to be insidious and cannot be proven to be facts. The contribution of such character problems in a clinician will typically remain a murky area where a patient has to learn to rely on their own discernment. Although in some situations an analyst's character difficulties may become so well known that some external validation may be acquired, frequently there will be little or no corroborating "evidence" from others. The patient must eventually make their own determination.

For a patient coping with such losses, both symbolic and real, complexity mounts in a layering of demanding psychic tasks: mourning the lost good analyst, the past as the patient knew it, their former self, and a lost future; overcoming melancholic submission to a persecutory object; risking new relationships—to others and to the self—in order to contend with the anguish of betrayal and to reconcile with the truth. As Dimen (2011) identifies, "My struggle in writing this account has been to balance my loss, grief, and fear of shame with the capacity to think ... and to grieve while speaking" (p. 39; this volume, p. 28). For the next analysis to be reparative, time must be fashioned into a web that can hold these intricate psychic maneuvers.

A grave disservice is done to the full potential of this new treatment to consider it as a "rebound relationship." I believe that the psychoanalysis of the unraveling of faith in psychoanalysis is possible. This is not merely an extended consultation, or a bridge to some hypothetical future treatment which can only occur after the "dust is settled." In its immediate confrontation with pain and loss, this analysis of victims of analysis is the opposite of escape and manic defense. As it unfolds in all its seeming paradox and futility, the next analyst must be able to hold "in trust" what may seem impossible for the patient. In so doing, we envision a future, seeded in the present, that will afford a space to look back. Later, perhaps *much later*, there will be another analytic goodbye—hopefully a *good* one.

Notes

1 This chapter originally appeared as an article in *Psychoanalytic Dialogues*, 25 (5): 557–571 (2015).
2 I will be using "ethical violations" as an inclusive term covering a spectrum of professional misconduct.

3 It should however be noted that, in an effort to protect the good object and to reject the reality of the loss, certain patients, including those who are clinicians, may yield to rationalizations put forth by the analyst. This situation may include continuing in treatment with a clinician who is publicly known to have committed a violation.

4 This question raises the issue of whether an erring clinician has been the recipient of misdoing in his or her own treatment, and is then participating in a transgenerational transmission of trauma (Faimberg, 2005b).

References

Botella, C., & Botella, S. (2005). *The work of psychic figurability: Mental states without representation*. Hove: Brunner-Routledge.

Burka, J. B. (2008). Psychic fallout from breach of confidentiality: A patient/ analyst's perspective. *Contemporary Psychoanalysis*, 44: 177–198.

Celenza, A. (2007). *Sexual boundary violations: Therapeutic, supervisory, and academic contexts*. New York: Jason Aronson.

Deutsch, R. (2011). A voice lost, a voice found: After the death of the analyst. *Psychoanalytic Inquiry*, 31: 526–535.

Deutsch, R. (2014). *Traumatic ruptures: Abandonment and betrayal in the analytic relationship*. London: Routledge.

Dimen, M. (2011). *Lapsus linguae*, or a slip of the tongue? A sexual violation in an analytic treatment and its personal and theoretical aftermath. *Contemporary Psychoanalysis*, 47: 35–79.

Eickhoff, F. W. (2006) On *Nachtraglichkeit*: The modernity of an old concept. *International Journal of Psychoanalysis*, 87: 1453–1469.

Elise, D. (2011). Time to say goodbye: On time, trauma, and termination. *Psychoanalytic Inquiry*, 31: 591–600.

Elise, D. (2012). The danger in deception: Oedipal betrayal and the assault on truth. *Journal of the American Psychoanalytic Association*, 6: 679–705.

Elise, D. (2014). Saying goodbye: Traumatic reverberations in the subjective sense of time. In R. Deutsch (ed), *Traumatic ruptures: Abandonment and betrayal in the analytic relationship*. London: Routledge, pp. 199–215.

Elkind, S. N. (1994). The Consultant's role in resolving impasses in therapeutic relationships. *American Journal of Psychoanalysis*, 54: 3–13.

Faimberg, H. (2005a). Apres-coup. *International Journal of Psychoanalysis*, 86: 1–6.

Faimberg, H. (2005b). *The telescoping of generations: Listening to the narcissistic links between generations*. London: Routledge.

Ferenczi, S. (1949). Confusion of the tongues between the adults and the child—(The language of tenderness and of passion). *International Journal of Psychoanalysis*, 30: 225–230.

Hampton, C. (Director) (2003). *Imagining Argentina* [Movie]. USA: Arenas Entertainment.

Harris, A. (2009). "You must remember this". *Psychoanalytic Dialogues*, 19: 2–21.

Kantrowitz, J. L. (1992). The analyst's style and its impact on the analytic process: Overcoming a patient-analyst stalemate. *Journal of the American Psychoanalytic Association*, 40: 169–194.

Levin, C. (2014). Trauma as a way of life in a psychoanalytic institute. In R. Deutsch (Ed.), *Traumatic ruptures: Abandonment and betrayal in the analytic relationship*. London: Routledge.

Levine, H. B. (2010). The sins of the fathers: Freud, narcissistic boundary violations, and their effects on the politics of psychoanalysis. *International Forum of Psychoanalysis*, 19: 43–50.

Ogden, T. (2000). Borges and the art of mourning. *Psychoanalytic Dialogues*, 10: 65–88.

Ogden, T. (2004). The analytic third: Implications for psychoanalytic theory and technique. *Psychoanalytic Quarterly*, 73: 167–195.

Ogden, T. (2005). *This Art of psychoanalysis*. New York: Routledge.

Perelberg, R. J. (2006). The controversial discussions and apres-coup. *International Journal of Psychoanalysis*, 87: 1199–1220.

Perelberg, R. J. (2008). *Time, space and phantasy*. London: Karnac.

Winnicott, D. W. (1958). The capacity to be alone. *International Journal of Psychoanalysis*, 39: 416–20.

Part 3

Boundary trouble in the analytic community

Chapter 7

Don't tell anyone[1]

Joyce Slochower

I was a young analytic candidate in the early 1980s when I had my first encounter with sexual boundary violations. A good friend, in analysis with a respected male analyst 20 years her senior, confided that he had been making explicit sexual advances toward her. She shut them down but continued with him in treatment, remaining silent both with him and about him.

If she had been traumatized by this experience, she kept it to herself. Her matter-of-fact silence confused me; I wasn't able to assimilate—let alone articulate—how I felt about all this. Instead, I tried to file away what I knew and held it in a space apart. This was, I thought, most likely a single incident in the career of a widely esteemed analyst. What would be gained by creating trouble for someone to whom so many were devoted? There seemed to be no way to hold his talent in tension with his transgressions and I sidelined the latter.

It turned out that my friend had been far from alone in her experience. Rumors—some vague, others quite specific—began to surface, communicated in whispers intermingled with both horror and prurient pleasure. My friend's analyst and another similarly senior person had breached sexual boundaries with both supervisees and patients. Decades later, we came to know that these were neither rumors nor isolated occurrences.

Nearly all of us have been privy to gossip—and fact—about boundary violations (sexual and nonsexual) within and outside our particular institute community. Yet only a tiny number of these violations have come under public scrutiny; even when they do, they are almost never openly discussed, let alone made public in wider forums. Most often, the event is treated more like a lurid story than a phenomenon requiring serious exploration.

Psychoanalytic theories have their origins in ideas about sexuality's psychic elements. So how ironic—and how unsurprising—that we've enacted incestuous boundary crossings since our professional beginnings. While there's a large body of literature on the dynamics of the violator and victim (Celenza, 2007; Dimen, 2011; Gabbard & Lester, 1995; Gabbard & Peltz, 2001; Margolis, 1997; Pepper, 2014; Pizer, 2000; Sandler & Godley, 2004), far less has been written about the communal side of this phenomenon. What does happen, psychologically speaking, to those of us who are not directly involved? What do we do with—and about—what we know?

We psychoanalysts may represent a clinical/theoretical Tower of Babel in many respects, but one thing binds us together: despite our commitment to protecting our patients, analysts have been engaging in sexual boundary violations since this field began. While the larger professional community is enormously disturbed by these events, we've done little to address the problem; in fact, we've mostly colluded to keep it out of sight, if not out of mind. While we don't quite fall prey to the kind of malignant dissociative contagion that Sue Grand (2000) spoke about, we tend to deal with what cannot be encompassed by retreating from it.

Sexual boundary violations—and their perpetrators—are ghosts that haunt us within (and of course outside) the psychoanalytic world. Loewald (1960), borrowing the term "ghosts" from Freud (1900)—and indirectly from Homer—noted that

> [G]hosts of the unconscious, imprisoned by defences but haunting the patient in the dark of his defences and symptoms, are allowed to taste blood, are let loose. In the daylight of analysis the ghosts of the unconscious are laid and led to rest as ancestors.
>
> (p. 249)

We haven't surfaced, let alone analyzed, our ghosts. Unlike ancestors that can be laid to rest, the ghosts of sexual boundary violations have an impact that is at once insidious, unnameable, and profound (Kalb 2015). These ghosts hover—unmetabolized—at the edge of our communities, coloring our feelings about our profession, our institute, and our colleagues (Margolis, 1997; Honig & Barron, 2013). Periodically popping into the clinical encounter, the shadows of both violator and victim becomes "not-me" elements that disturb, disrupt, and even derail us.

It's not surprising that sexual boundary violations tend to record across analytic generations; their victims (like victims of other trauma) are especially vulnerable to reenacting, in reverse, the assault they experienced. Too often, the victim is left feeling abandoned, shamed, or blamed, alone to metabolize the experience; rarely is there a recognizing group to witness, let alone take action on behalf of the victim and against the perpetrator.

But our communal failures don't reflect indifference. If anything, it's our near-absolute inability to encompass sexual breaches that renders us passive. We don't know what to say, whom to tell, or what to do. Deeply disturbed, we feel helpless and often immobilized.

The fact that sexual breaches are frequently committed by those with professional power only exacerbates our conundrum. The violator has *gravitas*. He[2] may even have been a psychoanalytic "great," someone we idealized. Like the father in the 1950s American TV serial "Father Knows Best," we believed (and wanted to believe) that he knew best. How could he have ignored, indeed flaunted, our code of professional ethics, acted as if the rules did not apply to him? We feel shocked and demoralized. His behavior shakes up, even dismantles, our professional ideal and we become not merely distressed but disillusioned.[3]

Our need to idealize the violator makes it tough to absorb the scope of his breach. We half-rationalize. Perhaps his therapeutic brilliance allowed him to ignore boundaries without compromising his healing capacity (Slochower, 2011). Perhaps he really *was* acting in the best interest of the patient, at least most of the time.

If our idealization enables the violator, it comes at a high personal price: abandoning own sense of ethical agency—an ethical sensibility with both personal and professional derivations—we fail to name what we know. We become collaborators—passive participants in something we abhor. An exaggerated asymmetry (Aron, 1996) effectively ties our own hands and renders us smaller, less wise, less aware than we are (Grand, 2010), while elevating the stature of the idealized other. Certainly, the actual violator bears primary responsibility for what he does, but we enable him by virtue of our silence. Our idealization thus has a malignant underbelly. It obfuscates what we need not to see and not to know. It invites our passive participation in the sexual breach and, in this sense, it renders us complicit.

Yet our idealizations aren't something we can altogether do without. We need to believe in our mentors and in the field of psychoanalysis as a whole. Steadying us in the face of clinical uncertainty, our ideals inspire and sustain us; they give us something against which to evaluate ourselves.

We want—and need—to believe in the field's (and our own) curative potential, in our capacity to set aside the excesses of personal need in the best interests of our patients. Psychoanalytic ideals remind us of the importance of professional ethics and integrity, self-reflectivity, and the honesty of the field as a whole. In some respects our ideals represent a wedge against the kinds of delinquency I've discussed elsewhere (Slochower, 2006, 2014), against what Irwin Hirsch (2008) calls "coasting in the countertransference." They ought to serve as a barrier to sexual and nonsexual boundary violations.

But they usually don't. If anything, our ideals have made it near-impossible for us to face either their excesses or their vulnerability to collapse. Too often, the space between our ideals and actuality silences us; it invites compartmentalization, denial, even disavowal. "It's not possible that he had sex with the patient, it's a nasty rumor perpetrated by those who envy him." "She wasn't a patient, she was just a supervisee." "It was a single incident, not such a big deal." At other times, we find more complex (but equally troublesome) ways of rationalizing what happened: "Sometimes people really fall in love. The patient is his age and they're both in the field; they made a mature, conscious decision to move the relationship into a different arena." Or even, shocking in its cynicism/naïvety, "Come on. It's not as if he raped her."

When evidence of harm makes these kinds of rationalization impossible—for example, when the analyst is decades older than the patient or when the patient falls apart or presses charges—we may move disavowal in a different direction. We maintain our idealization by blaming—really pathologizing—the victim, and emphasizing the analyst's innocence and benign intentions. "The patient is really borderline, unbelievably seductive. I bet she hallucinated half of it, turned his kindly touch into a sexual moment." "He thought he was helping her and she seduced him into playing out her abuse history. He's naïve but really he's a good guy. And she is extraordinarily self-destructive."

Despite the denial embedded in these idealizations (and denigration of the patient), there's often at least a bit of truth. Patient victims often bring their own abuse history into the treatment relationship; those dynamics contribute to its sexual *denouement* and make it easier for us to blame her. Adding to our emotional confusion is the fact that analysts who breach professional boundaries are rarely guilty of cold, calculated abuse. Most are probably not psychopaths and most aren't entirely defined by their action; they may be brilliant writers and/or may do sensitive, skilled therapeutic work with other patients.

Analysts—themselves vulnerable to fantasy—sometimes lose track of their own need or wish for intimacy, rescue, or idealized love. As Gabbard (2017) reminds us, sexual violations are typically the endpoint of a slow slide down a slippery slope with a particular patient—not with all patients. Should we utterly blacken the name and destroy the reputation of someone who also resides outside the realm of analytic failure?

Our need to protect the violator's stature often reverberates at a more abstract level because the wish to preserve a professional ideal collides with the need to call a spade a spade. What if "telling" damages our community's place in the wider psychoanalytic world? What if we disrupt, even dismantle, the experience of those analysands, supervisees, and students who were, in fact, helped by the analyst? In declaring that the emperor has no clothes, will we take down the—our—kingdom?

To further complicate things, whistle-blowing is its own wild card. What if naming names triggers excessive punitiveness on the part of ethics committees and the larger community (Celenza, 2007)? What if we do more harm than good? And will we be punished for telling, if not by the perpetrator, then by those who surround and want to protect him? Often (though not always) the violator is someone with professional power; we fear his (and his supporters') capacity to retaliate. We're silent because we're scared. Our anxiety may even make us doubt what we know.

All kinds of legal constraints coalesce with these more personal anxieties and shut us down. In the United States, state law defines whether anyone other than the victim-patient can report a sexual violation;

in many states, those who "know" via hearsay cannot initiate action. Furthermore, both the whistle-blower and the institute itself are vulnerable to libel suits when names are named; those in positions of administrative power are silenced by their own legal counsel.

Frequently, our hands are tied; there's nothing we can do with what we know or suspect. Scared, fearful of making trouble, feeling impotent, we become doubtful. *Are* we sure? After all, we weren't there. What if we're wrong? Helpless, frustrated, we sideline what we know.

When reality becomes undeniable and we're confronted with what we cannot exclude, our idealization shatters, replaced by bitter disillusionment. "He's a sleazeball." "He's losing it." "He thinks with his dick." We effectively excommunicate the analyst, eject him from our psychic as well as literal midst. In part we do this because the analyst's behavior has, in fact, been reprehensible and deserving of ostracism. But I think another dynamic is often at work here: as we denigrate the analyst, we simultaneously find a way to protect our idealization by relocating it elsewhere: "He's not a real analyst." "He's no hero of mine; X, on the other hand, would never behave in this way. It's him I emulate."

Those who commit boundary violations often justify their actions by invoking a clinical theory that seems to rationalize away the rejection of the ordinary analytic frame. The patient's vulnerability and need, sexual or emotional inhibition, require it. The breach often begins when the analyst responds to the patient's trauma history and the intensity of her baby needs with a sense that extraordinary measures are required. Gabbard and Lester (1995) describe how nonsexual physical holding can gradually transform into a sexual liaison as the analyst finds himself caught up, submerged by the power of his (and his patient's) sexualized desire to save the patient. Rescue fantasies merge with underlying grandiosity and disavowed rage, precipitating a gradual slippage toward sexual transgression, a slippage apparently supported by the analyst's theory of clinical action.

Some have suggested (e.g., Bernstein, 2003) that particular theories (e.g., object relations models) especially invite boundary breaches because the power of the reparative maternal metaphor pulls the analyst toward action.[4] However, I'm convinced that any clinical theory can be misused in this way; no model represents an impermeable protection or theoretical safe haven against them.

Here are two dramatic instances in which other clinical theories were used to justify boundary violations. These examples are not intended to be representative of this phenomenon. They reflect particularly egregious and flagrant examples of sexual acting out. More often, sexual boundary violations evolve fluidly out of a growing emotional involvement with a patient. But these specific examples illustrate how the analyst can misuse theory to justify a boundary breach.

A young woman's Freudian analyst regularly masturbated her to orgasm in the name of activating her "dead libido." His theoretical investment in the power of drives was used perversely as a rationalization for sexual acting out. This analyst's grandiosity, supported by his stature in the community, protected him from scrutiny, let alone censure.

Another patient, in analysis with an Interpersonalist, described how her analyst frequently took her to lunch, after which he kissed and fondled her. The analyst believed that free social/sexual interaction would help his shy and self-deprecating patient feel better about herself and awaken her sexual longings. The patient was aware of feeling awkward and self-conscious, yet also pleased about the special place she had in her analyst's life. Only years later did she come to recognize how traumatizing these experiences had been.

Although no analytic theory justifies these kinds of boundary violations, no analytic theory entirely protects us from their pull. In fact Sue Grand (2017) suggests that our theories may actually be implicated in our misbehavior. By privileging the therapeutic import of erotics in the transference, we create a situation of "seductive excess" that slides only too easily in the direction of actual seduction.

If there is any protection against this slide, it lies instead in community—in our willingness to see and name these breaches collectively. Yet it's the rare psychoanalytic community that has effectively addressed this issue with its members, before we even consider the larger psychoanalytic world. While violators are sometimes forced to leave their institute, most often they reestablish themselves elsewhere. Their leave-takings tend to be kept quiet; the community either remains unaware of what happened or is publicly muzzled because of concerns about legal ramifications. Ultimately, this transgressive element becomes part of our professional legacy, lodged in a kind of psychoanalytic collective unconscious.

At one of my institutes we continue to not name a beloved mentor, now long deceased, who is widely known to have committed multiple sexual boundary violations. We admire his vision and his writing; we don't know how to reconcile his brilliance with his misbehavior. It's yet more impossible for us to name violators who are still alive and working among us. And so, when recent boundary violations at one of my institutes came to light, intense gossip *and* public silence dominated. In part, this is because the administration was legally constrained: fear of lawsuits and other financial consequences led attorneys to insist on complete discretion. But unavoidable though these constraints may be, they mystify—indeed gaslight—the wider professional community and, particularly, candidates in training.

We're not silenced only by legal constraints, though. Social and personal concerns also muzzle us. We worry about rumor-mongering, about making trouble or getting into trouble, about hurting a colleague, his patient, or a friend. Whispered gossip is so often our only relief or release. We find an Other, or a few others, with whom to share what we suspect or know. But gossip is a weak word to describe this. The Hebrew equivalent—*lashon hara* (evil speech)—perhaps more accurately captures the very charged bad feelings (and intent) that this kind of gossip embodies. Rather than serving as an emotional envelope within which to contain, process, and work through disturbing feelings, gossip intensifies our sense of charged anxiety and distress. It leaves us disrupted rather than relieved; it provides no opportunity for emotional exploration or working through.

Gossip takes place almost exclusively between friends or in very small groups; larger groups usually preclude this kind of exchange. Indeed, when two sexual violations—one old and one current—came up in a class of ten that I teach, both were energetically discussed while we all avoided naming the faculty members. Several people declared that it would be libelous to do so (even though we all knew whom we were talking about and that these were facts, not rumors). The conversation turned instead to a transgressor from a different institute whose story had been publicized in the press. It's safe to name him; he was "other," neither personally beloved (idealized), nor powerful in our institute. When it comes to our own, we usually remain publicly mute.

Our silence may appear to protect our community, but it doesn't. If anything, it supports a kind of group illusion/delusion that makes it nearly impossible for us as individuals—and as institutions—to contain or metabolize violations without doing major damage to our professional self-image and group identity. To our family.

And paradoxically, even as I try to surface this dynamic here, I may simultaneously enact it. I describe really disturbing events but I don't name the institutes I'm referring to or those about whom I'm speaking. I leave you, the reader, guessing. Do I mystify more than clarify? Do I arouse curiosity and anxiety, thereby perpetuating the problem even as I try to unpack it? Do I inadvertently create yet more silent, silenced witnesses?

I'm tempted to name a name, to actively break into this collusion. It would have to be a name that's safe, the name of someone deceased or someone already named in the press, someone who couldn't sue me or my institute. On one level, doing so would be relieving; I would be naming the elephant in the room.

But on another level, I would feel more disturbed than relieved. Naming the perpetrator could have a destructive impact on his former patients—those he didn't abuse—or on his colleagues and students. What would be gained by naming someone who's no longer a danger to his patients? It's those I *cannot* name who remain a danger; it's the perpetrators who are alive and active I'm really worried about. And even here, naming names is problematic. In the process of identifying some, I'd be leaving others out, creating some scapegoats while inadvertently protecting other transgressors. There seems to be no exit.[5]

There is something else to consider. How will you—the reader—experience all this? What if you yourself were a victim of or a witness to a sexual violation? What if I break into your disavowal—if it's *your* analyst, colleague, or friend who was, or is, a violator or victim? Will you feel anger at the violator for breaching your trust? Exposure as your secret is partially unmasked? Guilt because you remained silent about it? Shame over not reporting your abuse or the abuse you witnessed? Jealousy and hurt (over *not* having been chosen as a "special" patient or confidante)? And if you are "only" a witness, how upset are you entitled to feel? After all, it didn't happen to you.

When I first began working on this chapter, I naïvely assumed that I would be addressing bystanders and witnesses—those who dwell outside the arena of actual violations. Only later did it dawn on me that some readers might have (or might be currently) committing a boundary violation. Will this paper open up reflective space, make room for you to own what you did or are doing? Or will I alienate you, leaving you more defensive and angry than ever?

When I presented earlier versions of this chapter at conferences, I was concerned about whether a large group setting could contain the feelings this material might evoke. Large groups provide neither a sense of cohesion nor emotional safety; we need to limit how much we expose ourselves in them. We also need to remain mindful of the vulnerability of the larger group, which is easily threatened by the disclosure of sexual boundary violations. Indeed, I found that these group discussions regularly evoked memories of boundary violations that had occurred in the community—and sometimes to a group member herself. Strikingly, many reported that they had "forgotten" all about the boundary breach until that moment; some contended with significant distress in a context that didn't feel altogether safe.

A published paper might solve the group problem. We read alone and can, perhaps, metabolize alone. We don't need to deal with the Other, at least not at first. But with aloneness come other risks. We confront our suspicions or our secrets in private space. We're isolated from those who might share our experience; we're vulnerable to a microform of the loneliness that accompanies trauma's absent historicity and accountability (Grand, 2000). That loneliness perpetuates our collective silence and, once again, invites disavowal.

Disavowal is a formidable defense, one that reflects the magnitude of the traumatic disturbance it sidelines. And I know this from the inside because I encountered my own disavowal while writing this chapter. It's a story I never repressed or dissociated, but one that became lodged in a space so covered over that its impact was apparently forgotten.

About 25 years after I finished my first analysis, I learned that my former analyst had left her husband for a patient. My ex-analyst and I were still in touch, and I (rather naïvely) tried to communicate my distress to her. Unsurprisingly, she didn't welcome this conversation and became extremely angry and defensive. The interaction was difficult and disappointing, but it was what happened next that represented a real boundary breach.

A few days later I received a very long and hostile phone message from my ex-analyst's partner (whom I didn't know). In it, she not only defended my former analyst, but made it clear that she knew quite a lot about me and used that knowledge to attack me personally. Her viciousness left me shaken. Clearly, my ex-analyst had shared personal information about me with her partner. Her partner's retaliatory, threatening phone call evoked a mixture of hurt, outrage, and vulnerability as I tried to digest the fact that my analyst had betrayed my trust.

Probably because this treatment relationship was decades old and I had come to see my former analyst in a shaded rather than idealized way, I was less upset with her than I might have been. Still, it's astonishing to me that, until I began writing this, I hadn't realized that a second boundary violation had been committed—against me. My analyst betrayed her patient-lover first, but she also betrayed her other patients and ex-patients—including me. She'd up-ended my professional ideal twice by breaching sexual boundaries with her own patient and then failing to honor the privileged nature of our relationship. I had managed to sideline the fact that I had been both witness and victim. How difficult to metabolize, even thirty years on.

Former patients who learn of, but are not victims of, boundary violations are perhaps in a position similar to that of a nonabused child whose sibling is being abused. While often she or he has no emotional choice except to keep the secret, the peripheral traumatic element is assimilated on a procedural level where it festers and disturbs.

At times, a socio-political residue informs our silence: it's the horror of being informants, grown-up "tattle tales." In the United States, our reluctance in part reflects the traumatic shadow of the McCarthy era. Finger-pointing sullies us; we cringe at its implications. Indeed, many of us are identified with the position of the Other and with the ethical autonomy inherent in that stance. It's not an autonomy that easily moves us to whistle-blowing.

Whether or not we were red-diaper babies, though, in one way or another, we resist becoming informants. Personal, political, and realistic concerns inform that silence. We want to protect ourselves and our community from scandal. We don't want to make trouble, join the establishment, or collaborate with the powers that be.

And then there are more personal sources of conflict about speaking up. Does our anxiety (often unconscious) about our own badness and destructiveness make whistle-blowing feel like an act of aggression or duplicity rather than one done on behalf of the victim and the wider community? After all, who among us has never committed a boundary violation or permitted themself a sexual fantasy about a patient? Who has never harbored hostile fantasies about a colleague or worried about her or his negative impact on the other? To name a transgressor stimulates our own bad-analyst feeling (Epstein, 1999), associated anxiety, and guilt about our own misbehavior, however minor and whatever its particulars.

Here's another complicating element: despite the fact that psychoanalytic writing has long acknowledged the presence of erotics in the countertransference, our own sexual fantasies edge uncomfortably close to enactment when we contemplate the actuality of sexual violations. While these violations disturb us, an element of sexual charge often coexists with that distress. Most of us have never engaged in sexual boundary crossings, but I would bet that nearly all of us have had moments when we wished we could. Thinking about or gossiping about a colleague's sexual acting out is disturbing, but it may simultaneously be exciting.

The colleague who enacts the forbidden provides us with an opportunity to vicariously experience what's prohibited, all the while reinforcing our subjective sense of purity. Do we register a double response of horror *and* a kind of perverse titillation? Do we split, locating sexuality out there where it doesn't threaten our own good-analyst feeling?

I suspect that both shame and pleasure are embedded here—a response to trauma that melds with a more ordinary erotic excitement and leaves us feeling at once ashamed and affectively elevated. We gossip, allowing ourselves the charge of an erotically colored shocking story while remaining above the fray. Is our gossip a kind of emotional masturbation—stimulating but lacking a climax or finality that would contain and settle things?

Certainly, our excitement is not uncomplicated. In part it's informed—driven, in fact—by underlying feelings of erotic horror (Kumin, 1985), grief, identification with the victim, anger, and a sense of powerlessness. But alongside all this—or perhaps in response to it—we find it tough to relinquish the perverse pleasure inherent in keeping and gossiping about these erotic secrets.

I'm suggesting that we in the community fail to contain violations because we're invested in them. But in mystifying what is known, we confront a different danger—the feeling that we're complicit, that we are, in part, collaborators—both as individuals and as a professional community.

It seems to me that, at bottom, our very complex feelings about boundary violations reflect our powerful, mostly unconscious need to retain an exalted analytic ideal. That exalted ideal precludes doubleness and thus is vulnerable to shatter. If we are to move beyond this impasse, we need to encompass the possibility that truly reprehensible professional behavior can coexist with a capacity for good analytic work and/or intellectual brilliance.

Can we find a way to create our own version of the South African Truth and Reconciliation Commission (Moskowitz, 2013)? There, the victims of unspeakable violence confronted their abusers. The possibility of genuine restorative justice was created when harm was fully acknowledged and, in some instances, amnesty from prosecution was given.[6]

So here is a wish/fantasy: that we, as psychoanalytic communities or institutes, could create a restorative justice system for both the victims and perpetrators of boundary violations. Then we could begin to directly but privately approach our colleagues when we think they might have committed—or might be committing—boundary violations. And that we could do the same with those we suspect are victims.

The victims of major boundary violations often write about their experiences in essays and books (see especially Dimen, 2011; Deutsch, 2014), while also protecting the violator's name and institute or other setting in which the breach occurred. This is, I think, a first step toward the kind of restorative process I am thinking about. But it doesn't go far enough.

Can we imagine creating a protected, "safe" space in which such a process could happen publicly? In which perpetrators could acknowledge what happened as a first step toward rehabilitation? Could we create a reflective rather than a punitive atmosphere within which victim and perpetrator could speak to each other and acknowledge harm done? In which state law and local governing associations like the American Psychological Association could grant amnesty from criminal instances where full disclosure, remorse, and reparation occurred? Can we even fathom such a process as being separate from legal action and banishment?

I'm not sure. But to even contemplate doing this, we need to acknowledge what we know. Aloud. To speak. Together. This means accepting that some of our exalted analytic heroes were—and are—also violators. With the fact that we who would *never* breach a sexual boundary nevertheless commit small but disturbing analytic infractions (Slochower, 2003, 2014).

We psychoanalysts have got much to be proud about—and much to be ashamed of. How ironic that we who embrace the clinical value of paradox and emotional complexity have such difficulty holding our ideals flexibly! We're too often pulled to negate the nonideal because the threat of traumatic deidealization is unbearable. If we are to confront our silence and its dynamics, if we are to address the experience of victims, perpetrators, and witnesses and attempt any kind of repair, we need to speak together about what we know, feel, and are afraid to say. We need to revisit our relationship to our personal and professional ideals and make peace with the limitations of this profession. Honig and Barron (2013) give us a model to follow in their description of an institute's responses to a sexual boundary violation. Pizer (2000) proposes that we require ongoing consultation across our analytic lifetime as a wedge against them. And certainly, this book opens a dialogue and places the issue in the public domain where it can be addressed.

I very much doubt that we'll ever succeed in putting a full stop on sexual—or nonsexual—boundary violations, but we might find ways to address their impact on the professional community and our participation in them were we less wedded to a rigid vision of the field and ourselves. We need to create settings in which these public conversations can begin, conversations that are neither purely condemnatory nor collusively negating of actuality. It's time, isn't it?

Notes

1 This chapter originally appeared as an article in *Psychoanalytic Psychology*, 34 (2): 195–200 (2017). It is based on papers presented at The Wounds of History Conference, New York University, 2013; the Israel Forum, Tel Aviv,

Israel, 2013; the American Psychological Association Division 39 Spring Meeting, New York, 2014; and the International Association for Relational Psychoanalysis and Psychotherapy, Sydney Chapter, Sydney, Australia.

2 For the sake of simplicity, I refer to the violator with traditionally "masculine" pronouns. While sexual boundary violations occur between female analyst-male patient pairs and also within same-sex pairings of both genders, the vast majority of such transgressions are committed in male analyst-female patient constellations, and it's on these that I focus here.

3 Of course, this isn't always true. Some violators are known to be corrupt, even psychopathic. Their breach may upset us, even leave us feeling cynical and bitter, but it's not surprising and doesn't alter our professional ideal (see Gabbard 2017).

4 Visions of maternal repair have come under especially sharp critique for inviting boundary crossings since Wynne Godley (Sandler & Godley, 2004) published his paper on his experience with Masud Khan.

5 In a discussion of her own experience as a patient, Dimen (2011; see also Chapter 2 in this volume) considers the dynamics of sexual violations and the powerful forces silencing patient, analyst, and institute. She, like me, refrained from naming the violator.

6 Beginning in 1995, the South African Truth and Reconciliation Commission provided an opportunity for victims of human rights violations during apartheid to publicly describe their experience. Those who had committed human rights abuses could also petition for amnesty from prosecution in return for acknowledging their actions. Amnesty was granted to those who told the "whole truth" and whose crimes were "politically motivated." (Of course, these are subjective assessments.)

References

Aron, L. (1996) *A meeting of minds: Mutuality in psychoanalysis.* New York: Analytic Press.

Bernstein, J.W. (2003), Analytic thefts: Commentary on papers by Joyce Slochower and Sue Grand. *Psychoanalytic Dialogues*, 13: 501–511.

Celenza, A. (2007). *Sexual boundary violations: Therapeutic, supervisory, and academic contexts.* Lanham, MD: Aronson.

Deutsch, R. (Ed.) (2014). *Traumatic ruptures: Abandonment and betrayal in the analytic relationship.* New York and London: Routledge.

Dimen, M. (2011). *Lapsus linguae*, or a slip of the tongue? A sexual violation in an analytic treatment and its personal and theoretical aftermath. *Contemporary Psychoanalysis*, 47: 35–79.

Epstein, L. (1999) The problem of the bad-analyst feeling. *Contemporary Psychoanalysis*, 35: 311–325.

Freud, S. (1900). The interpretation of dreams. In J. Strachey (Ed. & Trans.), *The complete psychological works of Sigmund Freud* (vols. 4 & 5). London: Hogarth Press.

Gabbard, G.O. (2017). Sexual boundary violations in psychoanalysis: A 30-year retrospective. *Psychoanalytic Psychology*, 34(2): 151–156.

Gabbard, G.O. & Lester, E. (1995). *Boundaries and boundary violations in psychoanalysis*. New York: Basic Books.

Gabbard, G.O. & Peltz, M.L. (2001). Speaking the unspeakable: Institutional reactions to sexual boundary violations by training analysts. *Journal of the American Psychoanalytic Association*, 49: 659–673.

Grand, S. (2000). *The reproduction of evil*. Hillside, NJ: Analytic Press.

Grand, S. (2010). *The hero in the mirror: From fear to fortitude*. NewYork & London: Routledge.

Grand, S. (2017). Selective excess: Erotic transformations, secret predations. *Psychoanalytic Psychology*, 24(2): 208–214.

Hirsch, I. (2008). *Coasting in the countertransference: Conflicts of self-interest between analyst and patient*. New York: Analytic Press.

Honig, R.G & Barron, J. W. (2013). Restoring institutional integrity in the wake of sexual boundary violations: A case study. *Journal of the American Psychoanalytic Association*, 61(5): 897–924.

Kalb, M. (2015). Ghosts in the consulting room: Reluctant ancestors. *Contemporary Psychoanalysis*, 51: 74–106.

Kumin, I. (1985). Erotic horror: Desire and resistance in the psychoanalytic situation. *International Journal of Psychoanalytic Psychotherapy*, 11: 3–20.

Loewald, H.W. (1960). On the therapeutic action of psycho-analysis. *International Journal of Psychoanalysis*, 41: 16–33.

Margolis, M. (1997). Analyst-patient sexual involvement: Clinical experiences and institutional responses. *Psychoanalytic Inquiry*, 17: 349–370.

Moskowitz, M. (2013). Personal communication. April 17.

Pepper, R.S. (2014). *Emotional incest in group psychotherapy*. London: Rowman & Littlefield.

Pizer, B. (2000). The therapist's routine consultations: A necessary window in the treatment. *Psychoanalytic Dialogues*, 10: 197–207.

Sandler, A. & Godley, W. (2004). Institutional responses to boundary violations: The case of Masud Khan. *International Journal of Psychoanalysis*, 85: 27–42.

Slochower, J. (2003). The analyst's secret delinquencies. *Psychoanalytic Dialogues,* 13: 451–469.

Slochower, J. (2006). *Psychoanalytic collisions* (1st ed.). Hillsdale, NJ: Analytic Press.

Slochower, J. (2011) Analytic idealizations and the disavowed: Winnicott, his patients, and us. *Psychoanalytic Dialogues*, 21: 3–21.

Slochower, J. (2014). *Psychoanalytic collisions* (2nd ed.). Hillsdale, NJ: Analytic Press.

Chapter 8

Dissociation among psychoanalysts about sexual boundary violations[1]

Mark J. Blechner

Dahlberg (1970) published an important and brave exploration of sex between psychotherapists and their patients. He had difficulty getting it published, and the topic continues to be fraught with anxiety, suppression, and inconsistency. The primary inconsistency that has received little attention is the disconnection between the official and private attitudes of members of our profession. The gap between public and private views about sex between psychotherapists and their patients is causing a great deal of distress and confusion.

If I had been asked 30 years ago what my views were about sex between analysts and patients, I would have answered simply that it must be absolutely forbidden. The reason is the essential pact that we clinicians make with our patients. For their own good, they can and should talk about whatever feelings emerge in the transference, including sexual feelings. We clinicians guarantee that it is safe to do so; we will use our patients' revelations to help them explore their psyches, but we will not act on their sexual fantasies, or ours.

It is important to provide this safeguard. Without it, there can be no wide-ranging analysis of transference. And because we know that early experiences can be reenacted in psychoanalysis, it is especially important that we resist the temptation to violate this trust. For people who were sexually abused as children, the prospect of exploring these experiences in psychoanalysis and having such exploration lead to sexual reenactments can be doubly traumatizing.

The absolutist position

I would call my view the "absolutist position." There are many reputable people, past and present, who would agree with the absolutist position, including Hippocrates. The Hippocratic Oath includes the following passage: "Every house I shall only enter for the sake of my patients' wellbeing, refraining from every intentional harm and all seduction, especially from love relationships with women or with men, be they free or bonded" (Van Emde Boas, 1966, p. 215).

Renowned sex researchers Masters and Johnson (1970) were also absolutists and raised alarm about patient-therapist sex. Their patients, who generally had sexual problems, reported a startling number of psychotherapists who, recognizing the vulnerability of their patients, initiated sex with them. Masters and Johnson argued that therapists who have sexual relations with their patients should be prosecuted for rape. More recently, we have the unflinching viewpoint of psychologist Kenneth Pope and his colleagues (Pope et al., 1993) to consider, who wrote:

> Under no circumstances should a therapist ever engage in sexual intimacies with a patient. No matter what the situation. No matter who the patient. No matter what the patient has said or done. No matter how the therapist or patient feels. Therapist-patient sexual intimacies are in all instances wrong and must be avoided. In all situations, it is solely the therapist's responsibility to ensure that he or she never engages in sexual intimacy with a patient. The locus of responsibility for the therapist's behavior in this regard can never be shifted; it remains always and completely with the therapist.
>
> (p. 180)

This is the absolutist view; I still subscribe to it, but I have come to realize that many people, some respected clinicians, privately do not hold to the absolutist view. They usually do not publish their points of view, and so most people might be unaware that they hold them. For instance, I was involved in discussions of an ethics code for a psychoanalytic institute in which the issue of sexual ethics needed to be clarified. There were several analysts, some of them quite senior, who held what I would call the "relativist view." They said, "You know, sometimes those relations work out well. The patient and therapist marry, and the marriage is a happy one." I was at first startled by this argument; it seemed beside the point. The principle of adhering to sexual boundaries in psychoanalytic treatment is not dependent on whether the relationship works. It is based on maintaining the safety and integrity of transference exploration.

Even if one holds to the absolutist view, are there distinctions to be made? There are people who are well-meaning analysts who, in a single instance, fall in love with a patient and choose to spend their lives with that patient, whatever the consequences may be. They do it once; the relationship may work, or not, and the analyst may seek to remain part of the profession. Should they be differentiated from analysts who are "multiple sexual boundary violators," clinicians who repeatedly exploit the transference to seduce patients? The latter use their power within the analysis to try to keep this abuse secret, and they use their power within the profession to do the same and hold any judgmental colleagues at bay. In one instance, an analyst who committed a serious sexual boundary violation retained his position as director of a prestigious psychoanalytic institute for decades. Such analysts can have destructive effects on their patients, yet they may continue to sustain a positive clinical reputation. When their deeds are made public, they may blame the patient or exonerate themselves with justifications such as "the patient knew about transference," as if abstract knowledge about transference protects the patient from exploitation (Simon, 1991; Herman, 2012; Honig & Barron, 2013).

One could argue that multiple sexual boundary violators should be shunned by the profession and disciplined by the law. Yet in actual practice, many of them face no serious penalties, and quite a few manage to hold on to positions of authority (Gabbard, 1995). Courts of law are severe with sexual boundary violators, but the record of our profession enforcing its own principles is weak, uneven, and unfair. The punishment may be milder if the offending analyst is aggressive and threatens a countersuit, and harsher if the analyst is meek and repentant. Andrea Celenza (2007) calls this "rampant punitiveness" and has questioned whether some overly harsh and shaming punishments come from guilt about not having adequately prosecuted perpetrators who were more frightening.

Paradoxically, talking about sexual boundary violations can be punished more harshly than committing a sexual boundary violation (Dimen, 2011); several psychoanalysts who have spoken publicly about problems with sexual boundary violations in our profession have been threatened with punishment, as law professor Leonard

Riskin (1979) pointed out. The message seems to be "Keep quiet; don't talk about it."

The "supportive-of-sex-with-patients" position

There seems to be a reluctance to condemn and to punish sexual boundary violators. Is there another way besides ejecting them from the profession? One alternative might be to require that any practitioner who has sexual relations with patients must be open about it. Such a practitioner must re-certify as a psycho-sex therapist and inform patients in the first session that the practitioner sleeps with patients and that patients have a right to know this in advance. If they then choose to work with such a psycho-sex therapist, that is their prerogative.

At first glance, this proposal might seem preposterous, but it has some precedents. In 1966, psychiatrist James McCartney published "Overt Transference" in the *Journal of Sex Research* (McCartney, 1966). He argued that some patients need a real sexual experience within the treatment in order to proceed to mature heterosexuality. He notes that a man can sometimes find professionals who will allow him to work on his sexual development (by which I think he means prostitutes), whereas such resources are less available for women. Therefore, the psychoanalyst should fill in and give her what she needs. And he did that with dozens of his female patients. However problematic this proposal may be, McCartney deserves credit for being clear and straightforward—he was open about his approach; he even would meet the patient's husband or family at the start of the treatment to explain it.[2] In any case, after McCartney delivered his paper describing his practice, he was expelled from the American Psychiatric Association. However, McCartney's expulsion may have been imposed more to protect the profession and the organization than to punish a breach of ethics, because the Ethics Committee wrote: "There comes a point at which the offender so outrages social sensibilities that the peer group must act to protect its own integrity" (Riskin, 1979, p. 1008). If he had merely kept the information to himself instead of giving a paper on it, he might have been left alone. The message was: Keep quiet; don't talk about it.

We could call McCartney's position the "supportive of sex-with-patients" position. This position is officially an outlier in our field. We may assume that therapist-patient sexual relations are damaging. But how true is that? Do any patients find it benign—even useful—to sleep with their therapists? Those patients who have been damaged are more likely to go public with their experience, perhaps suing the therapist, perhaps going into treatment with another therapist. But if a patient finds the sexual relationship with the therapist useful, we are much less likely to hear about it.

At one of my lectures, I mentioned this problem and wondered aloud about whether we were not hearing from people who had benefited from sexual relations with their therapist. After my talk was over, a woman came to speak with me. She did not identify herself by name, but she told me, "I am one of those people. I went into therapy with a sexual problem; my therapist had a sexual relationship with me, and I no longer had the sexual problem, with him and afterwards. So for me the experience was useful." Martin Shepard (1971), outspoken about the "supportive of sex-with-patients" position, claimed that "as many people are aided by intimate involvements with their therapists as are hurt" (p. 207). The fact is, though, that Shepard was wrong. Research shows that sexual boundary violations are harmful much more often than they are helpful. A survey of the literature (Taylor & Wagner, 1976) found that 47 percent of patients who had sexual contact with their therapists found it harmful, 32 percent found it mixed, and 21 percent found it helpful. Pope and Vetter (1991), in a more systematic survey, found that it was harmful for 90 percent of patients who had sex with their therapist during treatment.[3] For those who had sex after the treatment was terminated, 80 percent found it harmful.

The percentage of psychotherapists who have had sexual contact with their patients has been estimated to be between 2.5 percent of women and 9.4 percent of men (Pope et al., 1986), which is almost one in ten male therapists. Why are sexual boundary violations so frequent? There are many answers; the simplest answer is that the therapists are unable to find satisfactory relationships outside the consulting room. Dahlberg (1970) noted that sexual boundary violators tend to be older, widowed, single, divorced or in troubled marriages, and lonely. The average age of the therapists he studied was 50, and the average age of the patients with whom they had sexual relations was 30. We all have sexual and romantic needs, and if our needs are not well satisfied in our lives outside the consulting room, how likely are we to seek satisfaction within the consulting room? If we are not physically or emotionally attractive to most people, or have our own inhibitions or character quirks that make romantic relationships difficult for us, how tempting is it to use the rose-colored haze of the transference to feel more attractive to a romantic partner lying on the couch? The answer will depend on many factors, including character, superego strength, fear, and one's education and role models.

Role models—there we have another problem. Part of the trouble is that sexual transgressions are so common in the history of psychoanalysis. The list of psychoanalysts who have had sex with patients or married them reads like a *Who's Who* of our field: Carl Jung, Sándor Ferenczi, Erich Fromm, Frieda Fromm-Reichmann, Wilhelm Reich, Victor Tausk, Otto Fenichel, Harry Stack Sullivan, Karen Horney, and many others. I know of no instance where Freud had actual sexual relations with a patient. In his writing, Freud took the absolutist position (Freud, 1910, 1915), but in practice, Freud violated his own principles, especially in the Frink case. Horace Frink, an American psychiatrist, went to Vienna to be analyzed by Freud (Edmunds, 1988; Warner, 1994). Frink was married but was having an affair at the time with one of his patients, Anjelika Bijur, a very wealthy woman. Freud encouraged Frink to leave his wife and marry his patient, which was disastrous for everybody concerned. So, starting with Freud, we have a long-standing dissociation between the official condemnation of sexual relations between analyst and patient, and a hidden acceptance or even support for them.

The "empathic-sentimental" position

We teach the theories and principles of the major figures in psychoanalysis and rarely mention when they had sexual relations with their patients. Perhaps our training programs need to acknowledge this fact and open up more of a discussion with psychoanalytic candidates about sexual feelings in treatment. We need to teach and take seriously Searles's (1959) observation that sexual and romantic feelings and fantasies are common in the psychoanalyst, especially towards the end of a successful treatment. Searles wrote:

> Since I began doing psycho-analysis and intensive psychotherapy nine years ago, I have found, time after time, that in the course of

the work with every one of my patients who has progressed to, or very far toward, a thoroughgoing analytic cure, I have experienced romantic and erotic desires to marry, and fantasies of being married to, the patient. Such fantasies and emotions have appeared in me usually relatively late in the course of treatment, have been present not briefly but usually for a number of months, and have subsided only after my having experienced a variety of feelings—frustration, separation-anxiety, grief, and so forth—entirely akin to those which attended what I experienced as the resolution of my Oedipus complex late in my personal analysis—specifically, about five years ago.

(p. 180)

Searles provided an unusual perspective on erotic countertransference: if understood and handled correctly, it is not necessarily a problem. It may be a sign that the psychoanalyst has done good work, and it is near the time for termination of the treatment (Brockman, 2008; Blechner, 2009). We need to discuss why sexual boundary violations have occurred so often in the history of our profession and the unconscious attitudes that may support such boundary violations, even while they are officially condemned. One of those attitudes is that many analysts feel empathy for romance and true love. We could call this the "empathic-sentimental" position, and it competes, sometimes unconsciously, with the absolutist position. Psychotherapists want people to be happy in their love lives, and it is often a goal in treatment. Consider the example of Frieda Fromm-Reichmann. She had been raped during her medical studies, a terrible trauma (Hornstein, 2000, p. 69). At the age of 36, when she was still Frieda Reichmann, she had never been married and had no children. This was considered shameful for a woman, certainly for someone from an Orthodox German-Jewish background. Frieda began psychoanalyzing Erich Fromm, an attractive, brilliant man who was 11 years younger than her and came from a similar religious background. She claimed they fell in love, ended the analysis, and married. Some people felt or continue to feel, "Isn't it wonderful that Frieda got a chance at love with Erich?" Yet most people also avoided speaking about it, betraying their ambivalence. Hornstein notes in her biography of Fromm-Reichmann: "I found it extraordinary that every person I interviewed knew this fact [that Erich had been Frieda's patient before marrying her] but claimed never to have discussed it" (p. 401, n. 24). Their belief seems to have been: Keep quiet; don't talk about it.

Hornstein (2000) is herself ambivalent about the relationship; she alternates between ethical concerns and the empathic-sentimental position. She says that almost everybody fell in love with Erich and suggests that Erich seduced Frieda. Lawrence Friedman (2013), in his biography of Erich Fromm, suggests that Frieda seduced Erich. The fact that there is a debate about who seduced whom in a psychoanalytic treatment reveals the tendency to romanticize these situations in the empathic-sentimental position.

Daniel Mackler (2006) has taken a different stance in "An analysis of the shadow side of Frieda Fromm-Reichmann." In the absolutist tradition, he writes:

> It is the patient's inalienable right to *try* to seduce his therapist, just as it is the therapist's inalienable emotional responsibility to analyze the (not-so-) hidden message in the patient's behavior— for the sake of her patient's growth. If the therapist goes along with the patient's attempted seduction—no matter what the time period or what the therapist's analytic style—it is really the therapist seducing the patient in disguise, in an equally disguised attempt to have the patient meet her own ancient unmet childhood needs.
>
> (p. 10)

From this point of view, no matter what the situation, the analyst is letting down her or his patient if there are sexual relations, and the patient may be traumatized in ways that may not immediately be obvious. Dahlberg (1970, p. 121) cites Raymond Sobel: "The determinants of whether the therapist acts out are his inner states rather than the seductiveness of the patient. The latter is always with us."

Fromm-Reichmann seems to have espoused this viewpoint herself. In her classic text, *Principles of Intensive Psychotherapy* (1950), she stresses near the beginning of the book how important it is for the psychotherapist to be sure to have adequate sources of personal gratification in life outside the consulting room, in order to avoid seeking such gratifications from patients. She writes:

> Sexual gratification has been quoted as another goal of satisfaction in man's life. The therapist has to safeguard strictly against using the patient, actually or in fantasy, for the purpose of lust, so that sexual fantasies with regard to the patient or the partners whom the patient mentions, or identifications with the patient or his partners regarding their sexual experiences, do not interfere with the psychiatrist's ability to listen … A psychiatrist who is lonely must see that his own need for physical contact does not interfere with his coming to the correct conclusions about patients' needs.
>
> (pp. 9–12)

In summary, we need to be clearer about where we stand as a profession on sexual boundary violations. We need to relax the unspoken but powerful ban on discussing this issue, in current clinical work and in the history of psychoanalysis. Our message must shift: Don't keep quiet; speak out! We must resolve the dissociation between what we say publicly and think privately and what we believe unconsciously. Only when we deal with this gap can we hope to confront sexual boundary violations honestly and effectively.

Notes

1 This chapter originally appeared as an article in *Contemporary Psychoanalysis*, 50 (1–2): 23–33 (2014).
2 It is hard to believe that the husbands or families of female patients gave consent for such treatment and agreed to pay for it.
3 This is quite close to the finding of Dahlberg (1970). In his relatively informal survey, in one case out of nine (11%), the sexual interaction between psychoanalyst and patient had no apparent harmful effect.

References

Blechner, M. (2009). Erotic and antierotic countertransference. *Contemporary Psychoanalysis*, 45, 82–92.

Brockman, R. (2008). The slippery slope: Touch in dynamic psychiatry. *Journal of the American Academy of Psychoanalysis and Dynamic Psychiatry*, 36, 403–414.

Celenza, A. (2007). *Sexual boundary violations: Therapeutic, supervisory, and academic contexts.* Lanham, MD: Jason Aronson.

Dahlberg, C. (1970). Sexual contact between patient and therapist. *Contemporary Psychoanalysis*, 6, 107–124.

Dimen, M. (2011). *Lapsus linguae,* or a slip of the tongue? A sexual violation in an analytic treatment and its personal and theoretical aftermath. *Contemporary Psychoanalysis*, 47, 35–79.

Edmunds, L. (1988). His master's choice. *Johns Hopkins Magazine*, April, 40–49.

Freud, S. (1910). The future prospects of psycho-analytic therapy. In J. Strachey (Ed.), *The standard edition of the complete psychological works of Sigmund Freud* (vol. 11, pp. 139–152). London: Hogarth Press.

Freud, S. (1915). Observations on transference-love. In J. Strachey (Ed.), *The standard edition of the complete psychological works of Sigmund Freud* (vol. 12, pp. 157–171). London: Hogarth Press.

Friedman, L. (2013). *The lives of Erich Fromm.* New York: Columbia University Press.

Fromm-Reichmann, F. (1950). *Principles of intensive psychotherapy.* Chicago, IL: University of Chicago Press.

Gabbard, G. (1995). The early history of boundary violations in psychoanalysis. *Journal of the American Psychoanalytic Association*, 43, 1115–1136.

Herman, C. (2012). Sex with patient caused no harm, doctor says. Suit alleges negligence, violations of consumer law. *Commonwealth Magazine.* January 26.

Honig, R. & Barron, J. (2013). Restoring institutional integrity in the wake of sexual boundary violations: A case study. *Journal of the American Psychoanalytic Association*, 61, 1–28.

Hornstein, G. (2000). *To redeem one person is to redeem the world: The life of Frieda Fromm-Reichmann.* New York: Free Press.

Mackler, D. (2006). An analysis of the shadow side of Frieda Fromm-Reichmann. *International Society for Psychological & Social Approaches to Psychosis Newsletter*, 7 (1), 10–12.

Masters, W. & Johnson, V. (1970). *Human sexual inadequacy.* Boston, MA: Little, Brown.

McCartney, J. (1966). Overt transference. *Journal of Sex Research*, 2, 227–237.

Pope, K., Keith-Spiegel, P. & Tabachnick, B. (1986). Sexual attraction to clients: The human therapist and the (sometimes) inhuman training system. *American Psychologist*, 41, 147–158.

Pope, K., Sonne, J. & Holroyd, J. (1993). *Sexual feelings in psychotherapy.* Washington, DC: American Psychological Association.

Pope, K. S. & Vetter, V. A. (1991). Prior therapist-patient sexual involvement among patients seen by psychologists. *Psychotherapy*, 28, 429–438.

Riskin, L. (1979). Sexual relations between psychotherapists and their patients: Toward research or restraint. *California Law Review*, 67, 1000–1027.

Searles, H. (1959). Oedipal love in the countertransference. *International Journal of Psychoanalysis*, 40, 180–190.

Shepard, M. (1971). *The love treatment*. New York: Wyden.

Simon, R. (1991). Psychological injury caused by boundary violation precursors to therapist-patient sex. *Psychiatric Annals*, 21, 614–619.

Taylor, B. & Wagner, N. (1976). Sex between therapists and clients: A review and analysis. *Professional Psychology*, 7, 593–601.

Van Emde Boas, C. (1966). Some reflections on sexual relations between physicians and patients. *Journal of Sex Research*, 2, 215–218.

Warner, S. (1994). Freud's analysis of Horace Frink, M.D.: A previously unexplained therapeutic disaster. *Journal of the American Academy of Psychoanalysis*, 22, 137–152.

Chapter 9

Do we really need boundaries?

Juan Tubert-Oklander

The concept of a "boundary" is far from clear, even though we use the term freely. A boundary is a line that splits a whole into two or more separate domains. It is a frontier that simultaneously separates and joins two territories or countries, each with its own language, customs, laws, and values. Such a topographical metaphor was essential in Freud's (1915) understanding of the mind.

Boundaries are needed for any perception or thought to develop. They also introduce an order into emotional experience, personal relations, and society. When two or more people cohabit in a shared space, conflict and misunderstanding are bound to emerge, and this requires that the relationship be ordered, by means of rules and values. This is the essence of ethics, which is a reflective thought about how we should act for the greater good.

In psychoanalytic practice, such order is introduced by the setting, which implies boundaries. A psychoanalytic session cannot take place anywhere and its temporal limits and procedures are well established (Freud, 1913). But the most important boundary is that which differentiates and separates the two parties, while at the same time creating the conditions for a meaningful communication and relation between them. Analyst and patient differ in their roles, their contributions to their common work, and their rights and obligations.

So, the analytic relation and process become possible as a result of the initial *asymmetry* that is introduced by the contract and setting and preserved by the analytic discipline and work. But the unconscious, on account of its own organization and functioning, knows nothing about boundaries and contracts, and enters the relation on completely *symmetrical* terms. This is true for both patient and analyst. Considering that the largest part of the latter's contribution to the treatment is per-force unconscious, it follows that most of the analytic relation and process will be necessarily symmetrical, unbounded, and non-ethical. It is up to the analyst, standing in the no man's land between asymmetry and symmetry, to strive to preserve the former, while always taking into account the latter.

This is a necessary consequence of the radical differences between the logic of the unconscious and that of consciousness. Ignacio Matte-Blanco (1975, 1988), who made an extensive analysis of the logic of both mental systems, pointed out that the logic of the unconscious is *symmetric*—that is, reversible—while consciousness is ruled by an *asymmetric*—hence irreversible—logic. But human beings are not just unconscious and primary process; consciousness and secondary process also exist, so that thinking always follows a double track. This is what the author calls "bi-logic", that is, the confluence and alternation of both kinds of logic, both symmetric and asymmetric:

> Bi-logical structures are most abundant. They are seen in the various ways of conceiving and living all aspects of human life, religion, art, politics, and even science, in the differences between psychoanalysts, and in every other aspect of life. Once one gets used to seeing them, *one cannot avoid the surprising conclusion that we live the world as though it were a unique indivisible unit, with no distinction between persons and/or things. On the other hand, we usually think of it in terms of bi-logic and, some few times, in terms of classical logic.*
>
> (p. 46, emphasis added)

The fact that most of what happens between analyst and patient is necessarily unconscious determines an evolution of the analytic process that is by principle unknown and uncontrollable by both parties. The only thing an analyst can do about it is to ride the wave, together with the patient, and try to somehow modulate the process by means of the partial understanding of it that emerges from the analytic dialogue (Tubert-Oklander, 2013). What is, of course, under the analyst's control is his or her own behavior, although this control cannot be based only on a strict compliance to rules, but rather on the identification and understanding of his or her own unconscious strivings that would lead him or her to disregard, break, or subvert these rules.

Now, the unconscious is a most complex continent, and it includes all sorts of polar mental phenomena—selfish and altruistic, crassly sensual and highly spiritual, childish naïvety and ancient wisdom, rash impulsiveness and silent contemplation... It is only natural that, when one of these poles has been instated in consciousness on an exclusive basis, the other, which has been relegated to the unconscious (repressed), should violently strive to break this boundary and gain access to the realm from which it has been excluded. This is particularly so in the case of those trends that have been repressed on moral grounds, such as libidinal and aggressive impulses, but it is also the case with other parts of the personality that have been repressed and denied, as a consequence of education, social norms, or idiosyncratic experiences. For instance, a woman who has been taught since the cradle that she is not, and should never be, an intelligent human being, and hence should duly show a proper respect for the superiority of hallowed males, may well show a return of the repressed (her intelligence) in the form of a complex theoretical system, namely, a highly elaborate delusion.

This psychopathological digression shows that boundaries can be either healthy and progressive or pathogenic. Which is the case for the basic ban of any sexual contact between analyst and patient? Is it a much-needed boundary, such as the incest taboo, which is claimed to be the very basis of civilization, or is it an anachronistic moralist remnant of millennia of unwarranted repression, both social and psychological? Some writers have held, on the basis of a misunderstanding of Freud, that all these taboos should be overcome in order to attain the true human freedom, provided by a full satisfaction of drives. If this were the case, we should revise the ethical injunctions that regulate our practice. But what if it were not?

The psychoanalytic community has been deeply concerned about the danger of the sexual acting out of an analyst with a patient, ever since Freud learned about Carl Jung's involvement with Sabina Spielrein (Carotenuto, 1980/1982; Tubert-Oklander, 2011). Nonetheless, the fact that it often happens has been widely concealed, until quite recently. Why is this so? The very fact that two members of a larger group meet together in a closed space in order to engage in an intimate communication is unconsciously interpreted, by both the group and the two persons involved, as a sexual meeting. This is what Bion (1961) called the "Basic Assumption—Pairing". Besides, the very fact that the psychoanalytic procedure demands a loosening of the boundary of repression invites the emergence of the repressed, particularly those passions that are forbidden and declared inexistent by society. This is one of the reasons for the special prominence of libidinal and Oedipal strivings, and the corresponding institution of the incest taboo, although there is also an emergence of aggressive and homicidal impulses, envy, irreverent defiance of authority, and autonomous thinking, all of which have been previously repressed.

So, it is not surprising that the two people who engage in this intimate relationship, in which there is a loosening of the usual social and psychological controls, should be driven both by their own emergent sexual and erotic feelings and by the pressure of the unconscious fantasy of their community about the emotional meaning of such meetings.

Freud's response to these perils was to upgrade his obsessional defenses, crystallized into a strict ritual setting. Like Moses, he fought sin by means of injunctions. But it is well known that this kind of control only succeeds in strengthening the forbidden impulses, so that analysts are always in some danger of going overboard in this matter.

Of course, there is a much better solution, which is the deepening of the training analysis. The underlying rationale is that analysts who have become conversant with the ways of their own unconscious are in a much better position to identify their unconscious strivings and abstain from acting them out with their patients. But the question remains, why should they abstain in the first place? The answer to that cannot merely consist in invoking the conventional moral principles of a code of professional conduct (what we call "deontology"), but it rather requires a major ethical reflection. And such a reflection should be part and parcel of every analysis, especially in the case of training analyses. Unfortunately, however, the wish to avoid any kind of moralizing in the analysis, in order to overcome the workings of a rigid and cruel super-ego, has led most analysts to eschew any consideration of ethical matters with their patients (Tubert-Oklander, 2011, 2015). This is based on confusion between *morals* and *ethics*. Morals involve the imposition of a code, often of a religious origin, without questioning or analyzing it, while ethics are a wholesale reflection on the origins and meanings of the values and norms that regulate our relation to others, groups, and society. The basic ethical questions are what is good and what is evil, what we should or should not do, and why. In other words, it sets up an—always temporary and revisable—axiology to serve as an orientation for our action (Beuchot, 2004).

And so, what is the basis for applying a "principle of abstinence" to the analyst? We may find an answer in the initial asymmetry of the analytic situation. An analysis always starts with a demand of help from the patient, directed to the analyst. No matter what any of us may think about the therapeutic or non-therapeutic nature of the analytic inquiry, it is a fact that analysands always come to analysis with the expectation that this will alleviate some kind of suffering or distress, help them overcome unnecessary limitations, and represent some kind of improvement in their lives. Thus, when an analyst accepts someone into treatment, he or she assumes the responsibility of caring for another human being who is temporarily his or her charge. So the analyst should, from that moment on, abide by the basic law of all helping relationships, which applies to parents, doctors, teachers, priests, babysitters, policemen, nurses, and governments, as well as analysts: *Thou shalt not abuse thy charges.*

When a person finds him or herself in a position to look after the welfare, or even the lives, of others who are temporarily in a vulnerable and defenseless state, he or she acquires an obligation to act in their benefit, and not exploit the transitory power derived from the situation in order to serve his or her own interests, passions, or ideals. This is a value judgment and, as such, it cannot be demonstrated, only stated and accepted, but it is the very value that makes analysis possible. As many analysts since Freud have pointed out, the only possible reason for the patient to exhibit her or his innermost self to the analyst, is that she or he expects to be helped, and trusts that the analyst will not harm her or him. If the analyst forsakes his or her pledge and betrays this trust, the result is that the analysis becomes iatrogenic, instead of being therapeutic (or any other word we may choose, in order to refer to the beneficial or noxious effects of the treatment).

But why should sexual boundary violations be considered a form of abuse? Is this not a case of consensual sex between consenting adults?

No, it is not. Consensual sex can only take place when both parties have the same status and degree of autonomy and self-determination, and not when one of them holds power over the other. And all helping relationships imply that one of the parties—the one on the receiving end of help and care—is dependent on the other, and this invests the helper with power. So, a sexual encounter between them is most inequitable, and this turns it into abuse. In this sense it is quite similar to sexual harassment in the workplace, a practice that has very little to do with sex and everything to do with power, just as in the case of the *jus primae noctis*. Hence, this brings us to a consideration of the political aspect of the analytic relationship, one that has been systematically neglected by our professional community.

Besides, any sexual relation implies some degree of ruthlessness and disregard for the other, when the urgency to attain one's pleasure takes command. So there is no way in which the analyst can still be thinking and acting in the best interest of his or her patient when actual sex becomes a part of the relationship. Once again, this means forsaking the analyst's pledge to care for the patient to the best of his or her ability.

So much attention has been given to the case of sexual boundary transgressions that this has obscured the high incidence of other kinds of abuse. The analytic relationship, with its unavoidable dimension of dependence and power, lends itself to harbor the aggressive, economic, political, academic, or narcissistic exploitation of patients. These cases are frequently much more subtle than sexual acting out, and they may remain unheeded by patient and analyst alike, but they are no less noxious and they subvert the analytic relationship and process.

Let us consider a few examples. For instance, what happens when the analyst is a major innovator and theoretician of psychoanalysts such as Freud or Melanie Klein? He or she is bound to have a most significant libidinal investment in his or her work and would most probably be tempted to use analyses to validate and develop this investment further. And the patients, enmeshed in a positive transference, would certainly comply. Nothing would seem more natural, so it does not seem at all to be an abuse, but it certainly breeds problems that act against the therapeutic aim.

In the case of Freud, Abraham Kardiner (1977) tells us that when Freud took him as a patient, in the early 1920s, he established *a priori* that the analysis would last six months. This seems to us a rather unusual practice, but Freud did not consider the treatment of future colleagues to be therapeutic at all, but only some sort of practical demonstration of psychoanalytic doctrine and technique, which would be completed when the analysand became fully convinced of the existence of an unconscious meaning of dreams, child sexuality, the Oedipus complex, and repressed homosexuality—in the case of men—or penis envy—in that of women. So far, so good, but Kardiner found his analysis unquestionably therapeutic, was sure that he needed more of it, and felt let down when Freud put an end to it as scheduled.

In the case of Klein, in her clinical practice (1961) she clearly and constantly emphasized the use of extensive and meticulous interpretations that aimed at the confirmation of her theories. Wilfred R. Bion (1980), a former analysand of hers and himself a major theoretician of psychoanalysis, recounted this as follows, in his New York seminars, in response to a comment that Klein seemed to be "ruminating out loud":

> I would not have called them ruminations, but I think she did give a constant stream of interpretations. Latterly, I would have thought that they were too coloured by a wish to defend the accuracy of her theories so that she lost sight of the fact that what she was supposed to be doing was interpreting the phenomenon with which she was presented.
>
> (p. 37)

If we reframe this in relational terms, we could say that she was most of the time listening to herself, rather than listening to the patient.

On other grounds, we are all familiar with cases in which various analysts have been known to exploit their influence on patients in order to obtain social, political, or economic advantages. I am reminded, for example, of the anecdote of a senior analyst (who told this episode himself, as something perfectly natural). He had been audited by the local revenue service, so he called a former analysand of his, who held an important political position, and "he immediately put an end to this nonsense". Many of us would consider this a form of abuse of the analyst's power.

Another case, which we know well, since it is part and parcel of the inner workings of our psychoanalytic institutions, is the use of training analyses as a source of political support for the training analyst in the association. The founders of our discipline were by no means free from this unsavory practice. Freud clearly used his students and analysands as political allies for the dissemination of his ideas (Roazen, 1975) and so did Klein, as Winnicott (1987) showed when he compared the two rival groups in the British Psychoanalytical Society—the Kleinian and the (Anna) Freudian—in a letter addressed to both their respective leaders, dated June 3, 1954, in which he urges them to put an end to the alienation of the two training groups in the institute:

> There is a comment that I would like to make at this point which is that there is a slight but interesting difference between the formation of the two groupings. In the case of Mrs. Klein's colleagues and friends it is true, whether by chance or otherwise, that inclusion in the group depends on the fact of having analysis from Mrs. Klein or an analysand of Mrs. Klein or an analysand of such an analysand. The only exception that I know of is Mrs. Riviere and I know of no analyst who has completed an analysis in the Klein group who is not included by Mrs. Klein as a Klein follower. In the case of Miss Freud's followers, the matter is more one of a type of education and it happens that this gives a less rigid boundary. *One could say that whereas the followers of Mrs. Klein are all children and grandchildren, the followers of Miss Freud all went to the same school.*
>
> (p. 72, emphasis added)

The Kleinian group was undoubtedly a politico-ideological group, but in psychoanalytic institutions politics is indistinguishable from family relationships, due to the power of transference.

But neither was Winnicott free from these tainted relationships, which usually follow a transgenerational course, as James W. Hamilton (2008) expounded in his analysis of the Freud-Strachey-Winnicott-Khan sequence:

> Winnicott [was] taking advantage of Khan's consummate literary talents by pressing him, as Sharpe and Rickman had done

previously, to edit his papers and books, converting him almost into a servant or a secretary. In so doing, Winnicott made Khan feel special, only to later disillusion him by withholding the literary executorship. Freud behaved similarly with his analysands James Strachey and Joan Riviere, who were Winnicott's analysts, by enlisting them to be his English translators as had Strachey with Winnicott in the production of the *Standard Edition* of Freud's work. Except for occasional lectures, Winnicott had been excluded from teaching at the British Psychoanalytic Institute by faculty opposition, a painful reality for him, and he was therefore more likely to identify with Khan's brilliance and see him as a proxy.

(p. 1026)

Hence, the question of abuse in analytic relationships, particularly between colleagues, is extremely complex. Muriel Dimen's (2011; this volume, Chapter 2) article analyses an instance of such an abuse, in this case a sexual transgression by her analyst that might be construed as a minor abuse, as such things go, but which becomes a very grave disruption in the context of an analysis. The author rightly points out that the most harmful aspect of the situation was not the sexual act itself, but the fact of silencing it, thus stalemating the core of the analytic process, although the dialogue seemed to continue well on other matters, creating an "as-if" analysis. This was mainly due to the analyst's narcissistic personality and to the patient's need to idealize him.

She also shows how this whole situation was also determined, to a large extent, by the patriarchal ideology of society, which acted through both patient and analyst, and to the particular historical moment in which this took place, one in which the collective fight for women's liberation and quest for a new place in society, albeit not free from an internal ambivalence, represented a major threat to masculine identity, power, and self-respect.

But there is still more to it. We have not yet answered the question of why the psychoanalytic community and institutions have usually concealed the existence of these boundary violations. Sometimes they are summarily ignored, sometimes the blame is put wholly on the patient ("a seductive hysteric", or something of that nature), and on occasion, the transgressor is quietly banished from the institution and nothing more is said on the matter. It is indeed striking that a group of analysts should act in such a way, so at odds with the spirit, knowledge, and practice of psychoanalysis, which is founded on truth. Why is this so?

One possible answer is that psychoanalysts have suffered, from the very beginning, a deep fear of the full impact of their discovery: the unconscious. This has unleashed a whole pack of defenses, both individual and collective. One of them has been the creation of univocal theory systems, which are accepted uncritically and claim to provide "everything you will ever need to know about psychoanalysis". This paralyzes psychoanalytical thought and creativity in those individuals, groups, and professional communities that uphold and impose them.

Another such defense is the creation of a narcissistic omnipotent image of the analyst as an individual, analysts as a group, and psychoanalysis as theory and practice. This is rationalized as something done for the benefit of the patient, who would lose confidence in her or his analyst if she or he were to discover the latter's insufficiencies; hence Freud's rejection of the idea, proposed by Ferenczi (1933/1949), that the analyst should acknowledge to the patient his mistakes, prejudices, or countertransferences. The Master only accepted the recognition of an error, say, an inaccurate construction, when it had already been corrected by a better one (Freud, 1937). It is obvious that he considered that the patient's confidence could only be based on the belief in the analyst's infallibility (or, at the very least, on that of psychoanalysis as a discipline), while Ferenczi thought that it came as a consequence of the analyst's truthfulness and courage to face unsavory truths about him- or herself (Tubert-Oklander, 1999, 2014).

There are grounds to believe that this manipulative tactic is aimed at defending the analyst, not the patient, from the anxiety generated by the unavoidable uncertainty implied in the analytic process, and from the shame and guilt derived from his own insufficiencies, failures, or transgressions. If the analyst feels that having been a patient is indeed something shameful and abject, it is only natural that he or she should overemphasize the differences between him- or herself and the patients, and actively deny any childish or pathological trends or experiences in him- or herself, thus turning analysis into an iatrogenic practice. Such feelings are not only the result of an insufficient analysis of the narcissistic character traits in the training analyses. They also appear to reflect a process of collective denial functioning at the level of psychoanalytic institutions.

It is quite shocking to discover that our psychoanalytic institutions tend to function just like a severe narcissistic patient, striving to preserve an idealized image of the group and projecting the shameful and abject image on the abused patients (rather like how the authorities tend to respond to rape victims), or to use the offender colleagues as scapegoats for cleansing the analytic community from sin.

Could it be that the tendency, which still continues in our profession, to marginalize the potential contributions of group analysis, is linked directly to our collective need to avoid scrutiny of the role of our training system itself in contributing to the problem of sexual boundary violations and other ethical transgressions? Michael Balint (1968/1979) wondered why psychoanalytic group psychotherapy never received the level of acceptance accorded child analysis within our profession, though child analysis also differs radically in many respects from the standard analytic situation.

> It will be an intriguing historical—and psychological—study to find out what prompted psychoanalytic opinion to adopt exactly the opposite attitude in the case of group therapy [from child analysis]. Although Freud himself adumbrated some alloying of the pure gold of psychoanalysis in order to make it suitable for the psychotherapy of the broad masses, and although almost all of the pioneers of group therapy were trained psychoanalysts, we, as a body, refused to accept responsibility for its further development—in my opinion, to the detriment of everyone concerned, above all of our own science.
>
> (Balint, 1968/1979, pp. 101–102)

Classical psychoanalysis posed a sharp opposition between "internal" and "external" and contended that psychoanalytic inquiry should only refer to the internal. Hence, any attempt to interpret human affairs in terms of the allegedly external—i.e., of group, institutional, social, political, cultural, or relational phenomena—implies leaving the strictly psychoanalytic field altogether. Many of the splits in the psychoanalytic movement were based on this issue, since those clinicians and theoreticians who emphasized the importance of such external factors were disqualified as "environmentalists" and traitors to psychoanalysis, and their arguments were rejected and devalued without any rational discussion (Tubert-Oklander, 2006, 2014). Could it be that this negative attitude toward group analysis reflects our need to avoid the analysis of the analytic group itself—particularly with respect to ethical misconduct? Perhaps our anxiety about the ways in which the group may be implicated in sexual boundary violations has something to do with this.

The discipline of group analysis, which flourished initially in Britain with S. H. Foulkes (1964) and in Argentina with Enrique Pichon-Rivière (1971; Tubert-Oklander & Hernández de Tubert, 2004), is more than a mere "application" of the psychoanalytic knowledge derived from our bipersonal practice to the conduct of therapeutic groups. It is in itself a form of deep therapeutic inquiry, in which the analyst maintains an analytic attitude in order to understand the internal functioning of the group and its members, as well as their insertion in the wider social context. This well-proven but marginalized psychoanalytic knowledge and practice offers a way for psychoanalytic institutions that have been traumatized by the occurrence of boundary violations to do something, in order to (a) heal the wound, (b) prevent further occurrences of such events, and (c) be prepared to deal with them if they do happen.

The working-through of the consequences of the trauma requires the use of group-analytic techniques, conducted by an external counsellor, in order to overcome the tendency for denial and secrecy, and to foster the open expression and analysis of the reactions, feelings, fantasies, thoughts, and defenses displayed by the community and its members. Self-direction by the group is not an option, on account of all the members' involvement in the conflict, and also because psychoanalysts are not usually very knowledgeable on the matter of group dynamics or group techniques.

Working-through and healing require a prolonged, open discussion of the whole matter. This is not easy in a large group such as a psychoanalytic community, whose members have intense transference bonds among them. Large groups are by nature regressive, and a traumatized one is even more so (Hopper, 2003a, 2003b). This is the main reason why there is a need for an external intervention by a qualified and neutral group analyst, who may be quite difficult to find. But such an extraneous intervention can only be temporary and should open the path for the development of new organs and procedures that foster the continuance of the process, created and administered by the members of the institution. This is indeed the key for the prevention and handling of new occurrences of such events.

Here we are faced with two major obstacles. The first one is the prejudice of the psychoanalytic community against group practices and concepts. Group analysts are not considered to be analysts at all (at least inasmuch as they work with groups and theorize about them, since many group analysts are also members of psychoanalytical associations). So this may be a case of the proverbial situation in which my friends cannot help me, and those who can help me are not my friends.

Then there is a factor that was mentioned by Dimen (2011) in her article: the shame of being in need of help. Just as patients—perhaps not all, but many—experience a horrifying sense of shame at being in a situation—which they feel to be demeaning—of having to ask for and receive help, a psychoanalytic community and its members may feel that it is demeaning to have to require help from outside. So, just like patients do, they insist on trying to solve the problem with their own resources, which has already proved to be ineffectual.

But this poses a momentous question: is the feeling of abjection at being (or having been) a patient a universal phenomenon, a psychopathological symptom, or a cultural trait? I flatly reject the first option and consider such a feeling an expression of the other two. I know that many patients, former patients, and even analysts feel like this, as Dimen aptly puts it, in the following terms:

> Analysts suffering the dissociated, unforgettable abjection of having been patients may indeed find themselves inducing that very feeling in their own patients, in order to cleanse themselves and, thus cleansed, to become pure and strong.
>
> (Dimen, 2011, p. 73; this volume, p. 64)

But if an analyst harbors this feeling and acts out his or her suffering through such interpersonal defenses, I would most certainly think that a deep narcissistic omnipotent character trait has been left untouched by his or her own analysis. This may have happened as a result of an unconscious narcissistic pact between the analyst in training and his or her training analyst, but it may also be a consequence of the unwarranted assumption, underlying many of our psychoanalytic theories, that a state of mental health and full maturity involves full autonomy and an overcoming of "dependence".

In this, we are also dealing with a cultural trait. Our present world's dominant *Weltanschauung* emphasizes competitiveness, demeans traditional virtues such as compassion, cooperation, and solidarity, and upholds the myth of Man as a lonely hunter, who provides only for himself and his own, and who should never again be, after overcoming the humiliating dependence of childhood, in need of anybody's help (Hernández-Tubert, 2011). This ideology subtly pervades all of us who have been reared in this society, and even psychoanalytic treatments.

Difficult as it is, I am convinced that a true analysis should include a critical discussion and interpretative dialogue on this tendency, and that something one should have learned, when terminating a psychoanalytical treatment, is to be able to depend on others, whenever needed, and know that none of us can deal with life without help, a help that we should be able to ask for, receive, appreciate, and be grateful for, but also be willing to provide to those in need (Tubert-Oklander, 2013). If we can accept this perspective, then a psychoanalytical institution that agreed to engage in the kind of open discussion and reflection needed in order to work through the trauma generated by such transgressions as those we are now dealing with, would probably achieve much more than that, and arrive at a deeper and better understanding of what our discipline and treatment are all about.

One final point, which I can only mention in brief here, since it would require a full article to develop, is the question of sex and power. In her final analysis of the story she has shared with us, Muriel Dimen (2011) suggests, as many others have done, that "For a long time, sexuality had dropped off the psychoanalytic radar" (p. 73; this volume, p. 64), and that it is high time for it to reoccupy the central place it held in the beginnings of psychoanalysis. In this, I respectfully disagree. I believe that the emphasis on sex has been used defensively to conceal a repressed and denied theme, that of power and its abuse, ever since 1897, when Freud suddenly abandoned his traumatic theory of neuroses. Without minimizing in any way the import of sexual strivings and conflicts, these should be analyzed side by side with relational and social concerns, and with that major theme that has been omitted by psychoanalysis, even though it generates all sorts of individual, relational, family, group, institutional, and social conflicts and symptoms: politics (Pines, 1998; Tubert-Oklander, 2014).

References

Balint, M. (1968/1979). *The basic fault: Therapeutic aspects of regression*, 2nd edition. London: Tavistock.

Beuchot, M. (2004). *Ética [Ethics]*. Mexico City: Torres Asociados.

Bion, W. R. (1961). *Experiences in groups and other papers*. London: Tavistock.

Bion, W. R. (1980). *Bion in New York and São Paulo*, F. Bion (Ed.). Glenlyon: Clunie.

Carotenuto, A. (1980/1982): *A secret symmetry: Sabina Spielrein betweeen Jung and Freud*. New York: Pantheon.

Dimen, M. (2011). *Lapsus linguae*, or a slip of the tongue? A sexual violation in an analytic treatment and its personal and theoretical aftermath. *Contemporary Psychoanalysis*, *47* (1): 35–79.

Ferenczi, S. (1949). Confusion of the tongues between the adults and the child—(The language of tenderness and of passion). *International Journal of Psychoanalysis*, *30*: 225–230.

Foulkes, S. H. (1964). *Therapeutic group analysis*. London: Allen & Unwin.

Freud, S. (1913). On beginning the treatment (Further recommendations on the technique of psychoanalysis I). In J. Strachey (Ed. & Trans.), *The standard edition of the complete psychological works of Sigmund Freud* (vol. 12, pp. 121–144). London: Hogarth Press.

Freud, S. (1915). The unconscious. In J. Strachey (Ed. & Trans.), *The standard edition of the complete psychological works of Sigmund Freud* (vol. 14, pp. 159–215). London: Hogarth Press.

Freud, S (1937). Constructions in analysis. In J. Strachey (Ed. & Trans.), *The standard edition of the complete psychological works of Sigmund Freud* (vol. 23, pp. 255–270). London: Hogarth Press.

Hernández-Tubert, R. (2011). The politics of despair: From despair to dialogue and hope. *Group Analysis*, *44*: 27–39.

Hamilton, J. W. (2008). D. W. Winnicott and Masud R. Khan. *Psychoanalytic Review*, 95: 1017–1034.

Hopper, E. (2003a). *The social unconscious*. London: Jessica Kingsley.

Hopper, E. (2003b). *Traumatic experience in the unconscious life of groups*. London: Jessica Kingsley.

Kardiner, A. (1977). *My analysis with Freud. Reminiscences*. New York: Norton.

Klein, M. (1961). *Narrative of a child analysis: The Conduct of the psycho-analysis of children as seen in the treatment of a ten-year-old boy*. London: Hogarth.

Matte-Blanco, I. (1975). *The unconscious as infinite sets: An essay in bi-logic*. London: Duckworth.

Matte-Blanco, I. (1988). *Thinking, feeling, and being: Clinical reflections on the fundamental antinomy of human beings and world*. London: Routledge.

Pichon-Rivière, E. (1971). *El proceso grupal. Del psicoanálisis a la psicología social (I) [The group process: From psychoanalysis to social psychology (I)]*. Buenos Aires: Nueva Visión.

Pines, M. (1998). *Circular reflections: Selected papers on group analysis and psychoanalysis*. London: Jessica Kingsley.

Roazen, P. (1975). *Freud and his followers*. New York: Knopf.

Tubert-Oklander, J. (1999). Sándor Ferenczi e la nascita della teoria delle relazioni oggettuali [Sándor Ferenczi and the birth of object-relations theory]. In Borgogno, F. (Ed.) (1999), *La partecipazione affettiva dell' analista. Il contributo di Sándor Ferenczi al pensiero psicoanalitico contemporaneo [The analyst's affective participation: The contribution of Sándor Ferenczi to contemporary psychoanalytic thought]* (pp. 261–287). Milan: Franco Angeli.

Tubert-Oklander, J. (2006). The individual, the group and society: Their psychoanalytic inquiry. *International Forum of Psychoanalysis, 15*: 146–150.

Tubert-Oklander, J. (2011). Dependence and betrayal: An analytic approach to professional ethics. Read in the Panel "The Unforgiven: Disruptions That Cannot be Repaired", *47th International Psychoanalytic Congress*, Mexico City, August 2011.

Tubert-Oklander, J. (2013). *Theory of psychoanalytical practice: A relational process approach*. London: International Psychoanalytical Association/Karnac.

Tubert-Oklander, J. (2014). *The one and the many: Selected papers on relational psychoanalysis and group analysis*. London: Karnac.

Tubert-Oklander, J. (2015). The collective resonance of ethical transgressions in psychoanalysis. To be read in the Panel "Ethical violations and the social context: The relevance of the group", *49th International Psychoanalytic Congress*, Boston, July 2015.

Tubert-Oklander, J. & Hernández de Tubert, R (2004). *Operative groups: The Latin-American approach to group analysis*. London: Jessica Kingsley.

Winnicott, D. W. (1987). *The spontaneous gesture: Selected letters of D. W. Winnicott*, F. R., Rodman (Ed.). Cambridge, MA: Harvard University.

Index

abjection (of patients, and analysts as former patients) 17, 51, 57, 64, 183
absolutist position towards sexual boundary violations 160–163, 166, 167
abstinence 17, 66, 95, 174–175
American Psychiatric Association 163
American Psychological Association 155
analytic ideal 155
anger 151, 152
anonymity: of former clinician 129–130; idealization of 80
anxiety: betrayal 126, 127, 128, 131, 133; boundaries 180, 182; communal side of boundary violations 147, 153, 154; Dimen's *Lapsus linguae* 34, 36, 45, 58–59, 61
approach-avoidance 130–131
Aron, L. 91n5
as-if: analysis 179; dimension of analysis 14, 96–97, 98, 101
attachment theory 10, 65
authority *see* power
autonomy: boundaries 174, 176, 184; communal side of boundary violations 153; Dimen's *Lapsus linguae* 11, 50, 51; professional 7

Balint, M. 181
Barangers, M. and W. 96, 97–98
Barron, J. W. 156
Benjamin, J.: domination 83; love 11; passivity 50; separation paradox 51; third object 49

betrayal 117–138; boundaries 175; communal side of boundary violations 153; community "disappearances" 135–136; Dimen's *Lapsus linguae* 28, 29, 53, 119–121, 123, 127, 128, 137; dismay in the countertransference 132–134; dissociation among analysts 160; losing one's past 125–128
Bijur, A. 165
Bion, W. R. 9, 17, 96, 174, 177
Blechner, M. J. 16, 160–168
Botella, C. and S. 118
boundaries 171–185
Breuer, J. 57
British Psychoanalytic Institute 179
British Psychoanalytical Society 178

category crisis 60–61
Celenza, A. 11, 12–13, 14, 77–91, 162
certainty 33–34
Chused, J. F. 105
closure 118
collusion: of analytic community ('collaborators') 145, 150–151, 155; communal side of boundary violations: boundaries 179–181; "disappearances" 135–136; dissociation 160–168; patient-analyst 44, 112, 133; silence 143–157
compartmentalization 146
confidentiality 135, 147–148
Cooper, S. H. 9, 47
Corbett, K. 59

For Product Safety Concerns and Information please contact our EU
representative GPSR@taylorandfrancis.com
Taylor & Francis Verlag GmbH, Kaufingerstraße 24, 80331 München, Germany

www.ingramcontent.com/pod-product-compliance
Lightning Source LLC
Chambersburg PA
CBHW050708280326
41926CB00088B/2876